Freedom and Grace

Edited by
Ivor H. Jones and
Kenneth B. Wilson

WIPF & STOCK · Eugene, Oregon

Wipf and Stock Publishers
199 W 8th Ave, Suite 3
Eugene, OR 97401

Freedom and Grace
By Wilson, Kenneth B.
Copyright©1988 Methodist Publishing - Epworth Press
ISBN 13: 978-1-5326-0859-9
Publication date 9/15/2016
Previously published by Epworth Press, 1988

Contents

	Contributors	iv
	Preface	v
1	Science and Theology from an Arminian Perspective *Christopher D. Wiltsher*	1
2	The Poet of Salvation *David A. Pailin*	20
3	God and Spirituality: On Taking Leave of Don Cupitt *John A. Harrod*	48
4	The Trinitarian Model of God *Kenneth B. Wilson*	65
5	Grace, von Balthasar and the Wesleys *Ivor H. Jones*	86
6	Experiencing Grace *Kenneth G. Howcroft*	103
7	Surgical Spirit *David G. Deeks*	127
8	The Catholic Spirit: The Need of Our Time *Ralph Waller*	145
9	Logic, Chronology and Context in Theology *Martin L. Groves*	157
	Postscript: The Freedom to Respond	184
	Notes	189

Contributors

David G. Deeks teaches Pastoral Theology at Wesley House, Cambridge

Martin L. Groves is a circuit minister in Halifax

John A. Harrod is Tutor in Systematic Theology and Philosophy at Wesley College, Bristol

Kenneth G. Howcroft is Ecumenical Lecturer and Lecturer in New Testament Studies at Lincoln Theological College

Ivor H. Jones is Principal of Wesley House, Cambridge

David A. Pailin is Senior Lecturer in the Philosophy of Religion at the University of Manchester

Ralph Waller is Chaplain of Westminster College, Oxford

Kenneth B. Wilson is Principal of Westminster College, Oxford

Christopher D. Wiltsher teaches Philosophy and Systematic Theology at Wesley College, Bristol, and lectures in the Department of Theology and Religious Studies at the University of Bristol

Preface

This volume began in 1985 when a group of Methodist theologians met to discuss the impending celebration in 1988 of the 250th anniversary of John Wesley's Aldersgate experience, and the state of contemporary theological exploration in the British Methodist tradition. The influence of Wesley has been significant for the Christian church, both in respect of the fact of his founding of the community of the people called Methodists, and in respect of the very practical approach which he took towards church order and the matter of doctrine. Whether he was genuinely a theologian and had anything distinctive to say about doctrine is a matter of debate, though many have wanted to point to the priesthood of all believers and the doctrine of perfection as emphases which, if not radically new insights, rightly concentrated attention again on essential catholic doctrines. However it was our judgment that, whether or not the Methodist church had a distinctive theological tradition in its origins, any ability it may have had to contribute to the development of human understanding in the future would depend on its theological creativity today. And what signs are there of that?

Given that Methodists have thought much about the Aldersgate experience on 24 May 1738, it is surprising how little John Wesley referred to it. Attention has been focussed on the event and on the vicarious reliving of it, as if this were the main matter of interest within the orbit of the Wesleys' influence, whereas what matters is the theological account which we give of and as a result of the experience. And in the case of Methodism what we are addressing are the theological concerns which inform the heart of that community which owes its origin to the Wesleys who had that experience. These essays constitute one approach to the question, 'What are the present theological concerns of Methodist theologians?'

Interestingly, there do seem to be some themes which have

emerged; for example, the freedom of God and of humanity, and the universality and prodigality of God's grace; while we would not wish in any sense to claim that these are uniquely of Methodist concern, we would claim that they are coherent with the origin and historical experience of the Methodist tradition. In a postscript these themes are explored in the hope that further reflection will be stimulated. As practical people have often seen too late, the future lies with the thinker not with the doer: we hope that the Methodist community is aware of this too.

The papers represent the result of several meetings, some of them residential, together with an attempt by the two editors to focus for the purposes of publication the outcome of our joint work. We are grateful to several Trusts and institutions for help and support, particularly to the Gibbs and the Ferguson Trusts, and to Westminster College, Oxford and Wesley House, Cambridge, where the meetings have taken place. The purpose of the publication is to enable Methodists to share in our reflections with the expectation that this may promote a fuller discussion of the Methodist tradition. We hope also that those of other Christian traditions may find the approach here of interest and some stimulus in the contemporary theological task.

1

Science and Theology from an Arminian Perspective

Christopher D. Wiltsher

An Arminian approach to Christian theology claims that by the grace of God all people may be saved through faith in Jesus Christ. This approach depends on claims about the nature of the world, about God's ability to act in the world, and about the nature of human beings and their ability to act freely. All these claims are open to question from the perspective of modern science. In this paper we ask how the scientific material at our disposal affects the Arminian claims, and how the Arminian claims affect our handling of scientific data. Our conclusion is that modern science and an Arminian approach to Christian theology are not only compatible but mutually illuminating.

Introduction

Living as we do in an age dominated by the work of scientists, Christian believers of the present day find themselves faced often with theological questions arising from that work, especially work in the natural sciences. There are various ways of coping with such questions: some believers seek to ignore them altogether, some try to hold apart their science and their religion, and some try to bring together their Christian beliefs and the knowledge derived from science about the cosmos in which we live.

This paper adopts the last approach. We begin from the assumption that Christian theology and the natural sciences offer different ways of interpreting the phenomena of the world in which we live. The phenomena of the world, for our present purpose, are the occurrences which are part of the stuff of ordinary existence: the bubbling of heated water, the falling of leaves when the wind blows, the combination of leaf and water to produce a drink are all simple examples of a phenomenon. There are also more complex examples: the interaction of subatomic particles is also a phenomenon for this purpose.

Such phenomena are public occurrences which may be observed by anyone and they provide the raw material for the intellectual disciplines of the sciences and theology, which attempt to describe and interpret the world. Description and interpretation go hand in hand, for the very words used to describe a phenomenon carry interpretative colouring associated with their use on previous occasions. Part of the interpretation is drawn from the framework of ideas within which the interpreter works, and it is here that the chief difference between the scientist and the Christian theologian emerges. The scientist as a matter of principle describes and interprets the phenomena of the world without reference to God, while the Christian theologian as a matter of principle describes and interprets the same phenomena in the light of a belief in God.

This is not to suggest that the disciplines are mutually exclusive, or that it is impossible to be both scientist and Christian theologian. It is to say that the scientist as scientist and the theologian as theologian must work within the basic framework of their disciplines. However, scientist and theologian are using the same raw material and attempting to describe and interpret the same phenomena. Consequently, inferences and conclusions drawn within one framework may be illuminating within another, even though the presuppositions are different.

On this view one would expect the sciences and Christian theology to have interesting and significant things to offer one another, by way of illumination, correction and limitation. It is significant that the relationship is one of mutual instruction. We reject those views which seek to construct Christian theology in the image of science, or to pretend that theology supplies a wider framework within which scientists can do whatever they like without affecting theology, or to suggest that what theologians say has no consequences for the sciences.

There is no space here to develop or defend this approach to science and theology. We shall take it as given, and regard this paper as in part an illustration of this approach at work.

However it is worth noting one underlying theme of this approach which should appeal to followers of John Wesley. On this view, both science and Christian theology are seen as, in part, attempts to make sense of human experience of living in the cosmos. The theological reflection follows the experience, as does the scientific theory. This does not mean that the theory may not guide the account of the experience, or even affect what is experienced; it does mean that scientific theories and theological doctrines are human constructions which reflect human experience. Methodists have always taken experience as a basic resource for their theology.

Methodists are said also to adopt an Arminian approach to theology. That is, Methodists are claimed to take as basic theological principles the main points of the followers of Arminius, even though few Methodists would immediately connect their basic stance with that Dutch gentleman. The roots of Arminian doctrine can be traced to a conflict with the strict views on predestination of followers of John Calvin. Put briefly, the Calvinists claimed that God had elected some people to be saved and the rest to be damned; while the Arminians claimed that through the grace of God all people might be saved. When the difference is stated thus, most Methodists would recognize themselves as Arminian.

This gives us a focus for our discussion in this paper, in this particular volume. What we are interested in is the question: in what ways are an Arminian approach to Christian theology and the sciences mutually instructive? We shall attempt to answer the question by considering four specific areas of debate between Christian theology and the sciences.

First it is necessary to note the particular emphases of an Arminian approach to Christian theology, and some of the relevant theological consequences of such an approach.

We may express the basic tenets of an Arminian approach thus.[1] God has chosen, from before the creation of the cosmos, to elect for salvation all people who have faith in Jesus Christ. This choice is an act of divine grace. Human beings are incapable of responding to this act and finding salvation by themselves, but may do so through the grace of God in Jesus Christ. Their response to God's grace is an act of free will, may involve a great change in the individual, and will certainly be demonstrated in the way they live. Having come to faith, people may be maintained in faith by God's gracious activity; but they may also, of their own free will, reject God and fall from grace.

We must note that this is of necessity only a brief statement of an Arminian approach. In the nearly four hundred years since

Arminius died many qualifications and nuances have been introduced. Nevertheless, for our purposes, this statement will suffice. From this basic position, certain ideas follow which are essential to the Arminian approach, but are also of importance for some questions of science and Christianity.

We may express these ideas thus:

1. The cosmos in which we live is the creation of God. Were this not so, there would be no certainty that God could save anyone, let alone all who have faith in Jesus Christ.

2. God had a particular purpose for human beings from before the creation of the cosmos, namely that some of them should be saved. This implies that in some sense the creation of human beings was part of the intentions of God before the creation of the cosmos began.

3. God is able to, and does, bring about occurrences within the cosmos, freely and graciously. Were this not so, neither the claims about God's activity in Jesus Christ nor those about God's influence on humanity could be sustained.

4. Human beings are capable of change in response to God's grace, through the operation of that grace and their own free will.

None of these statements is exceptional as far as orthodox Christianity is concerned and each may be claimed to give a correct account of the data available to us about the cosmos in which we dwell. However, the sciences appear to offer a different interpretation of the data, and one which challenges the four statements above. In the light of present scientific knowledge, it may be claimed that:

1. The cosmos came into being as a result of chance happenings, without any divine action.

2. Human beings have evolved by chance in such a way that they cannot be seen as special divine creations, nor as the objects of any divine purpose from before the creation.

3. The cosmos is governed by natural laws which leave no place for the action of God within it.

4. Human beings are animals with inherited characteristics and behaviour patterns, who are conditioned by and adapt to their physical and cultural environment. They cannot change by their own will.

These four claims seem to destroy the basis of an Arminian approach to Christian theology, by denying the possibility of God's free and gracious activity for and in human beings and the possibility of a free human response to the grace of God. We should not be too surprised by this, for Arminius lived from 1560 to 1609 and did not have the benefit of all the scientific work which informs these statements. Arminius believed in the creation of the world according to the account found in the book of Genesis, including the special creation of human beings, and he did not question the idea of divine intervention in the cosmos. His beliefs were consistent with the knowledge of the natural world of the time; but clearly modern scientific knowledge offers a different picture of the natural world, and therefore on the view of science and religion adopted here, demands a fresh theological response.

Our purpose is to try and outline that fresh response in the four areas mentioned. Limitations of space require that we concentrate on the main lines of our response, leaving aside qualifications and details; but this may be an advantage in making the main lines clearer. Working with a broad brush on a large canvas, we shall try to give some account of the data available to us, and to see how it may be interpreted from the perspectives of science and Arminian theology.

Creation

One of the triumphs of modern natural science is the putting together of a coherent view of the coming into being of the cosmos in which we live. The story can be read in many places,[2] and a fascinating tale it is. For our purposes only certain parts of the most widely accepted version need to be rehearsed.

The story is this. The cosmos as we know it orginated in an explosion of unimaginable intensity. In the first few tiny fractions of a second after this explosion, there was a swirling flux of energy in which particles of sub-atomic matter were coming into being and being destroyed by their opposites. For some reason there was an imbalance, and some particles were not destroyed. As the energy flux cooled rapidly, these particles were drawn together in the atoms and then the molecules which formed the basic elements of the cosmos. From then on the story is one of evolution, as the matter now in being cools and reacts and forms the stuff of the cosmos as we know it.

Behind this simple story lies a great deal of dedicated and careful research. It will be noted immediately that there is no obvious reason why the story thus told should be incompatible with Christian claims that God created all that is: for one could simply claim that God produced the Big Bang which began the whole process.

Indeed, it is possible to claim more. The nature of the cosmos is governed by a very small number of factors, physical variables which together control the ways in which the elements of the cosmos are brought together. A slight difference in any of these factors would have led to a very different cosmos from the one we know. That all the relevant variables have just the right values to produce the cosmos we know seems too much of a coincidence to some people, and they claim that God the creator must have chosen those particular values for the variable factors which would produce a cosmos able to sustain human life.[3]

Such a view is sometimes held to receive support from what has become known as the anthropic principle.[4] This, a careful statement of scientific theory, holds in its strongest form that the cosmos is so ordered that the appearance within it of intelligent observers was inevitable from the beginning of the cosmos.

Whether or not the anthropic principle supports the claim that God chose the values of the determinative variables to produce human beings does not concern us here. What does concern us is that the story of the coming into being of the cosmos, taken with the coincidence of the determinative variables, is not only compatible with, but seems to some to make more plausible the idea of divine creation. What we have here is a modern form of the traditional argument for the existence of God from premises about the design of the cosmos.

Unfortunately, the argument suffers from the same defect as all such arguments. Even supposing that the cosmos does show signs of being designed, even designed for a purpose, why should we postulate a designer? It is one thing to say: if there is a creator of a certain kind, then this is the creation we should expect to see. It is quite different to claim that our perception of the creation necessarily points to the existence of a creator.

Further, even if the argument for the existence of a creator worked, what kind of divine creator would be involved? According to one writer, a very lazy creator. In his book *The Creation*,[5] P. W. Atkins has set out to show that all the features of the cosmos we know, including the values of the determinative variables, can be accounted for by a theory of random events. For Atkins, the cosmos just happened as one particular fluctuation in a series; it just so happened that the necessary factors occurred in the right combination – a piece of chance which produced the cosmos as we know it. Atkins does not attempt to dispute the existence of a creator; he merely follows Laplace in saying that we have no need of a creator, for the idea of a divine creator adds nothing to the account of the cosmos.

We should recognize at once that Atkins is quite correct in what he says as far as scientific explanation is concerned. He has provided a consistent account of the coming into being of the cosmos which makes the idea of a divine creator redundant, as an explanation of the origins of the cosmos. However, we must also note that he has made two basic assumptions, both of which may be challenged.

First, that a plausible account of the coming into being of the cosmos has been given does not mean that a true account has been given. If there are two or more accounts which purport to account for the same data, then the decision as to which of them is correct remains to be made. A Christian account of creation may be true, provided it accounts for all the data offered by the natural sciences.

Second, Christian theology does not purport to offer an explanation of the coming into being of the cosmos by reference to God. Rather, Christians begin from the experience of living in a world which is believed to be the sphere of God's free grace. God is worshipped and adored as the origin of that grace. As a consequence, in trying to come to terms with the cosmos as it is, the Christian believer is compelled to make claims about God as divine creator: for logically, the claims that are made about the grace of God and its results for human beings demand that God is divine creator. On that basis, the Christian comes to claim that God created all that is, and to draw inferences from that claim. The account offered of the coming into being of the cosmos may then be exactly that of P. W. Atkins or it may be some other account; the choice between the accounts is likely to be made largely on scientific grounds.

Largely, but not entirely, for from an Arminian perspective, not every account of the coming into being of the cosmos will be acceptable. Thus as we noted, it is essential for the Arminian approach to Christian theology that the cosmos is God's creation. Consequently, any account of the coming into being of the cosmos which denies the idea of an origin for the cosmos will be unacceptable.

Again, an Arminian approach to Christian theology requires a cosmos in which God is able to act decisively at any time. In so far as the account offered is an account of the coming into being of a determined cosmos, with the whole process controlled by inescapable and unchangeable laws, the Arminian must protest. The protest is most easily expressed in the claim that creation continues, both through the activity of God and through the activity of entities within the cosmos.

On the other hand, an account such as that given by Atkins points up one area in which an Arminian approach may need to change. The Arminian approach requires that the cosmos is the result of an intentional act of divine creation, while other interpretations of the data suggest a much less purposeful origin. But how necessary is it for Christians to claim that God intended to create this particular cosmos? Perhaps, for example, God was playing creatively and this cosmos emerged. Clearly if this suggestion were adopted there would be implications for the Arminian approach to the salvation of humanity, and these we shall look at later. For the present, we simply note that a theological interpretation less committed to claims about the eternal purposes of God may provide a better account of the data at our disposal than the traditional Arminian approach.

Thus in questions of the coming into being of the cosmos our science and our Arminian theology illuminate one another. The theology does not give a detailed account of the coming into being of the cosmos, and the science does not rule out the possibility of a creator. Our theology does lead us to insist that a complete account of human experience demands the idea of a creator who created and is creating the cosmos, and so puts definite constraints on the kind of scientific theories which are plausible in this area. Our science puts definite limits on the claims which can be made theologically about the God who creates and the divine intentions in creating.

Evolution

Let us turn from the coming into being of the cosmos to the coming into being of the human species. One of the best-known episodes in the history of science and religion concerns the controversy over the origins of the human being. It is widely believed that the publication of *Origin of Species* by Charles Darwin[6] marked the beginning of one of the great battles between science and Christianity, a battle in which Christianity was heavily defeated.

Such a simple picture does not do justice to the complexities of the debate, and makes far too sharp a division between scientists and religious believers. There were eminent scientists who rejected Darwin's theory, and eminent religious believers who accepted it. However, it is clear that in the last hundred and fifty years, one of the main components of Darwin's theory, the doctrine of evolution, has come to be widely accepted among scientists and religious believers alike as offering the best basis for an understanding of the origins of the human race, as well as the origins of other species. We should note that the doctrine of evolution was only one part of Darwin's theory, and other parts of his theory, such as the idea of the survival of the fittest, are less widely accepted. Even the doctrine of evolution is only widely accepted as a broad principle: there is considerable debate about some of the details of the doctrine, as well as about the mechanism of evolution.[7]

For our purposes the debates about the details do not matter. What we need to note is that the most widely accepted scientific account of the origins of human life sees human beings emerging on the earth in the same way that other species of animal emerged, by a process of change in genetic material together with some adaption to the environment. Genetic material is the means by which information about the characteristics of the species is passed from one generation to another. As a living cell reproduces itself, genetic material is copied from the parent cell and reproduced in the offspring, so shaping the new cell. This copying process can be inaccurate, with the necessary information not being copied exactly. An inaccurate copy will produce a cell different from the parent, which may or may not survive; if it does survive, it may give rise to a new species of living creature. Whether or not the copying of genetic material is accurate seems to be a matter of chance. Hence it seems that there is a randomness about the change of genetic material which is significant: for if changes in genetic material take place at random, then species, including the human being, developed by chance.

Behind this account lies a great deal of knowledge of the genetic material which all living creatures have in common, and much study of the features which different species of animal have in common. The account is not complete. There are many gaps in the story, which cannot yet be filled by hard evidence. We do not yet know how the inert objects of the earth somehow produced the first living cell, though there are plausible theories to account for this vital development. Moreover, we do not have anything like a complete account of the processes of adaption which determine how or why some cells survive and some do not. Nevertheless the account is sufficiently complete and detailed to be widely accepted, and to raise questions for Christian theology.

There are two aspects of this evolutionary account which pose particular problems for an Arminian approach to Christian theology: the random nature of the process, and the emergence of human beings in a way exactly similar to other animals. Arminians claim that God chose from before the cosmos was created to save all human beings who respond in faith to Jesus Christ. This implies that before the creation of any creature, God had decided to create human beings and had particular intentions towards them.

On the evolutionary account, this view becomes difficult to sustain: for if human beings developed from other elements of earthly life by a chance process, how could God have intended to create them? If human beings were not intended to emerge, how could God have formed an intention to save them before the creation? If human beings evolved like any other animal, what makes them so special that God has a desire to save them?

In the distant past, theologians accepted that all living creatures were created by God as we know them now, and human beings were distinguished by being given the breath of life by God in a way different from other creatures. On this view it is easy to talk of the intentions of God towards humanity from before the creation of the cosmos.

Such a view is still espoused by those who call themselves 'scientific creationists'. They hold that the account of the creation of human beings found in the Book of Genesis is accurate in detail and that the evolutionary account is wrong from both a religious and a scientific point of view. An important part of the scientific creationist case lies in showing that the evolutionary account does not adequately explain the data at our disposal and does not follow proper scientific methods. We do not have the space here to examine the scientific creationist position.[8] It does raise some important questions for proponents of an evolutionary view; but it seems to rest on views of science and the biblical material which do not command wide assent among scholars. Certainly the methods of scientific creationism are not those of the relationship of science and religion espoused in this paper.

An alternative approach to the problems raised by the evolutionary account has been the approach which accepts the evolutionary account, but claims that God directed the evolutionary process. In essence, this amounts to the claim that God intended to create human beings, and so arranged the process of genetic change that human beings evolved. Much of the argument turns on the nature of random processes, and the claim that what may seem a chance event in an individual case may be seen as part of a process with a direction when viewed on a population basis.[9]

All such accounts take seriously both the evolutionary account and the Christian claim that God has intentions towards human beings. The problem with them is that they leave a niggling feeling of doubt about the directedness of 'random' processes: even given the claims about the behaviour of populations, it is still a very strong claim that God directed the process to produce human beings: why should God take such an interest in us? This question is not answered: instead it is simply held that we know God does take such an interest in us.

However, in the light of the question raised above about the purposes of God in relation to the creation of the cosmos, we are encouraged to ask the question about God's purposes for humanity in a different form: what evidence is there that God took any interest in human beings from before the creation? There is none. That God chose to save human beings from before the creation of the cosmos is an assumption, and an assumption which is actually larger than is necessary for Arminian purposes. All that we need for an account of human salvation is the claim that God has decided to save human beings now that they exist. When God formed this intention is irrelevant.

On this view, we may accept an evolutionary account of creation, including the random nature of the evolutionary process, without losing anything of importance to our Arminian approach. For it does not matter exactly how human beings emerged or developed. What matters is that they have emerged and developed to a point at which God desires to save them and they are able to respond to God. Human beings are not saved because they are specially created: from an Arminian viewpoint, any human beings who are saved are saved because the gracious God chose to save them and they responded. Thus in this area, science has something to say to theology, but theology has little at present to say to science.

Divine action

Does God act in the world? If so, in what ways? Here we enter areas which have been hotly disputed, particularly in relation to claims that Jesus worked miracles, that miracles are performed now in the name of Jesus, and that God can and does alter the course of worldly events. One part of the dispute lies in the apparent claim of the sciences to give complete accounts of events, and to make exact and accurate predictions of events of the future.

The scientific case begins from the assumption that every event has a cause which can be discovered within the cosmos. The cause may be simple or complex and composed of a variety of inter-acting elements: the essential point is that the cause may be discovered within this cosmos. Since the cause of any event may be discovered within the cosmos, it must be susceptible to the careful methods of scientific examination and discovery.

Further, the sciences make the assumption that the whole of the cosmos operates under laws which can be established and enunciated and then used to discover the causes of events and to predict chains of events of the future. Essential to the working scientist is the idea that any experiment can be repeated with the same results: nature is consistent, and can be relied on to remain consistent.

Using these assumptions scientists have established a great number of laws which are used to explain and predict events within the cosmos. And they work. We all rely on them and use them without thinking in ordinary circumstances every day. One of the great strengths of the scientific enterprise is its success in explaining and predicting an enormous variety of events within our experience.

At first sight, this scientific case appears to amount to a strong case for a totally determined cosmos, one in which every event could be predicted if we had enough information. Some have indeed interpreted the scientific case in this way, claiming that all that stands between us and total prediction of events is the limitations of our own knowledge. In time, they assert, these limitations will be overcome.

Others have pointed to the history of science itself to suggest that whenever we think we are near to discovering everything, we find out how little we know; consequently, they suggest, the goal of total knowledge is simply beyond human capacity. Still others point to the sub-atomic world and the claims that there is a definite indeterminacy in events involving sub-atomic particles. Some claim that there is evidence of the exercise of choice in some sense by particles at the sub-atomic level. Whether or not this is correct, any indeterminacy of sub-atomic events, as distinct from indeterminacy of our measurement of those events, undermines any theory of a totally determined cosmos. So it is by no means clear that the cosmos is totally determined.

Nevertheless, science looks askance at any claims of intervention within the cosmos from outside the cosmos. Such intervention would not be susceptible to scientific examination, though its results might; and it would suggest that the ordinary laws governing the cosmos must be altered in some way, even if only temporarily. Further, the idea of unpredictable divine action cuts across the assumption that all events are, in principle, predictable.

In response to this, some Christians have claimed that God is active exactly in those sub-atomic events which are not determined, directing them, and so directing everything. This does not seem helpful, for it effectively says that every event is part of divine action and so robs the idea of divine action of any useful content. If the idea of divine action is to be of any use, it must be possible to say that there are events in which God has acted and events in which God has not acted. Much of the discussion has turned on ways of distinguishing these two classes.

Certainly an Arminian approach to Christian theology requires the two categories of events. For Arminians are committed to the proposition that God does act in the cosmos; but they are also committed to the proposition that God leaves at least some things to human free will, so that in some events God clearly keeps out. So an Arminian approach to theology demands a cosmos which is ordered and in which many things happen without divine action, but which has room for divine action.

It is not at all clear that a purely scientific approach to events within the cosmos could ever show that the Arminian approach is impossible. Having assumed from the start that the causes of all events are to be located within the cosmos, the sciences are unable to discuss the idea of divine action as a possible factor in any event. However, the sciences can provide interpretations which seem sufficient to account for all events within the cosmos, and so again make divine action an empty threat.

The problem here lies in the difficulty of saying what is, or is not, an adequate explanation of an event. For example, in human terms, is an explanation of someone's activity adequate if it gives no account of motives or intentions? For some purposes, such an account is probably adequate, but not for all purposes. Thus a non-interventionist account of events within the cosmos may be adequate for some purposes, but not for all.

However, the principal problem remains for the Arminian theologian. How do we distinguish examples of divine action from other events? The power of non-interventionist accounts lies partly in their ability in principle to account for all events by the same methods.

It is tempting to respond to the question by trying to list the characteristics of 'divine action'; but it is not clear that we need to. For what the Arminian claims is that God's grace is expressed in the cosmos: divine action is the expression of God's grace within the cosmos in some way. There is no reason why that expression of grace should not use the natural processes of the cosmos or work in accordance with the laws of the cosmos. What is necessary is that in some cases those natural processes should lead to states of affairs which exhibit the grace of God.

Christians claim that there is at least one example of such a process, in Jesus Christ. That many do not see Jesus as exhibiting the grace of God does not confound the Christian claim. But nor does the example of Jesus allow Christians to make large claims about the intervention of God in other events. It seems that we must be content to say that God can act in the cosmos, that God has acted on at least one occasion, and that the acts of God will always take place within and through the medium of the cosmos as we know it, and so will always be ambiguous. This does not give the Christian much, but it does give the Arminian sufficient for a consistent account of the data of human experience.

Here it seems that our science imposes great restraints on Christian theology, and our theology insists that science must not be too ambitious. Christian theology insists on the possibility of divine action in the cosmos, and claims to be able to produce at least one definite example; science excludes the possibility of divine action by methodological assumption, but offers no other means of ruling out such action.

The human animal

We have noted that it is essential to an Arminian approach to Christianity that human beings are able to respond freely to the grace of God, and to change. The kind of change sought is specified in a variety of ways, but it is always expected that the change will be expressed in the way a person lives. Thus the Arminian must insist that people can decide to live in a particular way, and are able to carry out their intentions, adopting particular attitudes and patterns of behaviour of their own choosing.

The data of human experience seem at first sight to support this view. We do commonly talk of deciding what we are going to do, we do expect to have some control over our own lives, and we claim and are claimed to be able to change our patterns of behaviour if we wish to. The change may be difficult, it may never take place because we are too lazy or insufficiently motivated: but that we can in principle change seems plausible. However, a different interpretation of the available data is possible which suggests that such changes as do occur in our behaviour patterns are the result of heredity or conditioning.

There are three main strands to this claim. First, it is claimed that our attitudes and behaviour are shaped in part by the genetic material which we inherit from our parents, which incorporates those patterns of living which have contributed to the survival of our species. These attitudes and patterns of behaviour have become so much part of us that they are now instinctive, and sometimes take control of us. The strength of this claim is a matter of debate, for while it is demonstrable that physical characteristics can be inherited, it is not so easy to show that attitudes have been inherited. Nevertheless, the power of instinctive behaviour cannot be denied easily, so if instincts are passed in genetic material from one generation to another, heredity does become an important factor in our behaviour patterns.

Secondly, it is claimed that our way of life is shaped in part by our physical environment. Here the claim is that our surroundings, in particular the surroundings in which we grow up, have a marked effect on our characters. Further, the food we eat, the presence or absence of particular chemicals, and all the factors which influence our physical well-being, are claimed also to make a difference to our attitudes and behaviour.

Thirdly, we may point to our social and cultural environment as an important factor in shaping our characters. The influence of those around us, our peers, our parents, those in authority over us, makes a difference. So does the opportunity for education, or lack of it, and the opportunity for exploring other cultures, discovering wider horizons, and so on.

The last two of these strands are widely accepted, and indeed are taken as given in much of the discussion of social planning. We expect that by changing the environments in which people live or work, we will make a difference to their future patterns of living. We further expect that some of the difference will be in matters of attitude and behaviour. The term 'social engineering' expresses both the hopes and fears of this approach to human life: hopes that the lot of many can be improved, and fears of manipulation to their advantage by those in power.

If these hopes and fears and the view of humanity which lies behind them are correct, then it seems that human beings are shaped by many factors beyond the control of the individual at least, and perhaps beyond the control of humanity. It thus becomes questionable to what degree we can change ourselves, or be changed in defiance of our conditioning and heredity.

Yet this is what the Arminian approach requires. Even if it is claimed that God's grace works through our environment and through other people and so on, it is still necessary to the Arminian that someone who has not responded to God's grace may decide to do so, may do so, and may continue to do so whatever the circumstances of the person's life or background.

It is clear that we do not need to deny that the various factors listed above are influential, nor even that we are conditioned in much of our pattern of living. What the Arminian must deny is that these factors, even combined, tell the whole story. We note that the problem is different for those who claim that God has destined some to be saved and others to be damned, for they can accept the idea of total conditioning, but cannot accept any change.

Can it be claimed that there is more to the account of our living than theories of conditioning or genetic inheritance would allow? The most usual way of tackling the problem is to claim that the whole is more than the sum of the parts, that is, the human being is more than an animal or mechanism. The essential difference, it is claimed, between human beings and other animals or machines is precisely the human capacity for thought and decision-making. However, it is not clear that human capacities in this direction are as distinctive as was once thought.

Even if they were, it is not at all clear that our problem would be solved. For thought and decision-making do not necessarily imply the ability to change one's pattern of behaviour at will or to adopt new attitudes. Moreover, it is not at all clear that human beings are the only animals to have something like free will.

A better approach, and one congenial to the Arminian, is to note that there are examples of people who do seem to have overcome their conditioning, do seem to have departed from inherited ways, do seem to have changed in unexpected and inexplicable ways. Such cases suggest that the story of conditioning and heredity is inadequate, since it can give no plausible account of them. An approach which insists on some element of free will can account for all the cases, so long as it does not try to say that conditioning and heredity play no part.

And that is all we need to make the claim that God brings about salvation. For some, the conditions of life may be such that they come to saving faith as a result of conditioning or heredity, without trouble; for others, there may be a struggle against heredity and conditioning and environment, and the influence of God's grace may be required. To claim that salvation comes by divine grace, it is not necessary to show that in every case God's grace is the only or most active factor in a person's coming to faith.

At this point we are departing from the traditional Arminian position. As we noted earlier, Arminians have claimed that only by the grace of God may someone come to faith. This claim is stronger than is necessary to support the idea that God intends to save and brings about the salvation of those who come to faith. All this latter idea requires is that God is able to bring about salvation in circumstances which are otherwise unpropitious.

In this area, then, scientific claims about the human animal as a creature fashioned by heredity and environmental conditioning suggest that the Arminian approach must be refashioned to some degree; but the Arminian approach also insists that the scientific account of human behaviour is incomplete.

Conclusion

We began this paper with the assumption that an Arminian approach to Christian theology and the scientific study of the cosmos and human beings within it are mutually instructive. Part of our purpose has been to see in what ways these two strands of human thought illuminate each other. In the four areas of discussion which we have briefly touched on, we have seen that the knowledge obtained through the sciences does help in the construction of our theology, and that theological considerations provide definite and significant pointers for scientists. Of course there is much detail to be discussed, but the mutual illumination is clear.

It was also part of our initial purpose to explore the fresh response required from Christian theology by the insights of modern science. We noted that our theological statements must take account of our knowledge of the cosmos, just as the statements of our guide Arminius rested on the scientific knowledge of his day. In what ways must an Arminian approach to theology be modified to be acceptable today?

We can best summarize the answer to this question by reformulating the four statements offered at the start of our discussion as consequences of the basic Arminian stance. These were:

1. The cosmos in which we live is the creation of God. Were this not so, there would be no certainty that God could save anyone, let alone all who have faith in Jesus Christ.

2. God had a particular purpose for human beings from before the creation of the cosmos, namely that some of them should be saved. This implies that in some sense the creation of human beings was part of the intentions of God before the creation of the cosmos began.

3. God is able to, and does, bring about ocurrences within the cosmos, freely and graciously. Were this not so, neither the claims about God's activity in Jesus Christ nor those about God's influence on humanity could be sustained.

4. Human beings are capable of change in response to God's grace, through the operation of that grace and their own free will.

In the light of our discussion we may now say:

1. The cosmos in which we live is being created by God.

2. God has a particular purpose for human beings (and possibly for other creatures), formed we know not when.

3. God is able to and does bring about occurrences within the cosmos, though probably through the natural processes of the cosmos.

4. Human beings are capable of change in response to God's grace, with their own free will and the grace of God playing parts in that change.

It is clear that we have modified the ideas with which we began. But have we lost anything of importance to Christian theology? The basic Arminian assertion was that all people might be saved because of God's gracious action in the cosmos, but that any particular person's salvation requires that person's response to the grace of God. Nothing in what we have discussed destroys that basic assertion. What is modified is our understanding of the grounds for God's gracious action. We conclude therefore that an Arminian approach to Christian theology is tenable in the modern world. We should want to go further, and claim that such an approach is highly desirable for Christian theology in the modern world: but that would require another discussion.

2

The Poet of Salvation

David A. Pailin

This paper considers how the doctrine of salvation may be understood so as to meet the twin criteria for theological understanding of significance and rational credibility. Having noted that many former ways of talking about salvation are now acceptable only to a declining cognitive minority, the relationship between divine salvation and human need, and the unacceptability of a number of traditional doctrines of salvation, are considered. After outlining the character of the cosmic, historical and individual threats to the significance of human being posed by its basic nature, the paper concludes by taking up a remark of Whitehead to suggest that God's saving activity may be significantly and credibly understood in terms of both preserving in the divine being what people have achieved and evoking in them creative responses to their situation.

> 'He does not create the world, he saves it: or, more accurately, he is the poet of the world, with tender patience leading it by his vision of truth, beauty, and goodness.'
>
> Alfred North Whitehead

The criteria of theological understanding

In his autobiography, *Some Day I'll Find You*, Harry Williams describes how he became 'disillusioned with thinking as a purely cerebral activity'. In accordance with 'the intellectual veneer' of traditional Christian understanding he considered that he was 'ransomed, healed, restored, forgiven', but in 'actual fact' he knew himself as 'sick unto death and little more than a slave'. Out of this self-awareness he came to realize that 'Christian truth' is only properly possessed when it has become 'part and parcel' of one's life: 'I saw that I could not truly say "I believe," unless it was another way of saying "I am."'[1] One consequence of this realization – and one from which many people have benefitted – was his decision that in his sermons 'I would not preach about any aspect of Christian belief unless it had become part of my own life-blood.'[2] In this way he hoped that he would speak to others of real faith for real life in the real world.

The approach adopted by Harry Williams describes one of the criteria of adequacy for theological understanding. This criterion is not wholly covered by the over-worked request for 'relevance', although it is important that theological understanding be relevant to the actuality in which people find themselves. To point out, for instance, that according to Matthew (1. 15f.) the great-great-great-grandfather of Jesus was called Eliud or that as a member of the tribe of Judah Jesus was a priest who is not of the succession of Aaron (Heb. 7. 11,14) is not likely to be regarded as information which illuminates the current character of the Christian life. What is required of a theological understanding is that it be 'significant'. In order to be taken seriously, that is, such understanding must affirm something that is recognizable as decisive for the fulfilment of human being in the world today. To affirm, for example, that God in Christ has conquered the cosmic orders of 'thrones, sovereignties, authorities, and powers' and led them as captives in 'triumphal procession' (Col. 1. 16; 2. 15) will not arouse interest in people who do not understand their existential predicament in terms of being in the thrall of such powers.[3]

At a popular level the demand for significance may be described as 'the Bright Hour Test' – namely, 'Can the mature ladies of the Bright Hour (or some such group), who may not have enjoyed "higher education" but who know from long experience what life is like, be reasonably expected to see that what the theologian is proposing, when appropriately presented, is fundamentally important for actual living?' In applying this criterion, though, it is important to take seriously the qualification expressed in the phrase 'be reasonably expected to'; an understanding must not be prematurely dismissed as having no significance because it is not immediately perceived to be significant. It may need time for reflection for its point to emerge. This test thus makes it necessary to balance present non-significance against the likelihood of significance emerging later.

Paul Tillich expresses the criterion of significance in a more sophisticated form when he states that only those propositions are theological whose object 'can become a matter of ultimate concern for us' in that it 'determines our being or non-being'.[4] In consequence of this view Tillich considers it important for theologians to pay attention to science and philosophy as formative factors, and to art and literature as symbolic expressions of the character of contemporary existence.[5] Through the insights gained from such studies they may discern how to relate the Gospel message of the 'New Being in Jesus as the Christ'[6] to the actual state of current human being.[7]

A second criterion for theological understanding is that it be 'credible'. The satisfaction of this demand converts theological proposals from attractive fictions, liable to be suspected of describing a desirable dreamland, into proper candidates for assent in thought and practice. According to Schubert Ogden this criterion requires of theological assertions that they meet 'the relevant conditions of meaning and truth universally established with human existence',[8] and so be 'credible to human existence as judged by common experience and reason'.[9] Although the ambiguity and polyvalent orderability of the world[10] renders the establishment of such credibility far from straightforward and indisputably conclusive, theological proposals must be warranted according to some recognized and appropriate canons of rationality if they are to be taken seriously. In the case of theology these canons include the requirements that the story that is told of the fundamental character of reality be internally consistent, comprehensively applicable, fruitful of further insights, pragmatically effective, and intellectually satisfying in that it makes sense of reality as we find it in our experience.[11]

It may further be suggested that Christian theological understanding, as such, must also satisfy a third criterion, namely, that it be derived from and in accordance with the foundational and normative expressions of the Christian faith. Ogden, for instance, maintains that a statement of Christian theology is only to be deemed adequate if its meaning is 'appropriate' to the 'apostolic norm'.[12] It must represent 'the same understanding of faith as is expressed' by 'the primary symbols' found in 'the "datum discourse" of the Christian witness'.[13] On the same lines it presumably could be argued that a 'Protestant' theology should be based upon and be in fundamental agreement with the foundational principles of that form of Christian understanding, and a 'Methodist' theology with those of Methodism (though a clearly defined and coherent body of such principles might be difficult to identify).

This demand, however, makes the mistake of confusing the classical sources of insight for theological understanding with the norms by which it is to be judged. All understanding emerges out of and to a large extent finds its warrants in terms of a particular intellectual background. This provides the materials for its thought and the plausibility structures which govern its reflections on those materials. To a considerable extent, therefore, all forms of theological understanding are moulded by the canons of significance and credibility presupposed in their cultural and religious backgrounds. In this respect all such understanding is inescapably relative. It is not surprising, therefore, that theologians who belong to different cumulative traditions of the Christian faith produce recognizably different presentations of it. For example, whether or not they are happy to affirm its underlying motifs, theologians who have been brought up in a community regularly using Methodist hymnody to express its faith cannot help being affected by its motifs in their thought. Consciously or unconsciously those ideas will mould their religious reflections.

Their underlying goal, however, should not be subservience to their background tradition but faithfulness to the truth. Only so will the resulting theological thought be properly faithful to their tradition, whatever it might be. The living tradition of a faith which is to be treated seriously – and its survival as such suggests that a number of people do consider that it is sufficiently important to be treated seriously – does not appear and develop out of a childish desire to be different. It arises out of the conviction that this form of understanding offers a more adequate apprehension of the truth about ultimate matters than any other that is available. Since, though, the criteria which brought it about are those of significance and credibility, it is by those criteria that its alleged insights are to be entertained, developed and judged. Augustine urged Christians to plunder pagan philosophy and acquire its perceptions of the truth for their own use.[14] Christian theologians should recognize that commitment to God as the God of truth demands a similar attitude to the sources of insight contained in the Bible and traditions of the church, including those of their own confession. What Coleridge suggests in the *Confessions of an Inquiring Spirit* concerning the authority of the Bible applies to all sources of theological understanding: their authority lies in their power to 'find' us by confronting us with what significantly and credibly fits 'our nature and needs'.[15]

Traditional expressions of the doctrine of salvation

Bearing in mind, then, these criteria and traditional sources of theological understanding, I want to consider what sense it may now be possible to make of the doctrine of salvation? Paul, for instance, writes that 'since we have now been justified by Christ's sacrificial death, we shall all the more certainly be saved through him from final retribution', and that God 'chose to save those who have faith by the folly of the Gospel' of the 'doctrine of the cross'.[16] In the eighteenth-century John Wesley reportedly stirred crowds with the message that God saves people 'from original and actual, past and present sin' and so from 'fear of the wrath of God' by pardoning them 'for the sake of the propitiation made by the blood of His Son'.[17] The faith of generations of Methodists since then has been formed in part through singing such hymns as Charles Wesley's

> Father, whose everlasting love
> Thy only Son for sinners gave,
> Whose grace to all did freely move,
> And sent Him down the world to save:
>
> Help us Thy mercy to extol,
> Immense, unfathomed, unconfined;
> To praise the Lamb who died for all,
> The general Saviour of mankind.
>
> The world He suffered to redeem;
> For all He hath atonement made;
> For those that will not come to Him
> The ransom of His life was paid.

What are we now to make of such language? As a young local preacher I was exhorted to preach to people with more awareness of the realities of life than I had dreamed of in the fourfold message that 'all men need to be saved, all men can be saved, all men can be saved to the uttermost, and all men can know that they are saved' – a sexist summary of the doctrines of justification, sanctification and assurance which the Wesleys proclaimed. It is questionable, though, whether these notions made much impact in the 1950s. While it may have provided some who had been brought up in a community using such language with a way of understanding their experience, most people had not been conditioned to interpret life in these terms and were probably left bemused and unimpressed by the language. A generation later it is even clearer that such language belongs to the members of a declining cognitive minority. And even among them its primary role may be the emotional one of providing slogans and rallying cries for the faithful remnant rather than that of describing the final character of their reality.

Human needs and divine salvation

Some critics have used the point that talk about salvation is significant only if it relates to what human beings currently consider to be their fundamental needs and the divine remedy for them to argue that both the idea of God and the notion of divine salvation are human inventions. Theists are thus accused of comforting themselves with what is an unrecognized illusion of a solution for what they consider to be their basic wants (which also may be illusory). David Hume speculating on the origin of religion and Sigmund Freud considering its psychological character suggest, for example, that the notion of God, as the projection of a 'father-figure' offering protection against threats of hostile forces, is a notion for which there is no known corresponding reality.[18] According to this view texts like 'If God is on our side, who is against us?'[19] are expressions of what people wish to be the case rather than descriptions of a reality which justifies their confidence.

It should not be overlooked, however, that the results of adopting such a hermeneutics of suspicion are not always justified. The fact that a remedy for some complaint is desired does not mean that one does not actually exist. My expectation that aspirin will relieve my headache is not to be rejected as an illusion simply because I hope that it will have this effect. Similarly, at the fundamental level of human being, hopes expressed in notions of divine salvation may be warranted because the character of the ultimate reality corresponds to what satisfies those hopes. The fact that we hope for there to be a saving God does not entail that there is no such being.

On the other hand, while theists may be justified in believing that a saving God exists, they may nevertheless misapprehend the nature of God and of divine saving activity because they fashion it on the basis of their own perception of their needs. The result may be compared to the situation in which a person thinks that she wants a new job in order to fulfil her potential, whereas those who know her better than she knows herself recognize that what she really needs is to come to terms with herself. Her problem is not the job but herself! Because of the possibility of such misapprehensions Karl Barth argues that human analyses of human needs should not provide the basis for notion of the character of divine salvation. Otherwise the result will be the construction of an idol. The knowledge of the need of salvation as well as of its divine remedy must be derived from what God reveals to be that remedy. The existential question of human being is thus to be grasped through extrapolation from the divine answer to it.[20] On reflection, however, this response to the problem of human misunderstanding turns out to be fundamentally unsatisfactory, since the way in which we make sense of whatever may have been revealed as a divine remedy will itself be moulded to a large extent by what we already consider to be our need of it. It is illusory to consider that reference to supposed revelation can free theological understanding from such human conditioning.

It is in order to prevent theology from becoming either an illusory 'apologetic theology' which derives its answers from the questions posed by human existence, or a Procrustean 'kerygmatic theology' which trims the questions to correspond to the answers supposedly given by divine revelation in the Gospel, that Tillich advocates 'the method of correlation'.[21] According to this method significant and credible theological understanding is established by making the fundamental questions of human being, as perceived through 'an analysis of the human situation', interact with the answers provided by 'the Christian message'.[22] Although Tillich himself views revelation as 'the ultimate source of the contents of the Christian faith',[23] the method of correlation itself does not depend on the adoption of such a position. What happens, though, when we attempt to perceive the meaning and significance of the notion of salvation in this way, namely, by seeking to take account of the mutual interdependence of 'existential questions and theological answers'?[24]

The Poet of Salvation 27

The unsatisfactoriness of some traditional views of salvation

Consideration of traditional perceptions of salvation indicates that in many cases at least they are no longer significant or credible. It may be pointed out, for example, that some views of salvation refer to transactions whose basic structures are unacceptable as ways of considering the relationship between the divine and the human. It is not compatible with a proper understanding of the holiness, ultimacy and perfection of the divine to imply, for example, that God is as touchy about his honour as an insecure feudal lord, or as entangled in the rules of a sacrificial system as a petty bureaucrat in the red-tape of administrative regulations, or as compelled to pay a ransom to a usurper as a politician seeking the release of hostages.

Such objections, however, may be countered by holding that they largely depend upon a fundamental mistake, namely, that of treating models as literal descriptions. Although various doctrines of the atonement have been developed upon the basis of this mistake, it is arguable that the primary use of such notions as those of the satisfaction of honour, sacrifice, and ransom is not to describe either the state from which we need to be saved or the means by which salvation is divinely effected. It is to express the quality of the resulting state. Being 'saved', that is, is being said to be somewhat analogous to the feeling one would have on being reconciled after estrangement, on having fulfilled the correct procedures for a relationship with the holy, and on being freed from captivity. Since, therefore, the significance of the models is to indicate what salvation is like, not how it is achieved, it is to perpetuate a misunderstanding of the point of these models to object that they ascribe to the divine-human relationship initial states and procedures which are grossly inappropriate for thought about the divine.

A more important objection to traditional descriptions of salvation, however, is that they refer to states of affairs which are no longer considered to be matters of fundamental concern whose solution is credibly ascribable to divine activity. In some cases this is because what is implied to be the character of the state of salvation is in fact contrary to what is now understood to be the creative purposes of God for human being. Dietrich Bonhoeffer expresses the basic point of this criticism in a letter of 8 June 1944 in which he condemns 'the attack by Christian apologetic on the adulthood of the world' as pointless, ignoble, and unchristian. It is 'pointless' because it pretends that people have problems which they do not have and treats adults as if they were dependent and adolescent; it is 'ignoble' because it tries to 'exploit' people's weaknesses for purposes alien to their proper being; it is 'unchristian' because it identifies the will of Christ with that earlier stage in human religiousness when faith was considered to be a matter of obedience to law.[25]

Bonhoeffer's remarks about certain forms of apologetics apply also to various views of salvation. They are to be rejected because they imply an understanding of God's will which is the antithesis of the recognition that God is the creator of persons, not the manipulator of puppets. To see the goal of salvation, for instance, as a state of abasement in which the saved rejoice that now there is 'None of self, and all of Thee'[26] is to contradict the creative love and purposes of God. It is to treat the aim of salvation – the making 'whole' of the self – as a matter of the effective destruction of those who are supposedly 'saved'. Although some people may so despair of their own being that they consider what amounts to personal suicide to be the true end of faith, this is no justification for holding that God is similarly depressed about their possibilities.

Other traditional notions of divine salvation are to be rejected on the grounds that they apparently ascribe to or expect from God the realization of states of affairs that are no longer credibly considered to be matters of divine agency. While, for instance, the Jews may have seen their deliverance from Egypt as due to divine activity, today it seems more reasonable to expect liberation from unjust regimes to come through political activity. The likely outcome of telling the oppressed only to pray, hope, and wait for God to free them is to condemn them to continued servitude. If the divine concern for justice is to be implemented in this world, it will be by human activity. As Gustavo Gutiérrez puts it, 'The Gospel does not provide a utopia for us; this is a human work.' It will involve 'active, effective participation in the struggle' of the exploited against the oppressors.[27]

Even less theistically acceptable are notions of salvation which imply that cosmic forces compel God to pay for the release of human beings. Ideas of such a transaction not only contradict the ultimate status of God; they also assert an ontology which is no longer credible. Underlying other notions of salvation is the assumption that God may be expected to provide protection against various physical threats to human well-being. Unfortunately such expectations not only are what Freud classes as illusions (the product of our wishes) but also to a large extent at least, seem to be delusions. Whatever may be the positive meaning of references to divine power and of such phrases as 'Give us today our daily bread', believing in the reality of the former and praying the latter do not prevent people from being tortured and from dying of starvation. It is blasphemous, furthermore, to suggest that the fates of those who do so suffer and of those who do not are due to the divine will. Such a view makes God a monster. Manifest partiality is not coherently ascribable to the object of unqualified adoration. So far as want, disease and warfare are concerned, people must accept the responsiblity for finding and, where necessary, forcefully implementing the remedies.

If the locus of divine salvation is shifted from the cosmic, the natural and the historical to the individual's personal relationship with God, problems still arise. It is no longer convincing, for example, to regard salvation in terms of paying off debts incurred through breaking divine commandments. It was not always so. John Pearson, for example, wrote in the seventeenth century that God, having 'the Sovereign power and absolute dominion over all men', has laid down a Law which is to be 'a perpetual and universal rule of humane actions'. Those who violate it are 'thereby obliged in all equity to suffer the punishment due to that obliquity' as debtors 'to the vindictive Justice of God'.[28] The human need of salvation is thus understood to arise from the fact that compensation is due to God from those who break the rules which have been divinely imposed on human beings.

Such a view is no longer acceptable. It fails to grasp the proper nature of moral goodness – and of sin as the failure to actualize it – and it presents an unwarrantable notion of the divine. To think of God as open to, let alone as requiring, compensation when someone infringes the divine rights is to turn the sacred into a petty and grasping litigant. Similarly, to consider that God regards the divine honour to be impugned by sin and angrily demands satisfaction demeans the worshipfulness of God.

Another view of salvation sees it as the receipt of divine forgiveness for wrongs done primarily to other human beings. David, for example, may harm John but, feeling guilty and repentant, he seeks and receives forgiveness from God. It is not justifiable to criticize such a view simply on the grounds that it presents a way of evading the unpleasant business of seeking to do justice to and to accept forgiveness from those who have been injured: genuine repentance involves this. Notions of guilt and forgiveness, furthermore, are complex issues which cannot be explored in detail here. Nevertheless it is arguable that that reference to God as the source of forgiveness in some cases at least is inappropriate. It is the individuals who have been directly harmed and the community which has been disrupted who must pardon if social harmony is to be restored and guilt released. Where this is no longer fully possible (as when those who have been harmed have died), the important human response to the torments of those feeling guilty, whether justified or not, is to assure the repentant by word and deed that they are accepted – and to provide counselling to help them to accept themselves. At best, therefore, reference to the divine is a way of expressing the community's forgiveness; at worst it reflects a failure to perceive the significance of sin for human lives.

While, though, evil is to be taken seriously in terms of human affairs, it is important to avoid the inhibiting scrupulosity which comes from regarding God as a 'ruthless moralist' who notes every tiny speck of evil and makes an issue of it. In this respect Alfred North Whitehead shows more insight into the divine than many moralizing evangelists when he remarks that God, operating 'in quietness ... by love,' is 'a little oblivious as to morals'.[29] The positive freedom of love is more in harmony with the divine creativity than the negative restrictiveness of fear of offending.

The answer to despair about human affairs, then, if it lies anywhere, may be held to lie in human thought, will and action. Enormous as the task may be, salvation will not be solved by people looking to God 'to do something' but by human actualization of the divine will. Physical wants will be met, if at all, by radical measures to control the population explosion and to establish a fair distribution of the resources available. Diseases will be eradicated, if at all, through the insights gained by medical research. The threat of armed conflicts will disappear, if ever, as political systems are made responsible to those who belong to them and political leaders learn how to become mature enough to work through disputes in ways that are sensible of the common good. Moral guilt will be answered by acceptance and counselling in the human community.

While, however, threats to physical and moral well-being may thus be diminished, the finitude of human being can never be eradicated. At the individual level the average length of life may be extended but death will eventually occur. As for the human species itself, there are no good reasons for expecting that it will persist for ever and some excellent reasons to expect that, even if it does not destroy itself, eventually a natural development (such as a mutation in a virus) will occur which will defeat innate and scientific powers to contain its fatal spread. These comments may seem too obvious to be worth making, but it is manifest that while for some naïve believers divine salvation applies to every aspect of human existence, for many more it still provides a basic confidence that 'in the end' God may be trusted to prevent 'the worst' from happening.

The human situation and the need of divine salvation

What in this situation is to be made of the notion of divine salvation? Is it a symbol that has died and no longer has authentic significance for current living? Does it express an illusion that has no substance? Either conclusion might leave theism as an interesting intellectual issue — like that of the discovery of the smallest prime number which has more than ten thousand digits — but it would also imply that theism is no longer to be regarded as significant for human being. All the talk about divine salvation that has comforted and excited believers over the centuries is exposed as a placebo which is materially inert. For some the coming of age of humanity brings the realization that belief about God's saving activity must go with other childish comforts like teddy bears.

This is how Sigmund Freud presents the human situation when he holds that we should stop hiding the truth in symbolic disguises. What he says about children applies all the more to supposed adults; they must be given 'a knowledge of the true state of affairs'.[30] Regarding psycho-analysis as one of the sciences, he thus affirms at the end of *The Future of an Illusion*: 'No, our science is no illusion. But an illusion it would be to suppose that what science cannot give us we can get elsewhere.'[31] In the heady atmosphere of the late sixties Sir Edmund Leach similarly affirmed in his Reith Lectures that it is 'about time' that humanity recognized its 'divinity' in that science now makes possible 'total mastery over our environment and over our destiny'. This is something to rejoice over rather than fear. We must realize that we cannot any longer trust 'God, or Nature, or Chance, or Evolution, or the Course of History'. We have the power and responsibility to 'take charge of our own fate'.[32] A century after his birth was announced, it seems that Nietzsche's 'overman' has finally arrived and is ready to take over. There is no God and the idea of God is redundant. *A fortiori* the notion of divine salvation refers to what has neither reality nor significance.

Such analyses of the human situation may, though, be judged to reveal either the shallowness of some current forms of human self-understanding or despair about the possibility of discerning any deeper significance for human life than that which is warranted by the kind of activity envisaged by Nietzsche, Freud, and Leach. In response to this situation it may be argued that the notion of divine salvation does have significance. This is because it meets fundamental threats to human being for which human activity can provide no answer.

When properly understood this argument is not open to rejection on the grounds that it merely seeks to identify other gaps for which 'God' can be used as an alleged plug until human beings can find 'real' ways of coping with them. It is not claiming, that is, that while God is no longer credible as a solution to the problems of political and social and economic liberation or to physical and social ills or to fear of things that go bump in the night or whatever, nevertheless there still are certain identifiable contingent problems of human existence for which it is possible to posit divine salvation as a solution. What this argument does maintain is that whatever currently happens to be the contingent state of human being, with all its actual and potential insights and powers, there are certain fundamental threats to the significance of human being as such which can only be solved, if they are solvable at all, by reference to what transcends the empirical and the contingent mode of being in the world. It is at this point that the notion of salvation finds a legitimate claim to significance.

The problem of the significance of human being

The fundamental question about human being threatens its significance as such. Is it really possible to justify claims about the significance of human being – and this means of the lives of each of the persons constituting human being – in face of the cosmic, historical and individual challenges posed by its situation?

On a cosmic scale, it seems that human being is an extremely brief item in the story of a planet with a finite existence. Even if the self-destructiveness of some forms of human activity or a chance alteration in the natural order or the exhaustion of the resources needed to sustain life do not eradicate human being sooner, its planetry home will eventually be swallowed up by its sun in the process of cosmic evolution. So far as human life in the envisageable future is concerned, the fear of being cindered realistically applies to the chances of mental derangement in the commanders of nuclear weaponry. In time, however, the physical remains of all human beings, wherever they are dispersed, will be consumed in the inescapable crematorium of an expanding sun. Furthermore, in terms of the physical dimensions of the cosmos, neither the presence of human life on this planet nor the temporary existence of the planet itself appears to be more than one of the myriad things that happen for a time to be and then cease to be, leaving what eventually becomes practically undetectable traces. As Whitehead puts it, the physical universe, as it slowly decays, is being transmuted into a new order in which the world 'as we at present know it, will be represented by a ripple barely to be distinguished from non-entity'.[33]

To move from the physical and cosmic to the historical and human does not make it any easier to affirm the significance of human being with any warrantable confidence. Its history is the story of the successive forgettings of what once was actual. Undecipherable grave-stones and the mouldering rows of books in the stores of great libraries are humbling symbols of the oblivion which results from becoming past. While these objects do represent some kind of memorial to a few persons long dead, their very survival as memorials to the very few brings home the way in which for most people death leads to practically total extinction within a very few generations.

Admittedly each present emerges out of the past and is predominantly formed by its immediate predecessor. Occasionally, furthermore, some action in the distant past erupts unexpectedly in the present – as when a person rooting for potatoes comes across a pot of Anglo-Saxon coins, or a long neglected book is discovered to have important insights. For the most part, however, those who constituted presents now long past have to be totally ignored because they are gone without a trace:

> There are others who are unremembered;
> they are dead, and it is as though they had never existed,

as though they had never been born
or left children to succeed them.³⁴

It is indisputable, for example, that I exist because of the action of a paternal grandfather ten generations back – and that, barring cases of overlap, 1023 other people at that stage in my genealogical ancestry acted in ways that have resulted in my genetic structure. They existed but who they were and what was the quality of their lives is now almost certainly beyond discovery. If, together with countless others, I contribute to being their memorial, it is an unacknowledged memorial to the utterly unknown.

Viewed in this way the work of historians does not establish the significance of human being in general but rather the opposite. By prolonging the memory of a few supposedly important persons and events, it shows positively how little is the ripple that they leave and negatively how the vast majority have utterly disappeared. We may have the pyramids and the Great Wall of China and Stonehenge but of the vast numbers of individuals who built them and of those in the communities that supported them we know next to nothing. Eventually even major achievements like empires and civilizations have their day and cease to be as the records of them dwindle away.

As well as cosmic and historical threats to the significance of human being, there is also the threat to the significance of each individual which is posed by the accidental nature of their existing at all, the continual perishing of their past, and the inescapable, if unpredictable, finitude of their future. The particular configuration of a person's inherited genetic constitution, with all its implications for the probable course of his or her physical development, is the product of a fantastic number of accidents in the meeting and mating of his or her ancestors. There is no necessity for the actuality of any particular person. Furthermore, the reality of the self that I was in the past, say thirty years ago, has now gone. Each moment the actual self I am for that particular moment is constituted by massively inheriting the character of the self that was I the previous moment although, since to be a self is to be a living (i.e. a responding) being, with room for slight modifications to that datum. That momentary actuality, however, only comes to be through the perishing of its predecessor. To be an actual I is thus to be a point of actuality whose identity as a persisting me is an abstraction refering to a series of massively overlapping inheritances as well as to modifications to them in a series of successive moments of actual being.

As evangelical faith comfortingly points out, what an individual person is may, by conversion, come to be radically altered. But while I may now be relieved that I am not in various respects the self I was thirty years ago and am embarrassed when people only remember me as such, it is more disturbing to consider what I will be in thirty, forty, perhaps even fifty years from now. So long as I remain alive, there will be changes, maybe even fundamental changes as I reflect on what I am conscious of having inherited from my past, respond to my environment and make judgments about my future so far as it is in my power to influence it. As I now try to peer into the future, though, what the changes involved in living will effect is unclear in the near future and quite unpredictable in the distant. I may continue to grow as a person and die suddenly while still enjoying making creative contributions to life. Or in time I may slip into senility, become a parasitic dependent, consuming goods but neither contributing to the enrichment of the life of others nor able to enjoy life for myself. What is certain, though, is that, at least so far as life as this physical self is concerned, the process will have an end. Eventually one in the series of my moments of actuality will have no successor.

Doctrines of God which deny the significance of human being

In view of these threats, is it possible to maintain the significance of human being in general and of the life of individual human beings in particular? There is clearly no credible answer to be found by asserting the importance of each individual's contribution to fashioning the human future. The story of that future is unlikely to be relevantly different from the story of forgetting and perishing that characterizes the human past.

Neither is there any answer to be found by reference to God if the divine perfection is held to entail that God is to be described in such terms as *actus purus* (i.e. pure actuality, without any potentiality), unchanging and impassible in every respect, being wholly in a timeless present without past or future, and knowing only in the sense of contemplating the eternal and utterly simple essence of the divine being. Any one of these characteristics, if meant seriously as a description of the divine rather than as a way of paying misguided 'metaphysical compliments', entails the total devaluation of human being. If the deity be so describable, it follows either that human being is to be classed as an accidental series of incidents in the unwitting attraction exerted by the divine perfection on the created order, or that all human actions are necessarily timelessly present to the divine. In the former case the events of history and hence the lives of the individuals composing it must be held to make no impression whatsoever upon the divine and so cannot be held to have any ultimate significance. If this be so, the most reasonable response of human beings, as for those who felt the hopelessness of their situation in Albert Camus' *The Plague*, may well be to devote themselves to the pointlessly boring life-style of 'cultivating habits'.[35] In the latter case the contingent freedom of human being, and so the supposed worth of human actions, must be judged to be a grand delusion.

The classical understanding of God as 'the One and the Plenum and the Unmoved and the Sated and the Permanent',[36] as Nietzsche vividly caricatures it, may be modified, however, to make it possible to conceive of the divine as creatively active in a temporally ordered cosmos. If, though, this conception leads to God being viewed as an all-controlling creator whose agential power determines all that successively comes to be, then again human being must be considered to be without value. It may seem comforting to hold, with Calvin, that God may choose to bend 'the wills of men, that whatever the freedom of choice may be, it is still subject to the disposal of God'[37] or to sing, with slaves, 'He's got the whole world in his hands.' But if the notions of divine will and power are understood in such a way as to imply that the divine finally fixes everything, human beings – and the rest of creation – are but marionettes in the hands of a cosmic puppeteer. Whatever value may accrue to their actions is to be ascribed to the puppeteer who pulls the strings, not to the marionettes who dance accordingly. The childish wish for a Protector who is in total control, when taken to extremes, thus turns out to imply a denial of the significance of personal being.

Even if the notion of divine power is further qualified to allow some freedom of initiative to human beings but salvation is still held to be a form of divine intervention into human affairs, then human being remains radically disvalued. In the end the fate of each individual is a product of divine decision, and the worth of human being as 'saved' is dependent upon the divine will.

Human lives in that case have no ultimate significance. God's necessary action takes away their value just as the actions of the owner of a business, however fine the underlying intentions, devalues the decisions of its management if at all points the owner is supervising what is being done and at crucial points intervenes to exercise proprietal rights.

In view of the cosmic, historical and individual threats to the significance of human being and to the impossibility of 'saving' that significance by reference either to its intrinsic character or to traditional understandings of the divine, it may seem that the symbol of salvation must die for us. At best it may be claimed to express a deep longing that reality as a whole – and human life in particular – is not a pointless performance, a tedious struggle to avoid nothing that must end in nothing. At worst it may be condemned as part of a silly game by which people try to hide from the truth.

The saving activity of God

Such a conclusion, though, goes against what some consider with good reason to be the fundamental conviction of human being. Is there, then, any way in which the notion of salvation may yet be interpreted so that it 'lives' as a symbol which provokes an existential response? In other words, is there any way by which the notion can be theistically understood so that it warrants what Schubert Ogden identifies as the fundamental human conviction that 'our existence as such is finally meaningful' and absolutely secure.[38] In order to do this it must point to what he describes as 'the objective ground in reality itself of our ineradicable confidence in the final worth of our existence'.[39] In the final part of this paper, then, I want briefly to consider how a sentence by Whitehead on the saving relationship between the divine and the human suggests a significant and credible way of understanding salvation.

In the final chapter of *Process and Reality* Whitehead outlines his understanding of the relationship between God and the world. In the course of his remarks he states that God

> does not create the world, he saves it: or more accurately, he is the poet of the world, with tender patience leading it by his vision of truth, beauty, and goodness.[40]

In this evocative sentence there are two basic insights into the saving activity of God. Both are necessary for a significant and credible understanding of the ultimate salvation of human being and both indicate that such salvation is only conceivable in terms of God as the one to whom all being is finally referred. We shall consider each idea in turn.

Salvation as preservation

The first idea depends upon recognition of the temporal unendingness ('everlastingness') and unrestricted passibility of the divine. Whereas most theologians in the Christian tradition have maintained (perhaps 'assumed' would be more appropriate, for it is a view that it is taken for granted more often than it is defended) that divine perfection entails complete determinateness, timelessness and impassibility, Whitehead's concept of the 'consequent nature' of God includes the understanding that the process of reality involves free agency, that the temporal distinction between the potential and the actual is real for God, and that everything which occurs, without exception, becomes as such part of the divine experience. The genuine contingency of future events (which means that their actuality cannot be known prior to the decision which defines their occurrence) and the absolute aspect of the divine awareness (which means that God neither is ignorant of nor forgets what is knowable in any respect) thus combine to entail the final denial of the ultimacy of the perishing which threatens the significance of the reality of human being. Whitehead sums up this point when he states that God 'saves the world as it passes into the immediacy of his own life'.[41] The salvation of human being is thus to be seen in part as a matter of the preservation of its momentary occasions of actuality through their incorporation into the divine.

In this respect the divine may be said to 'save' human being in a way that is somewhat analogous to what is meant when we talk of 'saving' mementos, artistic productions, and souvenirs. In the human case, however, attempts to preserve creative achievements of the past and to provide evocations of the experiences of past moments are at best temporary and partial. Although some artefacts are remarkably robust, practically all are liable to eventual decay. In any case the perception of their value alters with changes in culture and may be liable to decline with familiarity. The wonder of the first time that they were seen is beyond human recall. More significantly, it is only a minute proportion of anyone's life, however much they stuff the loft with memorabilia, which has any tangible record. The experiences which constitute the actuality of a self perish immediately on being incorporated into the next moment of actuality and for the most part are very soon forgotten so far as conscious being is concerned. Even those that are remembered are only recalled more or less vaguely and approximately. It is difficult to be clear about how one felt at a particular moment a week ago – for even if it was somewhat memorable, its evocation links it with the experiences of its surrounding moments and is mediated through subsequent experiences then unknown; it is impossible to recollect at all how one felt in nearly all of the moments of one's being twenty years ago – that particular self has perished beyond recall even if there are diaries and letters to bring some of its occasions to mind in a general way.[42]

God, in contrast, loses none of the past. In the clarity of the divine mind, all actual occasions of experience – and so the individuality of each self through all the moments of its being – are preserved in the sharpness of the immediacy of their actual occurrence. Thus, while Whitehead properly warns against trying to know too much about how the world is transformed in God's experience of it, he declares that 'what does haunt our imagination is that the immediate facts of present action pass into permanent significance for the Universe'. It is fundamentally wrong to class every activity as 'merely a passing whiff of insignificance'.[43]

Charles Hartshorne puts forward a similar understanding. He holds that 'the permanence of life's values' goes beyond what we may contribute to 'our human posterity'. Our 'abiding value' lies in what 'we give to posterity' by being incorporated into the life of 'the Holy One' who 'survives all deaths and for whose life all life is precious'.[44] In another paper he sums up his position thus:

> ... our adequate immortality can only be God's omniscience of us. He to whom all hearts are open remains evermore open to any heart that ever has been apparent to Him. What we once were to Him, less than that we never can be, for otherwise He Himself as knowing us would lose something of His own reality; and this loss of something that has been must be final, since, if deity cannot furnish the abiding reality of events, there is ... no other way, intelligible to us as least, in which it can be furnished. Now the meaning of omniscience is

a knowledge which is coextensive with reality, which can be taken as a measure of reality,[45]

As Hartshorne makes clear, this understanding of the future does not entail, though (it may be added) it does not necessarily exclude, our endless persistence as experiencing and responding subjects. What it does entail is that nothing that each actual self ever achieves is ever lost. As that momentary actuality perishes, the subjective immediacy of the experience is lost but its objective quality has become a contribution to and is for ever embraced by the divine.

What, in that case, is the point of human being? On the one hand it is to enjoy moments of value in the present and seek to create further moments of value in the future. Each self and each community of selves has thus to balance the joys of present satisfaction against the richer joys that may be attained at the cost of present discomfort – and the satisfactions that are presently to be experienced in recognizing what those discomforts may render possible. The upshot, though, is not to be a carefully calculated cost/benefit analysis so much as a recognition that the being of each moment has value and is to be treasured as such.

On the other hand the point of human being is to contribute to the richness of the divine being. Our experiences of good are also experiences of good for God, and it is in God that they are fully appreciated and preserved. All this, according to Hartshorne, follows from recognizing that 'we are to love God unreservedly'.[46] The 'first commandment' in fact sums up all the rest for if we seek the highest satisfactions for the divine experience we will properly seek the highest satisfactions that are attainable for all persons, including ourselves. The incorporation of our experiences into the divine, furthermore, is to be regarded as a warm personal appreciation of them, not an unconcerned absorption of further data in the unconscious and unvaluing register of some cosmic computer. Teilhard de Chardin expresses the resulting understanding of the divine-human relationship when he states that 'God pushes to its furthest possible limit the differentiation among the creatures He concentrates within Himself' so that 'at the peak of their adherence to Him, the elect also discover in Him the consummation of their individual fulfilment'.[47] The notion that the proper end for human activity is to enrich the divine experience may be criticized on two counts. It may be urged, first, that what any individual can contribute to the divine is such a minute fraction of that experience that it is absurd to consider that it may have identified worth for God. This, though, is part of the absurdity of Christian theism. As Kierkegaard points out, 'Christianity teaches that this particular individual, and so every individual ... exists *before* God ... on the most intimate terms.'[48] Furthermore, while it may at first seem incredible to hold that God shares in our joys – and our sorrows – stories of the widow's mite and the lost coin are reminders that magnitude and worth are not directly, if at all commensurable. It may be our failure to grasp the greatness of the divine that makes the notion of divine appreciation of literally every moment of every thing incredible.

The second criticism argues that the view that the end of human being is to contribute to the divine makes God unworshipful. In a typically perceptive and vigorous comment, the Revd C. V. Corner wrote in a letter that this view presents

> a sort of capitalist God who by our efforts accumulates more and more capital: grows richer and richer from the work of his 'hands' and then just disposes of them. There appears to me to be an 'almightly' self-centredness here – a God whose ultimate interest is to amass benefits for himself ... and eventually, presumably, the world (universe?) ends with a bang or a whimper, and the God who has 'grown fat' on the profits of the ages is all that remains. Such a God does not evoke my worship ... [49]

While I agree with the principles behind this criticism, I am not convinced that it properly applies to what Hartshorne is putting forward about the divine-human relationship. I suspect that it fails to deal adequately with the difference between the human and the divine and treats God as a magnified case of the human in a way that is inappropriate. It may be necessary, for example, to recognize that the divine is enriched by our values and is everlasting while we are temporally finite – that, in other words, this is how things ultimately are. I do not see, though, that this justifies the accusation of 'self-centredness' in the divine in enjoying (and promoting) the joys experienced by others any more than it warrants the accusation that I am being selfish in rejoicing in the happiness of a friend when she has become pregnant. I am not taking that achievement from her and making it my own: I am happy because she is happy in finding this fulfilment of her being.

Furthermore, although this may be because I am blinded by a rather different political standpoint, I do not consider that what Hartshorne is advocating is a God who deifies the ugly face of capitalism. For one thing, it is arguable that human beings only find ultimate satisfaction in their individual achievements if they believe that they are contributions to a greater whole. According to Teilhard de Chardin, for example, self-examination reveals that 'no one lifts his little finger to do the smallest task unless moved, however obscurely, by the conviction that he is contributing infinitesimally (at least indirectly) to the building of something definitive – that is to say, to Your work, my God'. Although he admits that this may sound 'strange or exaggerated', he maintains that 'it is a fundamental law of their action'.[50]

In any case, whether or not Teilhard de Chardin is correct in holding that the satisfaction of human being requires the sense of being labourers in such cosmic construction, what Hartshorne presents is a fundamental alternative to the self-centredness of human being which has produced in much traditional religious thought the implication that 'heaven' is a state where each 'I' finds endless pleasures for itself. From this point of view Hartshorne's notion of objective immortality may be interpreted as applying to the totality of human being the insight that persons find satisfying joy for themselves in giving to and sharing experiences with others in genuine love without self-seeking thoughts of return. In the case of the divine-human relationship, however, what the self gives to God is what the self itself enjoys. At this point selfish and unselfish forms of love are sublimated in a giving of joy to the other which is the same as the joy which the self itself experiences.

The divine, therefore, should not be deemed selfish because God shares and preserves what we feel and lose. We are not deprived of anything appropriate to our finite nature by the divine retention of what inevitably perishes for us. Nor does the divine enjoyment of our experiences in any way diminish our enjoyment of them: on the contrary our awareness of the former, if anything, enhances the latter. Whitehead thus describes God as not only extending our purposes 'beyond values for ourselves to values for others' but also as providing that 'the attainment of such a value for others transforms itself into value for ourselves'.[51] In that case, as Hartshorne puts it:

All of one's life can be a 'reasonable, holy, and living sacrifice' to deity, a sacrifice whose value depends on the quality of the life, and this depends on the depth of the devotion to all good things, to all life's possibilities ... as belonging to God's creatures and thus to God.

The proper response to God is the satisfaction of one's present being in 'generous openness to others' and 'to the beauty of the world'.[52]

Salvation as creative response

In one respect, then, the salvation of human being is the knowledge that none of the experiences of our successive nows ever perish in God. It is the peace of knowing that present joys are for ever joys in God. There is, however, a second aspect to what Whitehead says about salvation. God not only 'saves' the world by experiencing it: God also judges it with 'the judgment of a tenderness which loses nothing that can be saved' and 'of a wisdom which uses what in the temporal world is mere wreckage'.[53] As the one who saves, that is, God promotes the actualization of good as well preserves the good which is actualized. The divine 'judgment' is to be understood, not as a destructive rejection of what is bad, but as an inspiring perception of the possibilities for using what has been, good and bad, for future creative satisfactions.

This mode of divine salvation is partly effected through the exercise of the creative freedom which essentially belongs to human being. Within limits appropriate to their nature, human beings are able to respond to what they remember of the past, including the immediate past of their awareness of their environment, and to what they anticipate to be the possibilities of the future. It is because of this 'memory and anticipation' that the process of human reality[54] is not a matter of 'complete conformity to the average influence of the immediate past'.[55] Having freedom to respond, human beings are able to use their situation, whatever it may be, creatively to give material expression to the formal 'ideals of perfection, moral and aesthetic' in the divine nature.[56] Unlike the frightened schoolchild trying to excuse the school report by asking whether the results are due to heredity or to environment, we have freedom to determine our responses to both. The fundamental structure of creation makes available to each the salvation of using what may seem at first to be 'mere wreckage' – a dismal inheritance and an unpromising environment – as materials for conceiving and constructing what is novel and good. This, in some respects, is what is meant by repentance ('re-thinking') and what is implied in the recognition of human freedom and responsibility which Wesley affirms as Arminianism against the Calvinistic determinism that others mistakenly consider to be a proper recognition of the ultimacy of the divine. Today a similar affirmation has to be made against the neo-Calvinism of popular (but mistaken) notions of scientific determinism.

The role of the divine in this aspect of salvation, though, is not simply that of an utterly general creativity which ensures the freedom of human beings to respond creatively to their situation. When Whitehead concludes *Religion in the Making* by describing God as 'that element in life in virtue of which judgment stretches beyond facts of existence to values of existence', he goes on to speak of God both as the source of 'all forms of order' and as confronting 'what is actual ... with what is possible for it'.[57] The latter phrases indicate that God's saving role is in some way to be understood as an activity.

While it is arguable that the divine is not credibly to be regarded as presenting a specific optimum goal to each person at each moment of the process of reality[58] neither is it theistically satisfactory to regard God as a remote originator and sustainer who merely observes and enjoys whatever happens. God's respect for the freedom of human beings does not entail a benign distancing that refuses all active involvement in guiding the processes of reality. Thus in *Process and Reality* Whitehead speaks of God's influence on events as lying 'in the patient operation of the overpowering rationality of his conceptual harmonization'.[59] The use of 'overpowering', though, should not be interpreted as implying that God overwhelms people so that they have no option but to conform to the divine will for what is best. Such a reading would be contrary to Whitehead's explicit denial that God acts as such a force – and would also be contrary both to human experience and to the creative purposes of God. The 'overpowering' must be taken as referring to the quality of the divine understanding of the most fruitful actions possible, not to its effect on human beings. The influence of the divine is exerted as a lure or a persuasion, not as a coercion. At the same time, it must be insisted, it is a real influence on what happens.

Whitehead perhaps gets closest to expressing this aspect of divine salvation as attracting as well as enabling grace when he describes God as 'the poet of the world, with tender patience leading it by his vision of truth, beauty, and goodness'. The imagery suggests that just as the poet takes humdrum words of daily conversation and uses them to evoke excitingly novel insights into reality, so the divine caringly employs the present to enrich the future. It is interesting to note, though, that when Whitehead later reflected on this phrase, he crossed out the 'leading' in his copy and wrote both 'persuading' and 'swaying'.[60] The image, that is, is not of a poet, however sympathetic, who takes hold of the data of the 'language' which our experiences provide and manipulates them according to the poet's own creatively novel insights. Nor does Whitehead's understanding envisage the poet as having in mind a material state of affairs which characterizes the final end of all processes and so of all reality.

What Whitehead is suggesting, rather, is an image of the inspiring spirit of God quietly, patiently but persistently stirring human beings to discontent with their present state, whatever it may be and however fulfilling it may have been on its initial attainment. This is done by arousing in them an awareness of the divine vision of truth, beauty and goodness as formal goals. These goals restlessly activate the creative being of the divine and are communicated to human beings so far as they open themselves (whether consciously or not) to the divine. In this way God is not only held to enjoy the actualized values in this world but also, as the transforming spirit, to exert influence for the creative production of more joy. It is an aesthetic interpretation of the reality of God which gives significance to the life of each person. God 'saves' as the one who both preserves all that has been and draws out of it new riches.

Whitehead's model of a poet, however, has some limitations as a way of envisaging this aspect of divine salvation and may profitably be augmented by others. Whereas, for example, poets are generally thought of as struggling to control the materials of words and structures to express the contents of particular modes of their awarenesses, novelists typically report that their characters develop their own personalities as they write about them. In this respect the divine activity as creator and as saviour – and the two terms refer to what is essentially one divine activity – may be compared to the way in which a novelist fosters and appreciates the growth of characters in a novel as they respond to their situations. Since, though, all the characters in a novel, however bizarre or surprising they may seem to the novelist, are the products of the novelist's imaginative projections, more appropriate for the divine-human relationship are models taken from human relationships where the persons involved have some – if limited – autonomy.

The saving activity of God may, for instance, be compared to the roles of play-group leaders and of theatrical producers, especially in the case of a certain kind of drama. The former, when imaginative as well as courageous, seek to stimulate the children in their own explorations of their potentials. They do not control their activity but, having provided an environment and resources, seek to excite the children into being creative. Enjoying what is then produced, they provoke the children to see how they can turn to further good use what has been produced and to try out other activities when they seem, for the time being, to have exhausted their possibilities of novel enrichment in what they have been doing. The activity of the producer of an improvised drama may similarly cast some light on the nature of divine salvation as creative response. Here too the role of the producer is not to attempt to determine the actors' every speech and movement but to encourage them to explore the characters which they have been given to portray. There may be no script and no known ending to the play: the producer's role is to stimulate the actors, given the outlines of a situation, to respond to it and to find enrichment through their use of what is so given.

The poet, the novelist, the play-group leader and the producer are models for understanding the nature of divine salvation. Each of them, as a model, is not to be pressed too far. They bring out, though, in a way that models of sacrifice, satisfaction, cosmic victory, ransom and expiation seem now unable to do (even if they ever were so able), how God's saving activity is for the flourishing, significance and fulfilment of human being. It may be presumptuous but the doctrine of salvation involves the claim that God is interested in the well-being of each individual. God 'saves' by preserving what people have achieved and by evoking in them creative responses to their situation.

The question

At the start it was held that theological understanding must be significant and credible. The works of Whitehead and Hartshorne suggest an understanding of salvation that is significant for human being today. Whether it is credible depends on whether it is a coherent, comprehensive, fruitful, effective, fitting, and convincing understanding of the life of faith as it is found in experience and judged according to general standards of human rationality. This must be a judgment for others to make.

3

God and Spirituality: On Taking Leave of Don Cupitt

John A. Harrod

This paper explores the relationship between factual beliefs on the one hand, and values and spirituality on the other, suggesting that the latter are not wholly and in every respect 'autonomous' in respect to the former. The paper 'takes leave' of the position defended by Don Cupitt by arguing that our spirituality and values are prompted by, and receive a rationale in terms of, our beliefs. Claims about God are thus not spiritual directives in encoded form, but rather truth claims; but truth claims which nonetheless have a proper purchase upon our values and spirituality.

Cartographers of philosophical country are not always agreed about the nature of the terrain. Whilst for some it is smooth, for others there are wide ditches that it is perilous to attempt to cross. Thus, Lessing maintained that between the truths of history and the truths of reason and theology there is an 'ugly, broad ditch' which we cannot cross however earnestly we attempt the leap.[1] On the one hand the 'accidental truths of history can never become the proof of necessary truths of reason'.[2] On the other, and more relevant to contemporary thought, theological and historical truth belong to diferent orders. Because they are about different issues, events in ancient history neither substantiate nor undermine theological belief, any more than the fact that Alexander conquered almost all Asia has any purchase upon our fundamental human understanding today.

More famous than Lessing's alleged 'ditch' between historical and theological truth – although the metaphor is not so frequently used – is the 'ditch' claimed to exist between our factual beliefs on the one hand and our values, attitudes and spirituality on the other. We may have our beliefs about the world and even about God. We may further have our values, our convictions about what is right and good, and our sense that certain attitudes and life-styles are worth nurturing. Between the two, however, there is no significant connection. Our values and spirituality are 'autonomous' in the sense that they are separate from our factual beliefs; although the nature and degree of this separation is not always made clear.

There is, for example, Hume's famous claim that a fundamental distinction must be drawn between 'is' statements and 'ought' statements. We might, he suggested, catalogue all the facts about a wilful murder. This catalogue, however, does not include the character of the murder as a vice. When we say that murder is a vice we are not saying anything further about the factual character of the murder. We are rather expressing 'only certain passions, motives, volitions and thoughts' on our part.[3]

> The vice entirely escapes you, as long as you consider the object. You never can find it, till you turn your reflection into your own breast.[4]

This led Hume to remark that it is one thing to make 'observations concerning human affairs', that is 'is' statements about what happens to be the case. It is quite another to make statements about what ought to be the case. This change from the 'is' to the 'ought' may be imperceptible. It is, however, 'of the last consequence'.[5]

Precisely the same phrase is used by G.E. Moore when he claimed that statements of the form 'X is good' are always synthetic and never analytic.[6] Thus it is one thing to offer an exhaustive analysis of the factual characteristics of something. It is quite another to say that that thing is good. When we maintain that something is good we are saying something extra and different. Moore's point may stand, whether the notion 'good' be thought of as a 'non-natural quality' or more plausibly as a category of evaluation.

The main concern of Hume and Moore is perhaps simply with the logical distinction between 'is' statements and 'ought' statements. At this basic level we must agree with their presentation. A distinction, however, is not a ditch, still less an 'ugly and broad' one which cannot be crossed. Some writers, however, have converted the distinction into a ditch; an example is R.M. Hare.

Hare says explicitly what is at best only implicit in Moore and Hume, namely that there is not simply a logical distinction between fact and value. More significantly, the latter are essentially separate from the former.[7] It is true of course that we call things good or bad because of some or other factual characteristic. Thus the notion 'good' is in Hare's terms 'consequential' or 'supervenient'.[8] It is we, however, who decide what characteristics are to be called good and bad. The facts themselves, are, so to speak, a plain canvas on which we paint whatever value picture we choose. Of course, if we are to play the 'language game' of ethics our prescriptions must be universalizable. Provided, however, we are willing and able to universalize our prescription (a considerable psychological restraint we must acknowledge) Hare insists that we are free to adopt any value position we choose.[9] Not only is there a logical distinction between facts and values, there is no legitimate movement – however loose or informal – from our factual beliefs to our values. A value stance is neither vindicated nor invalidated by an appeal to facts, even though we appeal to differing factual characteristics to justify differing evaluations.

Hume, Moore and Hare are writing as moral philosophers. What has been said about our moral stances may be said more generally, however, about our general dispositions and attitudes. It may be said, for want of a better term, about our 'spirituality'. The notion 'spirituality' is of course something of an umbrella word which can cover a number of things. There is no one 'correct' meaning, and writers are entitled to stipulate their own definition. Here the notion is given a fairly wide meaning. It denotes the dispositions and attitudes (the 'inner life') which we try to nurture and which we believe to be appropriate. It includes the values and obligations we hold to, but much else beside.

It is by no means certain, indeed, that 'moral issues' can be distinguished clearly from non-moral ones with a distinct divide in between. It is of course easy to instance issues that are clearly moral ones, for example the action of mugging a defenceless elderly lady in order to steal her pension for one's own selfish gain. It is also easy to instance issues that have no moral significance, for example whether I prefer vanilla ice-cream or raspberry ripple. Issues, however, do not always fall easily into the two categories of 'clear moral issues' and 'issues of mere taste'. Many matters are matters we debate with seriousness. We have firm convictions about them, but they are not obviously 'moral issues'. Thus, both Bernard Williams and G.J. Warnock remark that the boundaries of morality are blurred. Morality shades off only gradually into non-moral issues.[10] It is not surprising that much recent philosophical debate has centred on the question: What is a moral issue and how is one to be distinguished from an issue that is not moral?[11]

It is worth remarking that Christian theology has no vested interest in preserving a special area to be marked 'moral' since the whole of life, and not simply the moral bit, is seen as a response to belief in God. It is of interest to note that Paul's list of the harvest of the spirit in the fifth chapter of his letter to the Galatians is something of a mixed bag, some things falling clearly within the 'moral' camp, whilst others not.

The point to be made here, however, is that for some contemporary thinkers it is not simply our moral values that are autonomous, but also our spirituality generally. The Christian, in embracing certain values and in espousing a certain spirituality, sees these stances as being self-justifying. They have an appropriateness of their own, and neither receive nor require any rationale in terms of our beliefs about the way things are. Thus, now that the territory marked 'moral' is not as clearly bounded as has sometimes been thought, but runs into the territory marked 'attitudes' and 'spirituality', so the 'ugly broad ditch' extends into this territory as well.

I do not know if Don Cupitt would accept Williams' and Warnock's view that morality shades off only gradually into non-moral questions. There is no doubt, however, that Cupitt maintains that our spirituality is autonomous in relation to factual belief in a manner similar to traditional claims about the autonomy of moral values. He suggests that Kierkegaard did for religion what Kant did for morality:

> The religious demand is not something inferred from facts about the external world. It establishes itself autonomously and inwardly within the self as an inescapable claim upon the self.[12]

Cupitt rejects a 'realist' interpretation of theistic language, arguing instead that the doctrine of God is an encoded set of spiritual values.[13] He maintains that there is no positive reason for the realist's belief in God, that objective theism is probably incoherent,[14] and that in any case it is a threat to our autonomy and tends to foster intolerance.[15] The contemporary Christian is no more committed to objective theism than, say, to the doctrine of the verbal inspiration of scripture or a particular understanding of the atonement. This is because the Christian tradition is pluralistic and contemporary Christians simply put together whatever package commends itself to them. Furthermore, realists have no right to insist that their position is *the* traditional and orthodox one. The traditional position is neither clearly realist nor non-realist since it is only in modern times that this distinction has been clearly drawn.[16] He notes that in the Bible existential truth is often expressed as if it were factual. Scripture is 'pre-philosophical and is by no means unambiguously committed to any one particular view as to the kind of reality that God has'.[17] Thus, Cupitt maintains, it is just as valid an interpretation of scriptural utterances about God to regard them as encoded spiritual directives as to regard them as factual claims about a being other than ourselves.

Christianity then, he claims, is not concerned with what is the case. It is not about metaphysics. It is rather about the self and its spirituality. Religious truth is not speculative or descriptive but practical.[18] It is important to note that he does not regard his position as a reluctant reductivism, a kind of salvage job seeking to capture what can be saved from the sinking ship of objective theism.[19] It is at this point that he contrasts with, say, Ronald Hepburn.[20] Cupitt argues that even if *ex hypothesi* we were able to affirm certain truths about God, or about metaphysics generally for that matter, these facts would be irrelevant for our spirituality. Thus, just as Kant argued that the authority of the categorical imperative in no way depends upon the factual context of human life, so the spiritual values we espouse not only do not receive *but do not require* any rationale in terms of factual belief. Spirituality, like ethics, is autonomous.

> The crucial insight is that metaphysical facts can no more make religious values binding than they can make moral values binding. The religious claim upon us therefore has to be autonomous, in a way for which the best philosophical model and precedent is Kant's treatment of morality.[21]

Objective theism does not matter as much as people sometimes think. What matters is our spirituality. Such a spirituality is autonomous and 'cannot depend at all upon any external circumstances'.[22]

Cupitt then is commending a commitment to certain values and to a certain spirituality which is underived from and unsupported by any appeal to what may be the case about God and the world. Indeed, at points he even stresses the discontinuity between the 'spiritual' person and the world in which he or she may be set; so much so that one wonders what are the implications of his radical individualism for social ethics:

> On the view I propose, the Christian, the world is evil, and one can only be delivered from the world by principles of spirituality which are not of the world, but which inescapably and rightly set one to some extent at odds with the world ... For our highest good is to become spirit and we must do this in this life, for there is no other as far as we can tell. To become spirit we must transcend nature, and to do that we need to adopt a supernatural requirement which can lever us free from the world.[23]

Implicit in Cupitt's argument is the claim that there are three ditches separating the realm of fact from the realms of value and spirituality, although Lessing's metaphor is not one which he uses. The first ditch is linguistic. There is a fundamental difference in meaning between claims about facts and claims about values and spirituality. The second is logical. There can be no valid movement in argument from factual premises to conclusions regarding values and spirituality. The third and final ditch is no less fundamental. This is the psychological ditch. We choose our own spirituality. We see no need for support or rationale from the way things are. On the contrary, if our spirituality is rendered appropriate by the way things are then it is imposed upon us from without and so our autonomy is threatened.

> People increasingly want to live their own lives, to make their own choices and to determine their own destinies ... It is better to live one's own life, even if unsuccessfully, than to live a life which is merely the acting of a part written for us by someone else, and the principle holds even if that 'somebody else' is a god. Anyone who has tasted freedom knows that it would be a sin against one's own soul to revert to dependency.[24]

Thus, 'God has to become objectively thinner and thinner in order to allow subjective religiousness to expand.'[25]

Cupitt writes with a deeply impressive elegance, clarity, honesty and intellectual rigour. Furthermore, his position has many signal strengths which must be acknowledged. In drawing attention to the centrality of spirituality in the Christian life he is placing a salutary question mark against those interpretations of Christian faith, which, having no reverence for the secrets and mysteries of God, identify Christian faith with 'scoring the maximum on a doctrinal check-list',[26] as if we are saved by right belief or even worthy of punishment because of our failure to grasp some particular theological nicety. Theological realism, especially in the Western tradition which has placed less emphasis than has the Eastern upon the apophatic nature of religious belief, is sometimes characterized by an arrogant overconfidence combined with the claim that right belief in every detail is a central requirement for salvation. Cupitt's strictures against this are indeed most salutary.

Again, it must be recognized that there is an impressive nobility in Cupitt's espousal of a 'spirituality' autonomous and unsupported by – maybe even in opposition to – what the world is ultimately like. Cupitt remains committed to his chosen way 'though the heavens fall' and this commitment – even if all the odds prove to be against him – has a nobility to which we must pay tribute.

Cupitt is surely right also in reminding us that at least many traditional theological utterances, whilst utterly baffling when understood as statements of what is factually the case, nonetheless powerfully come alive when interpreted as expressing some spiritual value. It is a commonplace that many of the biblical narratives are to be understood in this way. Cupitt himself gives as examples the way in which some of the Old Testament prophets attacked 'objective' understandings of certain Hebrew institutions – cult, law, sacrifice, circumcision, etc. – and replaced them with an inward and spiritual equivalent. The internalization of a religious institution or doctrine, far from being a betrayal of the tradition, is in fact something that has gone on in the tradition since the beginning.[27] He also offers powerful and stimulating expositions of how the resurrection, the doctrine of God's omnipresence, the doctrine of providence, and the practice of prayer, may be understood as expressing spiritual values rather than as affirming or implying what is objectively true.[28]

That much in the Christian tradition needs to be interpreted existentially seems clear. The fact, however, that *some* things in the tradition should be so interpreted does not necessarily mean that *all* should. Furthermore, there is no reason why some aspects of the tradition may not be regarded as being *both* explorations of what is factually the case and *also* expressions of spiritual values. Thus, the realist could agree with the implications for spirituality which Cupitt finds in the notion of the divine omnipresence. Theological utterance is a very complex thing. We approach it with too blunt an instrument of interpretation if we assume that it must be either wholly and always descriptive or wholly and always expressive, and that the categories expressive and descriptive must be mutually exclusive. Some examples of religious language may indeed be regarded as disguised spiritual directives. This does not mean, however, that there cannot be a core which seeks to elucidate what is the case. Neither is it true to say that theological utterances cannot attempt both to explore what is true and also the implications of that truth for our spirituality. As John Hick remarked:

> If ... the entire range of religious beliefs were regarded as non-factual, none of them could possess the kind of significance which depends upon a connection with objective reality. Myths that are embedded within a body of facts bear this kind of significance secondarily and derivatively, but myths which live in a system which is mythological throughout merely define an imagined realm of their own ... what might be called valuable or significant myth is necessarily parasitic upon non-mythological beliefs, and ... if a set of myths becomes complete and autonomous it thereby forfeits its cognitive value.[29]

It must be acknowledged that in the strict sense Cupitt's position is unassailable. Taking refuge in the 'fact-value' distinction and in the claim that no spirituality or value stance can be formally required by any factual belief he embraces a wholly 'autonomous' spirituality, and since it is autonomous there is no point of purchase for criticism. Adopting a thoroughly non-realist view of religious language he avoids having to face the difficulties that attach to objective theism. At the same time, however, by seeing religious language as a kind of 'private language' he adopts a position which is invulnerable to criticism from outside since by his own definition religion carries no implications outside the borders of its own autonomous realm. As such it can be neither confirmed nor falsified by reference to anything outside it.

My aim in this paper is the relatively modest one of trying to suggest that an alternative position is not as untenable as Cupitt implies. In other words I wish to suggest that the Christian who maintains a realist understanding of theism may reasonably claim that certain value stances and a spirituality are prompted or encouraged by such belief. Hence, our values and spirituality are not completely autonomous. They receive a rationale in terms of our beliefs about the way things are.

We return then to the three 'broad ugly' ditches that confront anyone who attempts the perilous journey from the land of 'facts' to the land of 'values' and 'spirituality'. The first ditch is linguistic. It is maintained that there is a difference in meaning between sentences that purport to state facts and sentences that express commitments in value and spirituality. This linguistic difference is central to the arguments of Hume and Moore referred to earlier in this paper, and must be accepted.

The claim, however, that there is a difference in meaning between these two types of sentences is little more than a point about our use of language.[30] It ignores the more important questions about the relationship between our beliefs and values. To pursue the metaphor, this particular ditch – although indeed impossible to cross – merely cuts off a small corner of the territory. It does not run through the most significant areas.

We come next to the alleged logical gap between factual claims and claims about values and spirituality. Is this ditch as wide as many have claimed, so that it becomes completely unbridgeable? It may indeed be true that there can be no formal and logically tight process of inference from factual premises to conclusions about values and spirituality, so that one cannot argue from the former to the latter in the same kind of way as the logician or geometrist argue from certain premises to unassailable conclusions. To that extent there may be an unbridgeable ditch, although Philippa Foot does argue that there is a clear logical link between our conception of what is good and certain factual situations.[31]

Even, however, if we allow that there is no formal and logically tight movement in argument from factual beliefs to conclusions about values and spirituality, it does not necessarily follow that there can be no defensible movement at all. An argument can be rationally persuasive without being logically unassailable. A number of writers have maintained, without gainsaying the claim that there is indeed a difference between factual and value claims, that it is unreasonable to regard as utterly irrelevant for our values and spirituality our beliefs about the human condition and what the world is like. Value stances are not so completely autonomous as to be totally unrelated to our factual beliefs.[32] Thus certain factual beliefs may prompt or encourage certain positions regarding values and spirituality without formally entailing them. If this be allowed we cannot agree completely with Cupitt in his claim that 'our concept of a fact is the concept of a truth which is religiously and morally neutral'.[33] We may grant that this is so for many disciplines of study which necessarily confine themselves to their own subject matter. We may grant further that there is a whole range of fact which indeed appears to be irrelevant for our values and spirituality – the freezing point of water, the gestation period of elephants, the colour of daffodils, etc. We can conceive of moral dilemmas in which these facts might have to be taken into account; but as facts they themselves are morally neutral. It does not follow, however, that because many facts are indeed morally and spiritually neutral all facts must be neutral likewise. On the contrary it seems difficult not to experience certain facts as prompting a response. Thus A.C. Ewing argued that some facts are such that certain responses are 'fitting' and others not.[34] Also, I.T. Ramsey spoke of facts as giving rise to a value claim. 'The facts which are surveyed take on "depth" and become the occasion of a disclosure occuring around and through them.'[35] Helen Oppenheimer gives illustrations of this approach:

> We cannot simply say 'Yes I see' when confronted with a picture by Van Gogh, the story of the death of Captain Oates, the sight of a road accident, the announcement of a friend's engagement ... If we give it the attention it deserves it will implicate ourselves. It calls for some reaction and if this is not forthcoming we may be accused of failure to understand, however precisely we have noted the bare facts.[36]

She asks us also to consider the 'fact' that a child has fallen in water. Cupitt no doubt would say this fact is morally neutral; it is we who bring to it our scheme of values. Oppenheimer, by contrast, suggests the fact is such as to prompt a certain response:

> The existence of the child is not a bare fact but a compelling one: a human being, full of hope for the future, precious to his parents, lovable in himself, is struggling in the water and must be saved.[37]

Our concern in this paper, however, is not simply with our moral values – however the elusive area we designate 'moral' may be defined – but with our spirituality generally. Furthermore, our concern is not with factual belief in general but with theistic belief in particular. Following the hints set out above we now explore some of the ways in which theistic belief might encourage (or indeed modify) commitments regarding values and spirituality, without necessarily formally entailing these commitments.

Suppose, for example, it be a key feature of our values and spirituality that we respect the rights of others and attend to their needs when in a position to do so. Other people are not objects to be manipulated for our own gain, but persons in their own right, with feelings, needs, and hopes, like our own, and these we must respect. Now our beliefs in human dignity and in the obligations that go with it are indeed beliefs that 'stand on their own feet'. We see for ourselves their intrinsic appropriateness. To a large extent such a value commitment is autonomous, needing no religious or metaphysical sanction.

In order to affirm the basic autonomy of this value commitment, however, we do not need to deny the possibility of it receiving lateral support and reinforcement from our beliefs about what a human person *is*. Thus, the secularist has ultimately to accept that the human person is the product of a blind cosmic process. This does not make the secularist's commitment to human dignity, and the acceptance of obligations and rights, irrational. Nonetheless, this commitment receives no support in the beliefs that are held about what a human person is. For many theists, however, by contrast, the other human person is a child of God, sharing with us in the divine love. We are all brothers and sisters with a common father. Thus, our value commitment, which does indeed already stand to a considerable extent in its own right, receives powerful reinforcement from our beliefs. As Rashdall remarked, the love of God is a stimulant and complement to the love of others.[38] Likewise Austin Farrer a generation later suggested that 'what claims our regard is not simply our neighbour, but God in our neighbour and our neighbour in God'.[39] Indeed, despite the impressive commitment to humanistic values of many who have no religious belief, it remains a real question how long and for how many a wholly secular understanding of what a human person is can sustain our traditional values regarding human dignity and rights and our obligations towards one another.

Suppose, to take another example, it be a feature of our spirituality that we be 'at peace with ourselves'. This does not mean that we are smug and complacent, blind to our faults and unwilling to change or grow. It does mean, however, that we accept ourselves with our limitations. We set realistic goals for our lives and do not fret because we cannot be or do what is beyond our powers. We accept ourselves even though we do not have the gifts to become, say, a brilliant linguist or musician; even though we do not have the fund of wit that makes us the life and soul of every party, and so forth. Once again, this spirituality is 'autonomous' in the sense that its basic sense and appropriateness can be apprehended without any theological support. For the theist, however, it may receive reinforcement in the claim that we are accepted and forgiven by God. Those whom God has accepted may accept themselves. This would appear to be in line with Paul's claim that we may be at 'peace' because we are 'justified' by 'faith'.[40] The theme was powerfully explored by Paul Tillich a generation ago.[41]

Suppose again it be a feature of our spirituality that we have a sense that our living is basically worthwhile and purposeful, not that we have a facile optimism that denies the reality of deep tragedy and evil. Such evil and tragedy, however, do not allow us to become completely disillusioned and despairing, let alone cynical. Without giving way to a facile optimism – indeed such an optimism on the part of the privileged may appear insensitive and repugnant by the unfortunate – we have a fundamental attitude of hope and confidence.

A spirituality at least akin to this seems in fact to be recommended by Cupitt. He says that it is 'good that one should commit oneself to existence in religious hope' and that 'in spite of all the ugliness and cruelty in the world, it is good that one should at least sometimes experience and express cosmic awe, thanksgiving and love'.[42] Now it is difficult to see how such a stance in our spirituality can be completely 'autonomous' as if the 'spiritual' person (Cupitt's phrase) can pursue his or her existence in a way that is totally oblivious of the way things are. An attitude of hope and confidence is based on the belief and trust that the universe is such as to make such an attitude appropriate. Now the secularist might accept this, but go on to point out the empirical fact that – at least for those who enjoy the benefits of modern society – there is reason for such an attitude. The theist need not deny this, but will go on to claim that this attitude receives powerful reinforcement from theistic belief. God is the creator and giver of our lives. The doctrine of creation makes reasonable an attitude of hope and confidence.[43] We may even have hope 'for his kingdom to come'.[44]

Admittedly it is at this point perilously easy to parrot religious slogans, slogans that appear callous to those overwhelmed by tragedy. How theological belief at this point is to be formulated, and how our formulations are to have 'cash value' is a very complex issue and takes us beyond the brief of this paper. It is sufficient to claim simply that this aspect of spirituality is hardly completely autonomous. It requires a rationale in terms of our beliefs about the way things are.

These are but three ways in which theistic belief may reasonably be held to have purchase on our values and spirituality. It would be going too far to argue that such value stances and such components of spirituality are justified *only* on the basis of objective theism, so that if that belief evaporates so they will evaporate too. Particularly with regard to our ethical convictions it is important to maintain an at least relative autonomy. Our moral convictions stand 'in their own right' apart from religion. The same may be true of much of our spirituality. It is important to stress this since there is nothing that rightly raises the protests of secular moral philosophers as much as the bogus claim that there can be no morality without religion.[45]

One may affirm, however, an important autonomy regarding our convictions in ethics and spirituality without suggesting that they are so completely autonomous as to be unrelated completely to our beliefs about the nature of the world and the human situation. They receive a rationale – sometimes a reinforcement, sometimes a modification – from our beliefs. Our spirituality has many sources – social, emotional, contextual and rational. It will be influenced by personality traits over which we have only limited control. Nonetheless, in the mishmash of factors that affect our spirituality beliefs play a part, and indeed a reasonable part.

Cupitt's claim that our spirituality is autonomous in the sense that it 'cannot depend at all upon any external circumstances'[46] seems frankly incredible. If this means what it says people's spirituality will be unaffected by whether they be struggling against hunger and disease in Ethiopia or enjoying the benefits of modern Western society; by whether they be enjoying the surroundings of the English Lake District or be beaten up as prisoners of conscience under some totalitarian regime. It has been my claim that our values and spirituality cannot be completely autonomous in this way: and that in particular theological belief has a proper purchase upon them. Thus it seems likewise incredible to suggest that our values and spirituality should not be affected by whether we believe our human lives to be the transitory result of some blind cosmic process, or to be part of God's creation, and as such the recipients of his gracious, enabling, and fulfilling love.

Indeed, if we say that our ethics and spirituality receive no rationale or justification whatsoever from the factual context it is difficult to see how they can receive any rationale or justification at all. At times Cupitt may be taken as implying that we simply choose whatever spirituality and values happen to attract our own individual whims,[47] in which case presumably there are no grounds upon which we may arbitrate between the values and spirituality of, say, Nietzsche, Hitler, and Cupitt. I may reject the stances of Nietzsche and Hitler – I may reject them vehemently – but my rejection has no validity beyond that of being my *de facto* choice. Such statements of Cupitt must be read by the sympathetic reader, however, in the light of his more predominant claim that certain values are recognized by us as being authoritative in their own right. The autonomous person is persuaded of the intrinsic appropriateness of certain values and a certain spirituality.[48] If, however, this intrinsic appropriateness is not elucidated and supported by reference to factual belief, in what does its appropriateness consist? Cupitt seems to offer nothing more than a simple intuitionism by which we intuit certain values as authoritative for us, quite irrespective of our factual beliefs.

So much, then, for the claim that our standards should be autonomous in the sense of being unaffected by factual belief.

Cupitt insists, however, not only upon the autonomy of the standard, but also upon the autonomy of the agent. As Keith Ward has shown, Cupitt speaks of the autonomy of the individual in a number of different and not all of them easily defensible senses. For example, autonomy in the sense of complete self-government leads to anarchy.[49] Cupitt's fundamental claim, however, is that we should enjoy autonomy in the sense of apprehending for ourselves the appropriateness of our moral stances and spirituality. We are not to be inhibited by external constraints which we cannot make our own. He maintains that those who have tasted freedom will not want to give it away.[50] Repeatedly he attacks a God who infringes our autonomy, an 'objective deity who among other things antecedently prescribes our moral values and our spiritual itinerary from outside'.[51] He rejects 'an odious subjection to the will of another such as is incompatible with the dignity of a conscious rational self'.[52] By contrast our spirituality must be 'freely chosen and self imposed'.[53] There is thus a psychological ditch between our factual beliefs and our values and spirituality. To allow the latter to be guided by the former is to threaten our autonomy:

> We must choose our own religious values because they are intrinsically precious rather than because any external being commands us to adopt them and threatens us with sanctions.[54]

Cupitt here appears to be working with the headmasterly 'Because I say so' approach to religious ethics and spirituality. Certain actions are deemed right or wrong, certain spiritual stances are required of us, because of some inscrutable and heteronomous divine decree, received either tangentially through revelation or via some ecclesiastical authority. It is inscrutable and without rhyme or reason and so may appear to ignore our best interests. Even worse, it might be backed up by the threat of punishment. Religious values are thus imposed upon us in a manner that violates our dignity and freedom – our autonomy.

Alas, this pejorative description does accurately describe the way in which religion has sometimes been presented, and we must be grateful to Cupitt for his protest. The fact, however, that some formulations of a theistic ethic and spirituality violate human autonomy in this way does not necessarily mean that all must. The position defended in this paper gives no truck to the idea that in our ethics and spirituality we are constrained and inhibited by inscrutable divine decrees; still less that we have to keep to the straight and narrow for fear of punishment. It was suggested rather that certain beliefs about God encourage, reinforce and modify (whilst not necessarily engendering) certain stances. Our spirituality is a response, freely given, to the goodness of God. This hardly threatens our autonomy since we apprehend ourselves the fitting nature of our response. We freely respond to the goodness of God. Indeed, Cupitt's own 'spiritual' person does not simply choose whatever spiritual values happen to suit his or her particular whim. Rather, they are chosen because they are 'intrinsically precious' – even 'a priori'.[55] If this is no threat to autonomy it is difficult to see why the position of the theist that certain grateful responses to God are 'intrinsically appropriate' should be. Furthermore, in speaking of spiritual values Cupitt commends a 'receptivity to grace' and the cultivation of 'cosmic awe, thanksgiving and love.'[56] He does not regard this as a threat to our autonomy – why should it become a threat when the objective theist sees these things as having reference in what is ultimately personal? It is interesting that Cupitt does not see *human* relationships as inevitably threatening our autonomy when in these relationships there is a mutual respect for freedom and well-being. On the contrary it is in such relationships that we find so much joy:

> If love can become disinterested then it will be possible to reconcile love with the other's freedom. We will love in a way that is not oppressively jealous and demanding but which actually liberates the other, making the other more autonomous and not less.[57]

This is well said. What is odd is that he does not consider the possibility that if human relationships of a certain character may further our freedom, autonomy and well-being, so this may also be the case with our relationship with God.[58]

Of course, we may resist this suggestion on the grounds of a doctrinaire individualism. But Cupitt most emphatically does not embrace a proud and arrogant individualism which refuses to receive love and enrichment from others. He insists, not upon individualism, but upon autonomy. His concern for autonomy is a concern for freedom, dignity and well-being. We choose our own life-style and spirituality as intrinsically appropriate. It is not imposed upon us from without. In this paper, however, it has been argued that for the objective theist, our spirituality is not imposed upon us. Rather we see it as a fitting response to the attractiveness of God. Such an approach surely satisfies Cupitt's criterion. Objective theism need not be forced to admit that God inevitably threatens our autonomy. On the contrary, it may be claimed that he is the ultimate source of our freedom, joy and hope. Augustine was not obviously talking nonsense when he claimed that the service of God is perfect freedom. In ordinary human relationships of love we do not find others a threat to our autonomy. On the contrary, our lives find fulfilment in relationship with others. It does not seem unreasonable for the theist to claim that this may also be the case, analogically, with our relationship with God.

My conclusion, therefore, is that a proper regard for the relative autonomy of the stances we adopt in ethics and spirituality does not preclude the theist from finding in theistic belief grounds for both the support and the modification of these stances. Our values and spirituality, whilst being partly autonomous, are guided by and receive a rationale from our beliefs about the way things are. Furthermore, it is simply untrue that all conceptions of objective theism must see God as a threat to our autonomy, in the sense of our well-being and proper freedom and dignity.

None of this of course meets Cupitt's other charges against objective theism – its alleged incoherence, unreasonableness and so forth – but that is another issue.

4

The Trinitarian Model of God

Kenneth B. Wilson

It is argued that the Christian doctrine of the Trinity makes sense alongside discussion of what it is to be human. Traditional attributes of God are explored as claims about the Christian understanding of God in relation to himself. It is further argued that this understanding of their reference illuminates the concept of God's freedom and the Christian claim that in his creating he gives himself. It is not argued that the doctrine of the Trinity is necessary to Christian theology; rather that since we have no better model it merits continued attention.

Whatever it is that makes humanity human, it is certainly capable of the utmost diversity of expression. A recent visit to Israel combined with the preparatory and consequent reading which included much on the holocaust has done nothing to diminish my awareness of the full range of the marvellous, the admirable and the terrible things of which we humans are capable. Bruno Bettelheim, himself a survivor of the concentration camps and a celebrated Freudian psychologist, presented some views on this at a conference on the holocaust in San José and added to them in a later published essay:

> Millions of Jews were systematically slaughtered, as were untold other undesirables; not for a conviction of theirs, but only because they stood in the way of the realization of an illusion. They neither died for their convictions, nor were they slaughtered for their convictions, but only in consequence of the Nazis' delusional belief about what was required to protect the purity of their assumed superior racial endowment and what they thought necessary to guarantee them the living space they believed they needed and were entitled to. Thus

while these millions were slaughtered for an idea, they did not die for one. Millions – men, women and children – were processed after they had been utterly brutalized, their humanity destroyed, their clothes torn from their bodies. Naked, they were sorted into those who were destined to be murdered immediately and those others who had a shortterm usefulness as slave labor. But after a brief interval they, too, were to be herded into the same gas chambers into which the others were immediately piled, there to be asphyxiated so that, in their last moments, they could not prevent themselves from fighting each other in vain for a last breath of air.[1]

Our humanity is capable, it appears, of anything: the full extremes of good and evil are presently available and open to each of us. We may say, as Christians, that evil behaviour is in some way anything that we do which is contrary to the real nature we have as humans, and that it is destructive of everything therefore that is contributory to human flourishing and human welfare.[2] But as a matter of fact we cannot deny that such behaviour occurs and that it is human beings who choose to perform it. We might wish from time to time that things were different, but we alternate between trying to make them different by establishing what is good and in the common interest and believing that since things could not really be otherwise than how they are, there is no point in trying to make them so.

But with God the case is different. Whereas with human beings we have to say a person is capable of doing anything, and frequently chooses to do so, with God although he also is capable of doing anything, he only does what gives life to the world for which he is responsible. His freedom lies therefore in being always true to his own nature, rather than in having the freedom to deny it. This aspect of his being is not a paradox but a fulfilment of the free nature of his essential being. The point can, however, be stated paradoxically. Although God is the one and only truly free being (and in this lies his uniqueness) he is in fact not able to do anything which reduces the capacity of other beings to fulfil their own true natures.

The Christian traditon of theological enquiry has explored this apparent paradox with the aid of many models, but most illuminatingly and helpfully through the mysterious doctrine of the Trinity. What is it for God to be God? It is bound up with his freedom in relation to the world for which he is responsible and his freedom in relation to himself. It is with this exploration into the nature of God as he is in himself that we are concerned in this essay.

The doctrine has been a matter of some considerable interest in the last few years to theologians, but the context, theologically, philosophically and psychologically or sociologically, has not been conducive to a developed understanding.[3] It is not simply that yet again in the history of the church, theological enquiry has been more concerned with 'practical' as opposed to what are too frequently regarded as theoretical and therefore irrelevant matters, or that for a large proportion of its work philosophy has disregarded metaphysics, let alone theology. It arises from the implied judgment made regarding the place (or rather perhaps the lack of place) which has been allotted to the person in cultural enquiry at all.[4]

It is plausible to argue (and often assumed) that we should trace the watershed to Descartes. Affected as he was by the radical scepticism of Montaigne, he sought a point of departure for philosophy which would produce propositions which could not be doubted. The self-evidence of the existence of the self in consciousness, together with, for example, the principle of non-contradiction seemed to him to provide sufficient material from which to deduce the existence of God in order to guarantee the trustworthiness of the human experience of the external world. In addition, he believed mathematical reasoning to be applicable to the whole of science. But the self whose existence was affirmed was an unextended, unperceiving and isolated self which had no share in the being of any other person and no requirement of any other being for its own existence. Thus the God who was required in order to guarantee the trustworthiness of the world of human experience was called upon to do no more than affirm the experience of isolated human being; the social experience of social humanity, or the logical interdependence of the beings whose experience was formulated in language (itself a social construction) was not involved at all. The logical construct of such a God is no God at all in the Christian sense. The extension of mathematical reasoning to all areas of science has involved a further reductionism as science has been effectively thought to cover more and more of human experience.[5] The consequence is that in theology it has been difficult to maintain attention on the being of God and much easier to concentrate on the effectiveness of the church whether in recruiting members or in influencing policy in social and economic affairs. The person having dropped out in terms of philosophy, the divine has dropped out of theology, with potentially disastrous consequences for the way in which human being is thought of and treated in society.[6]

The tendency has been paralleled in psychology and sociology. The Freudian revolution put the self beyond the possibility of experience by others and yet rendered that private world the one which determined the nature of the individual's experience of the world and of others. By contrast, a chemotherapeutic approach to the treatment of mental disorder has paradoxically reduced the need to take account of the inner self except in so far as and when it impinges on the lives of others. And sociology, which by definition is not concerned with any explanation of society which assumes a reality for the person as individual, has tended to suggest that we can cope for all real purposes with a view of the individual which is a construct of social realities which has no other existence. Like Hume in the 'Treatise on Human Nature', contemporary society lives with a perception of what it is to be human which lacks the connections which enable us to make sense of it. *A fortiori* the same is true of our concept of God. We do not see him as he is in himself because we have lost sight of what it is to see him in relation to his world and to human beings in particular. Apart from placing him in that context we do not see him as he is in himself because to see him as he is in himself is precisely to see him in these relationships. The analogy with what it is to be a human person turns out once again to be illuminating.

In a valuable essay called 'Transubstantiation for Beginners', Gareth Moore OP writes;

> Just as a piece of paper becomes something different, becomes money, by being taken up into an institution, a range of practices, and just as the possibility of its being so depends on the existence of that institution and those practices, so a piece of bread becomes something different, becomes the Body of Christ, by being taken up into the life of the Church.[7]

The significance/meaning of an object is seen within the context of the relationships and practices in which it has a place. The same is true of a concept, as Wittgenstein long ago taught us;

only when the total language which embodies a concept is exposed to view, with all its assumptions, logical relations and implications, can the meaning and life of a concept be grasped. Far from it being the case that this theory reduces truth and meaning to 'mere language', it points to the way in which we embody the meaning we give to the world in our language.

The institution and practices of the church, in association with the theological enquiry engaged in by theologians and believers alike, embody the term 'God' in appropriate Christian religious language. In Christian reflection this embodiment has found its most cogent and stimulating expression in the trinitarian model. It has been found so difficult to understand the concept (so that it has been rejected by some, for example, on the grounds of contradiction) that the only justification for continuing to hold it has sometimes been held to be divine revelation. Since mere human beings would not have thought up what is so confusing and mysterious and since the equation concerns the very nature of God himself and therefore cannot be true simply if thought up by human beings as an explanation of their experience, it must owe its origin to the Deity himself. The latter is not a view which I wish to sustain; nevertheless it correctly identifies the fact that in any work which the theologian wants to do, he or she had better pay attention to the fact of God. A culture which through failure to grasp the reality of the person in relation, fails to give appropriate attention to the human person *per se*, will hardly have the emotional space or the actual ability to find or pay attention to God, let alone to God as he is in himself.

There are other features of the situation which require attention. The lack of acceptance of the subject, let alone the subjective, has profoundly influenced the way in which theologians have themselves thought, since in order to be understood in the prevailing culture they have themselves had to seek an objective, distanced position from which at least to appear to be talking.[8] Interestingly, Charles Taylor regards this as a major spiritual influence upon the contemporary scientific emphasis on objectivity.

... I believe that the attractions of this freedom come from more than the sense of the control that accompanies submitting nature and society to instrumental reason. They are also of spiritual origin, in a sense which is understandable from our Western religious tradition. In both its Greek and Christian roots (albeit a deviation in this latter stream) this has included an aspiration to arise above the merely human, to step outside the prison of the peculiarly human emotions and to be free of the cares and the demands they make on us. This is of course an aspiration which also has analogous forms in Indian culture and perhaps, indeed, in all human cultures.

My claim is that the ideal of the modern free subject, capable of objectifying the world and reasoning about it in a detached, instrumental way, is a novel variant of this very old aspiration to spiritual freedom. I want to say, that is, that the motive force that draws us to it is closely akin to the traditional drive to spiritual purity. This is of course highly paradoxical, since the modern ideal understands itself as naturalistic and thus is quite antithetical to any religious outlook. But I believe that in this it is self-deluded.[9]

The experience of the First World War and the consequent disillusionment with all things human encouraged Barth to bear witness to the freedom of God. Only by distancing him in this way could there be any possibility of rethinking the ways in which human beings could find their way in the world; no institution could encompass him, no institution consume him, the freedom of God was paramount. Indeed the motivation for the development of his interpretation of the doctrine of the Trinity was precisely the need to show that God had no need of the world since he was bound up in relationship with himself, but that nevertheless out of his own good nature he chose to bring the world into existence and could again freely remake it. However, the result of this emphasis on the freedom of God and the consequent motivation for the elaboration of a doctrine of the Trinity, was the diminution of the role of human being. Of himself he was nothing; of himself he could understand nothing, at least he could not understand anything with profit for himself; in himself he was valueless. Human being was empty apart from the meaning and purpose given to him by God. In order therefore to be an instrument of God's will, he had to rid himself of self, not simply of self-preoccupation.

Thus, both from the point of view of the scientist and from the point of view of the most considerable theologian of the twentieth century, Karl Barth, there is a paradoxical commitment to a position which by objectifying the world (whether

The Trinitarian Model of God 71

natural or God's) threatens to reduce the individual person to a cypher or instrument. But this is to misunderstand the basis of the search for God in which the Christian tradition is engaged, the nature of the self with which he is endowed, and therefore the language in which it is embedded. Far from the freedom of God reducing human being to subservience, it is the condition of the freedom of human being and *vice versa*. Far from the ability of man being founded on his capacity to objectify his experience and thus reduce to vanishing point his or her subjectivity, it is a condition of human understanding of the world and therefore of the world's nature *per se*, that description or explanation of the world is seen as a human description or explanation. What is most significant about it is that it is something that human beings are doing with their world of experience. Furthermore, of course, such a view means that it is open to us to take responsibility for the knowledge of the world which we possess, though maybe not such absolute responsibility as we see God undertaking.

We begin with the classical attributes of God. God is absolute in his knowledge, his power and his ability to give himself in love to the world which he has made. Despite the philosophical objections which amongst other criticisms have objected that the notion of omnipotence is unintelligible or selfcontradictory, the natural inclination has been to begin with an understanding of God as all-powerful since in God's power lies the possibility of the overthrow of all that is inimical to human well-being.[10] All the more is this the case if evil is conceived of as a power which is contrary to God and perhaps even personified in form as the Devil. Since God has all power and has both the intention to use it well and the knowledge to enable him to make complete and correct judgment, man has nothing to fear for his future. Furthermore, by taking God's power as the basis of the human understanding of God as he is in himself there is an acknowledged tendency to excuse mankind from real responsibility for his own situation. Since God could have made things differently but chose not to, there must be adequate reason for the way things actually are with the world. Who is man to question the purposes of the Lord of all? Thus the theological support is provided for the (perhaps unconscious) desire of human being to stand outside the possibility of taking responsibility for his world. God's freedom has as a consequence the loss of freedom on the part of human being. One expression of this may be the desire to objectify and lose the place of subjectivity in scientific enquiry as if its application in technological development has some value in itself apart from the purposes to which human beings put it.

In a famous essay, A.G.N. Flew argued that divine omnipotence was consistent with human freewill.[11] His thesis was essentially that if you knew sufficient about somebody you could predict with complete accuracy what that person in given circumstances would be likely to do; moreover this in no way reduced the freedom which the individual human being either felt or possessed to choose to do what he or she wanted to do. And this case concerned ordinary human relationships. With God, *a fortiori* the example of the being who had complete knowledge and therefore complete capacity to predict accurately what would occur, the case is simply clearer. Knowledge of the future by another has no logical implication against the reality of the freedom of that other person to do what he or she wants. But there has long been recognized that this is a confusion; or if not a confusion, to the extent which it is true it fails to deal with the material point. The confusion is between freedom conceived of as doing what one wants to do and freedom conceived of as being able to act in a way which causes another surprise because although all experience so far would lead one to expect that he or she would choose to do X, in fact the choice was Y. It is hard to see how there can be anything approximating to human freedom and therefore to a personal relationship if the knowledge which one possesses of another is always fulfilled in the event by the choices which the other makes. It may be the case that technically there is no logically necessary implication between the knowledge of the future regarding a person and that person's choices, but it is quite clear that even the parallel worlds of Leibniz fail to satisfy the criteria which as ordinary human beings we place against our desire to be free. We want to know that in the last resort we are capable of making a choice which only we could have known we would make. Where Flew is right, however, is to insist that predictability is necessary in all relations including human personal relationships; the latter in particular depend upon the fact that we can and frequently do with success predict one another's behaviour. Without the confidence that this is the case we should give up the effort to know one another at all. Persons do not depend upon unpredictability of their behaviour, but freedom depends upon the limit case that one could behave in a way that was unpredictable. But where Flew was also right was in the identification of knowledge as the clue to understanding God's capacity to relate to the world rather than power.

This is particularly obvious when the classical attributes of God are seen to be, in their first application at least, self-referential.

The assumption usually made in respect of God's absolute knowledge is that he knows everything that it is logically or empirically possible to know including therefore everything that will take place in the future. On that basis it is necessary to solve the specific question which Flew asks about the compatibility of divine omnipotence and human freewill. But such a view is inconsistent with the fundamental Christian claim that God is in relation to the world and can be known by us.

If on the other hand we begin with the assumption that divine knowledge is above all self-knowledge a few things fall into place. Self-knowledge, as we know from psycho-analysis, is the basis of our ability to make good and sensible choices. Many choices are inhibited or marred by the fact that they are, for example, unwittingly made in a self-regarding way. Unconsciously we choose to take a certain path in a career not aware that we are influenced more by the image which we are seeking for ourselves, than by the integral attractiveness of the opportunity and even less by a knowledge of our own real capacities. Or perhaps in the event we make what we believe to be a good choice only to discover that it leads us into a form of self-knowledge with which we cannot cope and which conspires to destroy us. Lack of self-knowledge is, as the Greeks were fond of saying, the most debilitating feature of any human being's life. Hence there was inscribed above the entry to the temple at Delphi 'Know thyself'.

With God, so Christians believe, the case is different: God knows himself. Indeed he knows himself utterly. The question may be raised whether God's knowledge of himself is all conscious knowledge, but the question of the distinction between conscious and unconscious is meaningless with respect to God. Since there are no experiences with which he is in principle incapable of coping, it makes no sense to assume psychological processes which would develop an unconscious;

and this is quite apart from the fact that it would be in principle impossible for God to have experience of which he was unconscious. Hence, there is no aspect of himself which a choice of his, or an action of another will suddenly reveal to him, the consequence of which would result in lack of confidence or a threat to his Being. There is no ignorance of himself which could lead to him making a choice which was self-regarding; after all there is nothing which he needs to protect. (Christian theologians have often unconsciously witnessed to this by their attestation that God has revealed himself, only by guilty self-delusion to draw back as if this was to claim too much.) Most, if not all, of our self-regarding actions are performed under the delusion that by hiding from ourselves we can hide from others. Since God has no need to hide from himself he has no need to hide from others. His revelation of himself is therefore complete, unconditional and always freely given.

A main consequence of God's knowledge of himself is that he has power over himself. After all, personal power is the consequence of being able to threaten another and this stems from another person's willingness to allow himself or herself to be threatened. The major reason for giving in to such threats, or more basically even to allowing that they are real threats, is the lack of sufficient self-knowledge to give one the confidence and strength to ignore them. God is above all in control of himself because of his absolute self-knowledge. No matter what others may do, no matter what thought regarding possible actions occurs to him, there is no external reason which could lead him necessarily to act contrary to his nature. He cannot be surprised into taking unpremeditated action, nor could he be persuaded so to behave; on the contrary, all influences which come to him result therefore in other-regarding behaviour, not in self-regarding behaviour. This is perhaps the heart of the argument, since it enables one to show that we are dealing with a being whose nature is always to be able to give himself for the well-being of that with which he is in relationship.

Thus the implication of self-knowledge is self-control and the implication of self-control is the capacity to give oneself in love of the other. Since there is no illusion of the self which God has to protect and to pressure which could persuade him to act contrary to his nature he is free to be himself. And crucially this is not the whole story, for not only is he free to be himself, he is free to be himself in relation to others. The key to this claim lies in the fact that God loves himself. This is not so much an additional claim which is being made, as an attempt to spell out what it is to have full knowledge of oneself and to be in control of oneself. The Gospels urge that we should be perfect as our Father in heaven is perfect and that we should love one another as ourselves. These two statements are grossly misunderstood and are responsible therefore for much illness and hardship. To deny oneself is to cease simply to act in a self-regarding way, but one cannot do that unless one takes oneself into account. Not to take oneself into account is to lose the capacity to grow in self-knowledge, to lose in fact the ability to control oneself and therefore to continue in the mire of self-love, rather than the true love of self. How catastrophic has been the church's acceptance of such subservience for man who has therefore been enjoined to seek his own prison rather than freedom. The gospel is of quite a different order. God's freedom to love himself enables him to give himself to others. Our hatred of ourselves and fear of one another has lead us to reject God and therefore to seek objectification in the other, which is the death of self.

The problem here is at least two-fold. On the one hand it has been assumed that the search for perfection by human beings is futile because in principle unattainable; on the other it is argued that only if one is perfect can one have, and know what it is to have, authentic relationships. My contention is that both points are mistaken. Because God has complete knowledge of himself, and therefore utter control over himself, his self-giving is entirely himself. Because human beings are the creation of such a God, they are capable of authenticatable relationships with one another because of their openness to him who wholly gives himself. The distinction is between an actuality of being in the case of God, and the potentiality of being in relation to the human.

The freedom to be oneself in self-giving for the well-being of others is the freedom God possesses and the freedom human being seeks as it essays to be itself.

It is often suggested that it is dubious whether God had the possibility of making moral choices, given that he was incapable of taking evil decisions. If, as is largely assumed, 'ought implies can', then the possibility of moral judgment requires that there should be a real opportunity to choose either good or evil;

apparently this is not a choice which is open to God. In strictly logical terms this may be true. However, as Barth saw very clearly, the original choice which God made (in anthropomorphic terms) was a moral choice in the sense that it had to be wholly free. Any suggestion that God was under constraint whether through inner compulsion, the nature of some pre-existent matter with which he worked, or through the influence of some countervailing agency with which he had to grapple, simply does not do justice to the nature of the case in respect of the Christian claim regarding the creation of the world. Whatever it was that God was involved in when he brought into existence the world of human experience, it was something over which he had absolute and complete control. In this sense the freedom of God is absolute and therefore raises the question of the morality of that choice. Of course, since God is non-temporal and therefore his relationship with the world is not one which from his point of view has beginning or end, we are in principle dealing with the identical question at every moment of the world's existence in relation to God, not simply the pretemporal moment of creativity.[12]

It is this point which gives rise so centrally to the problem of evil.[13] If God is omnipotent, omniscient and all-loving, then how is it that there is such evil and pain in the world for which he is assumed to be entirely responsible? Since he could have chosen not to create in the first place (and at any time) there is a moral question raised for us in respect of his responsibility. In this Sutherland is surely right. If we cannot accept the morality of that choice, given what we subsequently have learned about the nature of the world, then it is simply humbug to argue that what is clearly an immoral thing for a human being to have chosen to do, is somehow made right because it is chosen by God.[14] On the other hand the thesis offered above goes some way towards helping one to think constructively about the problem.

God's intention in creating was to bring into existence the conditions in which his creation could enjoy the same freedom as he enjoyed and thus enter fully into relationships with him. The apex of that creative process, so far as we can see, is human being, but given the way in which such a claim has been interpreted, care is necessary. The claim is inclusive, not exclusive. In the human the opportunity of choice is central to the fulfilment of its nature in a way which points to the possibility of making or marring the work of the creator. All creation may fulfil itself in relation to God through the representative role of the human, as is explicit in a developed understanding of the eucharistic offering. This freedom means that men and women work in relation to and in the context of the whole created order, not over against it to exploit it. However, such freedom could not simply be 'made', or given by God in an act of creating, it had to be learned through experience. No more than any other acquisition such as competence with mathematics, or the ability to enjoy literature, or the skill to play the violin, can the freedom to be oneself be 'created'. Therefore in creating the conditions in which this fulfilment could be possible God had to take the risk that the creatures themselves might not see the point, might choose otherwise even if they did see the point, might not be willing to make the necessary and appropriate effort. Suppose this choice was made contrary to the intentions of the will of the creator, then would God have been justified still in creating? Suppose he had known that such a choice would have been made, then would the case have been morally different? The clue lies in the fact that there is no reason why if God is to be God, that he should know the future in any precise sense. What is necessary is that he should know that whatever occurs and whatever choices are made, and over whatever period of time the processes occur, he is willing to see it through and bring ultimately to perfection the world for which he is responsible. And given that, as we have argued, God knows himself utterly, to the extent that no external pressure, influence or power could bring him to behave in a way which was contrary to his nature, he is always free to give himself wholly in love to the well-being of the world, and to human being in particular. This is precisely what the doctrines of the incarnation and redemption are about, embodied as they are in a particular understanding of the life, death and resurrection of Jesus whom we call the Christ; for it was meditation and reflection on them that led Christians to believe, and leads them still to go on believing, that the God who created the world was justified in choosing to do so, and therefore is worth worshipping. He has, it is asserted, done all that he could and all that it was necessary to do, in order to make a success of the world which he has made; he has committed himself to it. And he is (in continuous present tense) committing himself to it.

It is hard to believe that this is the case because the circumstances in which we find ourselves in the world seem so diabolical. And the situation as at 1987 when this is written gives no scope for easy optimism. Who could be optimistic in face of terrorism in Beirut, in Sri Lanka, in Northern Ireland? Who could be optimistic when self-regarding action on the part of communities and individuals with wealth offers so little to a world in which disease, unemployment, hunger and violence are so conspicuous? But this set of problems need not have been the case and need not be the case. It is a destructive illusion that evil and suffering were inevitable, let alone that they are inevitable. It is a matter of contingent fact that the circumstances we face are as they are, not a necessary consequence of God's choice in creating the world. Original sin, far from being the doctrine which claims that all humanity is inevitably sinful, asserts that human being has an irreducible responsibility for the evil and suffering of the world and an irrefutable opportunity to take responsibility with God for a new world which could come into being. Only if that is the case, we might argue, can it be said that God was morally justified in creating a world.

But God is free and so is human being. And the freedom of one is the necessary condition of the other, given the purpose of the world as Christians conceive it to be. Just as we have argued with regard to God that no circumstances could necessitate that he chose to behave in one way rather than another, so also in order to create the circumstances in which human beings could find themselves through giving themselves to one another, God chose not to require their response to him. Only because God was free was it possible for mankind also to be free. Had there been any anxiety on the part of God that human beings might make choices which would cause him to deny his own nature or to seek the destruction of the world in order to start again or to lose control of himself through the subtle and calculating way in which human beings might choose annoyingly to behave, then God would have had no alternative but to limit the beings with which he was involved. But such was not the case, so that we are faced with a world in which the full gamut of good and evil is open to us and the full maturity of human being also therefore.

There are limits, but they are only the limits of the creature in relation to the Creator. Thus our freedom is in a finite context and only in an eternal context because of our potential relation with the Creator who is eternal. In that sense, although human being can always take more responsibility for the world of which he or she is a part, because he or she always is true to his or her own nature, and is a part of a world and not over against a world, then responsibility is in fact limited. What we can be confident in is our own choices, provided we want to learn from making them and do not engage in them as nothing more than self-regarding activities. Given that we want to grow in knowledge of ourselves and therefore to gain control over ourselves with the consequence that we can more completely find ourselves in self-giving activity, then no choice that we make, however dire or catastrophic it may seem at the time, precludes this possibility. But learning is not inevitable; it only occurs if we wish it to and work for it to happen. It is reasonable to argue therefore that human beings are in fact affirmed in their freedom fundamentally by affirming that freedom in relation to God who is in his creating offering it to them. It might even be argued that the concept of sin is best understood as a logical way within the structure of Christian religious discourse to refer to the continuing freedoms and opportunities which are consistent with being human. It is the consequence of living within a finite world where freedom is limited that sin should therefore have to be coped with if the human being is to enjoy ultimately that relationship with God which is eternal. In this sense it is necessary to argue, as Christian theology has, that God's creative activity is redemptive and therefore in principle salvific. God saves mankind from sin; that is what is in fact meant by talking about the creative activity of God in Christ and why the Gospel of St John can talk of the creation of the world having been through the Word.

In approaching this it is crucial to recognize that creation and redemption are not in fact sequential acts, though conceptually they clearly have to be distinguished. Creation and redemption are two ways of characterizing the simple matter of the Creator's relationship with the Creation: it would make the point to say that God's manner of creating is redemptive. It is perhaps this very point which characterizes the distinction between the theological stances of the Synoptic Gospels and that of the Gospel of St John. Of course, this raises the difficult question of the historical role of Jesus. But in exploring the development of human enquiry about the human situation Christians can point not simply to the centrality of the life, teaching and death of Jesus, but also to the essential nature of his experience of God. That experience provoked the insight that the world could bear the full imprint of the nature of God without denying itself or becoming what it was not. The Creator's commitment of himself to his creation is fulfilled in the person of Jesus Christ.

It is the fact of God's freedom to be himself that guarantees the freedom to human being which is necessary if persons are to emerge through experience of one another, through knowledge of the world and above all through the acknowledgment of the freedom and grace of God in creating. Only because God is as he is can human being have the confidence to behave in the sorts of ways which are in fact necessary if he or she is to find out who he or she is. Exploration for self-knowledge is a demanding and potentially disturbing matter; it frequently leads us to want to hide from the future or to avoid any contact with the world. The encouragement to overcome this natural tendency to avoid difficulty and dis-ease would be all the greater were it not for the confidence which the Christian tradition proclaims regarding the nature of the God who is responsible for it all and who is committed himself to making a success of it.

If it was true that human cantankerousness could frustrate God's purpose or lead to his behaving in a way that was inconsistent with his nature, then human confidence in trying to be itself in relation to God would rightly evaporate. It is those children who are most worried about the risk of damaging their relationship with their parents because they do not know how they will behave who are most at risk and who most often find it difficult to become themselves: human relationship with God is as mutual and reciprocal as that of a parent with a child.

It is this notion of God as 'person' which is explored and developed and checked by the traditional model of expression, the 'Trinity'. Calculation has often seemed to some believers to be the basis of theology, so that numbers have had a particular fascination, whether they involve puzzling out some significance for the number 5000, the six days of creation or the mystical reference to the beast in the Book of Revelation. Mathematical dexterity has nothing to do with the Trinity. No one thought it had; nevertheless this is an important point to make, because some discussion of the issues appears to presume that it has. For example, the relationship between one and three, which can generate a large range of misunderstanding about the relationship between the persons of the Trinity, has nothing to do with the case.

The notion of a trinitarian formula is suggested by the liturgical form of command to baptize, familiar from the Gospel of St Matthew. Its clearest statement before the Council of Nicaea comes in the Adversus Praxean of Tertullian and he it is who is the first to use the term Trinitas. But it is important to notice the context here. Tertullian is defending the traditional faith against the arguments of Praxeas who was a patripassian.[15] Given that the whole question of the nature of God had been fundamentally raised again for the religious world by the claims which Christians were making about Jesus, it is not surprising that the question should from time to time be activated around the possibility of God's suffering. Did God suffer? And if so, in what sense? Since God was in Jewish terms inviolate and incapable of human experience and since the other major influence on the thinking of the early Christian community was that formed by Greek philosophical reflection, it is not surprising that this should constitute the primary problem for the church, at any rate in theological terms. Indeed, the Arian controversy was largely concerned with the same topic. If God has not assumed the suffering of the world, then of what difference is it that Jesus should himself have suffered on behalf of the world? The identity of commitment and work on behalf of both the Father and Son was necessary if the development of the understanding of God as the one who creates redemptively and whose being was essentially free was to be maintained. Of course there were ambiguities related to this, as the image took control of the problems. What exactly (the word 'exactly' is important because the idea was taken seriously even if the idea was irrelevant) was the relationship between the Father and the Son? But the image was intended to enable us to unpack the question of purpose for the world in the light of the dawning perception that what God intended he could not simply achieve on his own. The 'break' in the being of God was a response to the dawning realization that what was meant by 'person' (especially in relation to the agency of God with regard to the creation of the world) was a way of interpreting what was meant by commitment. God, who had to be conceived of as ultimately responsible for what he had brought into existence, had also to be unpacked in terms of the concept of 'god' which was bound up with a Jewish/Greek duality of systems which made the idea most complicated. The natural perspective for such a development was the normal experience of human relationships. And in that regard the assumption of agreed purpose of father and son, the attraction of the idea that father and son would have a common commitment which would not simply be determined by relationships but by interest and desire, was an image which carried weight. The necessity of distinction between the two was a witness to the requirement that co-operation could not simply be determined if it was to be significant for mankind, whereas the necessity of identity of substance was witness to the coherence of the result with the intention. While all things were conceivable for the future, since both God and human being were necessarily free, the ultimate purpose was in fact conceived of from the beginning and always within the grasp of a Father whose nature could never be destroyed by the behaviour of the world. The essential being of the God whom Christians were beginning to form a new conception of was inviolate and therefore he was always available to the world for which he was responsible. And this should be contrasted with the frequent assumption that somehow this constituted an irresolvable conundrum – a paradox. It is no such thing.

But that is not all. God's commitment of himself to his people, which Christians glimpsed through their experience of and reflection upon their experience of Jesus, had to be presented in a way which showed that the world to which God was committed in creation was not a world which was alien to him, but one which was as natural to him (in a different sense) as it was to the creatures with whom he was 'making' it. So that the growing into God of the world through its salvation by 'God in Christ' was not a new direction, but a reasonable and sensible progression. Indeed it should be regarded more in the way of a realization as a form of selfknowledge and therefore as fulfilment through discernment of the real nature of the power appropriate to the world than as a new direction which requires fundamental change or transformation. In this case the distinction was between God and the world as 'sanctified by the Spirit', as Basil the Great chooses to express it. The community of purpose is one which holds together the integrity of God's being in himself, which is a necessary condition of his capacity to give himself to the world, both of which are essential if the world is to fulfil the ultimate reality of its being through relationship with him. This image, of course, also accounts for the arguments over the priority of being and relationships which pertain between the three persons of the Trinity. God the Father must have some priority but only in the sense that if God is to be God then Creator is the category that has to be seen in relation to the Redeemer, and the Redemptor/Creator in relation to the assumption of the potential (because real) divinization of the creation. These are actual relations but not therefore historical or temporal and even for their actuality they depend upon the co-operation of the world itself before they are significant. Thus is God subject to the vulnerability of his own decision to create. These considerations question the reasonableness of regarding patripassionism as a heresy. Indeed it may be suggested that the capacity to suffer, far from being a weakness in the perfection of God or a challenge to the doctrine of his unchangeability, is a characteristic element of his Being, and the one which he recognizes in himself as the necessary condition of his self-giving love in creation.[16]

Human beings have to take seriously the reality of God if they are themselves to fulfil their own natures. The task is one of intellectual and emotional enquiry, not simply one of obedience to an externally defined will whose purpose can neither be understood nor interpreted. In this respect some of the categories of contemporary literary theory are significant. A novelist knows what he or she is about. But as soon as the task of writing has begun there follows the realization that the characters, the story line, has a life of its own. From that time onwards (and indeed from the beginning, one increasingly realizes) the matter of the writing becomes a co-operation between the author, his characters, the form of the novel, the nature of the language which is being used and a variety of other variables which cannot ultimately be controlled but can only be managed. But that is not all, since the purpose of writing a novel is to be read. In this regard the novelist has to be content that the ultimate meaning or significance of what he has done is beyond him to determine on his own. Quite apart from the tradition of fiction in which he or she writes, quite apart from the contemporary context which presents a variety of purposes for the novel, there is the individual reader. That reader is a collaborator in the pursuit of the meaning which the writer had in mind. The risk and the pain of the author is real, continuous but always potentially creative. How else would one be stirred by the poetry of William Dunbar, the fifty-first psalm or the novels of Balsac?

Thus the reality of the physical world raises the matter of

interpretation. The description of the world never satisfies and is not all. The account of the creation offered by Peter Atkins[17] is delightful but ultimately unsatisfying because it leaves out of account the remarkable face of the human capacity to enquire and explain in the way which he so brilliantly does. A rather different point may be made regarding the work of Richard Dawkins,[18] who clearly does find the wonder of the human understanding a delight. However, it is not apparently a question. And the world of human experience appropriately and necessarily raises questions; questions which are about meaning and purpose. The modelling which takes place in the human mind is as relevant to the uncovering of that meaning as the mere description; indeed, the merely descriptive itself cannot even avoid the allusion, the image, the analogy, the metaphor. All ideas and theories about the nature of the world presume a relationship with the world on the part of the merely human and raise questions about the astonishing fact that the world is intelligible to human being at all. But it very evidently is. Yet there are two explicit consequences of this. First, that the process of understanding brings about a difference potentially to the nature of the problem about which one is enquiring. Secondly, the behaviour which one decides to adopt also changes the nature of the experience which one learns from. From these two points it is clear that it is no idle remark to assert that human being is able through both the process of enquiry and the behaviour consequent upon that understanding to change the world of which he is nevertheless completely a part.

The argument in this essay is intended to illustrate the fact that the same process is true in relation to God and that indeed the process of understanding which human being undergoes in relation to God is necessary if man is to come to a full knowledge of himself. The creative activity which is God's is unintelligible as God's unless it is shared by human being. The activity of understanding and behaving which belongs to man is incomplete and unfulfillable apart from the freedom which is actually his because it is completely God's.

The doctrine of the Trinity is an attempt to come to terms with the problem that all arguments about the nature of God's relationship to the world have to be both necessary and contingent.

Is the doctrine of the Trinity a necessary doctrine in the future development of Christian doctrine? This cannot be said. On the other hand, it seems likely that at the moment we have no better model to do justice to the difficulty of talking about God's freedom in relation to the world he is responsible for; it is therefore worth a good deal more reflection before it is discarded.

5

Grace, von Balthasar and the Wesleys

Ivor H. Jones

The convergences between the two traditions represented by von Balthasar and the Wesleys are greater than might be anticipated. In both grace is understood as divine love radiating through human life and becoming for those who are serious in their following of Christ a renewal of their existence, so that in their lives God's glory is returned in humble rapture to its source. Such a convergence suggests intriguing possibilities for a programme for rehabilitation for the Wesleys, for a re-examination of some contemporary points of ecumenical friction, but above all for a fresh evaluation of the relation of divine grace and human freedom.

Divine grace as the source and goal of all human life and as the renewal and transformation of life in all its forms and structures is a crucial element in Christian theology, Orthodox, Catholic and Protestant.[1] That God's free, personal self-offering defines the entire enterprise of human life and history is for all three traditions a common affirmation of faith. There are different nuances and interpretations of that central element, but its place is virtually uncontested. Grace is a basic rhythm of Christian thought.

Among those nuances in the Christian understanding of grace there is one which has brought the three traditions into particularly close proximity. It can be summarized as follows and provides the core of the material for this article: the divine grace which defines all human existence is most truly affirmed in the act of adoration, is most effectively embodied in lives of personal self-offering, and in this way seeks the salvation of all.

Grace is the basic rhythm of Christian thought in as much as it is also the rhythm of Christian life, devotion and mission.

From this rich vein of Christian thought we select for study the work of three people, the modern Roman Catholic theologian, Hans Urs von Balthasar and the two Wesley brothers. Von Balthasar developed his formulation of the doctrine of grace in twentieth-century counterplay with the Catholic Maurice Blondel and the Protestant Karl Barth.[2] The Wesleys developed theirs against a very different background of eighteenth-century piety in which Orthodoxy, Arminianism, Puritanism and Evangelicalism all played a part.[3] Common points of reference, apart from scripture, are the Greek and Latin Fathers, and a long list of saints of the church, including mavericks such as William of St Thierry.[4] So despite their separation in time and setting von Balthasar and the Wesleys share significant sources and some important approaches to theology, not least in their understanding of the doctrine of grace, as they adore the One (in John Wesley's words) whose 'mercies over all rejoice' and look for their lives to be transformed by grace: '... this mission is the love of God and neighbour as revealed in Christ; it can be accomplished only by taking one's stand where he took his'.[5]

Von Balthasar differs of course from the Wesleys in a host of ways. There are aspects of his theology, such as Petrine authority and his devotion to Mary,[6] which lack a comparable emphasis in their work. This means that any comparison of them has to be kept in a proper perspective: far-reaching differences have to remembered. Not the least important of these is – and this point is of particular importance for the purposes of our study here – that von Balthasar's work, unlike theirs, is often set out systematically. As we shall see, this is one of the differences which makes it useful to compare them. For it is one thing to criticize the Wesleys; and quite another to take on the massive learning of von Balthasar. Nevertheless it remains a difficulty that we should have to compare the Wesleys with a systematic theologian, and we shall take account of this by treating each separately. What each has to say about grace will be presented in the contexts proper to each.

Not that von Balthasar's systematic approach to theology makes our study of grace any easier. There is no summary by von Balthasar of his understanding of grace, certainly not a summary comparable, say, with Rahner's articles on that subject.[7] In von Balthasar's case systematic theology is in the form of massive projects any part of which requires evaluation and comment in the light of the whole. The role of grace is just such an area. So it is not sufficient simply to collate the references to grace e.g. in his *Theodramatik* and his *Herrlichkeit*, although that is certainly instructive. It is the relation of these to the whole theological enterprise which is important and it is the place of grace in the whole enterprise which provides the interest for us in this study.

Significant for our purposes is that von Balthasar begins a major work, *Herrlichkeit* (The Glory of the Lord), with the Greek words CHARIS (often translated 'grace').[8] Charis/Grace has a distinctive context there: that God displays, irradiates, the splendour of his eternal triune love in that disinterestedness which true love has in common with true beauty (beauty being another meaning of the Greek word CHARIS).

> In so far as God's revelation appears as his free favour, which merits the name gratia not only by its own gratuitousness but by its interior quality ... and in so far as the content of this self-revelation of God's bears the name of doxa ..., to that extent the analogy suggests itself between aesthetic and theological revealed reality and its reception.[9]

I make three comments on the quotation: first, the power of 'the analogy between aesthetic and theological revealed reality and its reception' is specifically that it evokes the recollection of how our eyes can be opened by the grace/the beauty of what we see and suggests an appropriateness of this analogy to matters of Christian faith. Perception of that kind (so argues the Conclusion to *Herrlichkeit*, 'Verherrlichung als Aneignung und Rückgabe'),[10] draws us into an ever-deepening awareness of God's being and glory. Grace enables us to relish and enjoy the form of divine revelation and to be transformed by the Spirit into that likeness. 'A whole world of love-mysteries opens up to us, stretching farther and farther beyond our sight, to the ultimate grounds of the divine life which has neither beginning nor end.'[11] We share in the life of the Trinity and so can give back to God the glory which has been made our own. We have been 'made to travel through God's grace to the objective reality of God, who has first (see Rom 5.8) had mercy on us'.[12] We ourselves become part of that form by which the truth of Christianity[13] is made identifiable and through our lives offer God the glory with which we have been endowed, a glory which is the splendour of love, selflessly serving out of love.[14] In this way the initial analogy, 'the analogy of beauty', suggests a perception which is nothing less than God in infinite freedom venturing forth to meet humanity and humanity in finite freedom venturing forth to meet God. The 'Unspeakable' has opened itself to reverence and adoration.

Implied in what has been said is, second, that the language of revealed theology is the language of action and response: it is 'revealed reality and its reception'[15] The drama of revelation and response provides a two-fold perspective on grace. On the one hand revelation has its own distinctive authority.[16] According to the 'analogia libertatis' as von Balthasar uses it, God is absolute freedom, a freedom that keeps nothing back:[17] the divine nature is self-giving love and underlies the reality of a world where gratuitousness is basic (otherwise how could the undeserved, beauty for example, be intelligible?).[18] God freely gives himself, and this form of his self-revelation in its capacity to enthrall us gives it its distinctive authority, not least in that it also radiates across the length and breadth of temporal reality. It is above all this freedom which for von Balthasar renders so much of the theology based on Idealism inadequate. Certainly it provides an alternative basis for theology, and for understanding grace,[19] one which discloses grace at work in the world of culture, politics, religion and myth.[20]

On the other hand there is the response. Grace makes possible the reception of this revelation in finite freedom.[21] To expound this von Balthasar adopts models which are integral to his trinitarian theology: conversation, dialogue, event and drama.[22] They are elements in the communication of revelation as they are elements within the nature of the Godhead and within the consequent nature of reality as just described. To know means 'personal selfless involvement'.[23] So conversation is part of the learning process and carries with it the values of graciousness (Huld)[24] and humility. Drama adds other elements to this: encounter, reaction, event, decision, role and plot, the emergence of meaning (a significant feature of von Balthasar's structure of thought as we shall see later) and the imposition of meaning, and above all openness, openness to different circumstances, to re-enactment, to fresh audiences.[25] All these relate to the reception of the divine revelation, and are models for a learning process by which humanity can move from perception of the divine glory – encounter with the divine word as fire and grace – to the response of adoration. Such a response is therefore no restful contemplation of God in his glory; it is itself an involvement in the divine work of judgment and mercy. To receive the revelation is to work with that revelation and to be transformed in and through it.

A third comment: both the analogy of beauty and the analogy of freedom in convergent ways raise the issue, fundamental to the study of grace, of the relation of grace and nature. The analogy of beauty allows us to see grace perfecting nature. An example: in his treatment of faith and biblical revelation, von Balthasar considers circumstances (such as Old Testament visions) where the object of faith is the determinant:

> This absolute determination (and, hence, concordance) effected by the object of faith is an essential component of an aesthetics of revelation. In this we can see both an opposition to an inner-wordly aesthetics and a surpassing of it which perfects it, since the truly beautiful is not magically 'conjured up' from man's emotive states, but, rather, surrenders itself on its own initiative with a graciousness that man cannot grasp. Here lies the 'point of contact' between natural and supernatural CHARIS.[26]

There is a 'point of contact' between nature and the supernatural, but it is one in which the distance between the two is evident and the supernatural surpasses and points to a perfection of the natural. The analogy of liberty is employed similarly, since, according to von Balthasar, human freedom is the more perfected the more fully it gives itself up to infinite freedom, that freedom which holds limitless possibilities yet is always giving itself up entirely unreservedly for the other:

> In the case of that which is created, 'to be in grace' is granted when our basic response of progressively embodying thankfulness to God for our being constituted a person (Selbstverdankung) is brought to perfection both as origin and as goal. That state is not granted, indeed it is taken away, when the creature rejects that basis, being content with the retention of its own freedom of action, or, still further, seeking personally to provide a foundation for it, and taking the view that, because of its transcendental structure, it can itself open up the space of its own transcendence. It belongs with the nature of what is created and God's faithfulness to his own creative

intention that the creature should in the last resort be sustained and held in existence against its will, and supported by God, even though unconsciously, when it sets its goal not on God but, for all its transcendence, ultimately on some finite aim or other. But the creature's refusal to recognize the presence of the giver in itself sets up a barrier because of his finite freedom which positively thereafter excludes God's self-giving.[27]

Both of the analogies are christologically formed.[28] The analogy of beauty is concerned with form and content, the form of Christ and the determinant revelation of God in Jesus Christ, in particular in his cross. The analogy of liberty is concerned with the gratuitousness of God's self-giving in his Son, the incalculable cost of the Son's mission, its fulfilment in obedience on the cross, and the Spirit's boundless affirmation of the unity of Father and Son. In this sense the analogies have been formed christologically. This recognizes Karl Barth's arguments about the dangers in any other analogies than the 'analogy of faith'. They are analogies which point to the nature of grace as preparing the perfection in Christ of the created and enabling the created to testify in Christ to the Creator's glory.

Those three remarks on one of von Balthasar's key references to grace provide a brief survey of grace in one of its contexts: it concerns grace as associated with divine glory and as: 'God's gift of himself in revelation which always reminds man of his creatureliness and interiorly makes him understand why it is that he can receive God's truth and appropriate it to himself only through obedient humility and the distance of faith'.[29]

This leads to the second major area: grace and growth in grace. von Balthasar suggests a broad way and a narrow way. The broad way takes up one stand of previous discussion, the narrow way the other. This is how he characterizes the first:

> Since 'Adam' (that is, since the beginning of creation) and all the more since Christ, the world stands in the light of grace, nature as a whole is intrinsically finalised to supernature, whether it wants it or not, knows it or not. Natural knowledge of God, natural religious ethics stand under this secret sign, whose manifest character the Church proclaims and in a mysterious fashion is. (Is this not the meaning of the old patristic doctrine of the logos spermatikos?)
>
> Were we to put this thinking into practice, the chief directions of contemporary intellectual life, the great impulses of modern

times could also find a home in Christianity. 'The religious element in mankind' stands as a whole unconsciously in the light of grace and redemption; on every religious road man can find the God of grace. This is the christening of the Enlightenment and of liberal theology from Herbert of Cleobury down to the present day'... This is the christening of German idealism... the cosmos, biologically considered, is in evolution up to man and beyond him... Further, why shouldn't a Christian truth be hidden even in Marxist total-labour process as the return of mankind from its self-alienation... And again, is it not through fellow-feeling that man truly becomes man?[30]

The narrow way, the way to which von Balthasar's work is specifically committed, is described in terms of a priority: the greatest possible radiance in the world by virtue of the closest possible following of Christ.

At the point where the tension between being a Christian and being a person like others is at its strongest, indeed so strong that it must appear to the natural man as lacerating and 'psychologically' unbearable by every standard of closed and harmonious humanity, there is raised up not only the outer 'eschatological' (i.e. world-vanquishing) sign – a kind of stimulating irritant – but also the reality itself, either in its visibility or (as with everything weighty in Christianity) in its invisibility.[31]

This is what led von Balthasar to form 'secular institutes', as a link between laity and the traditional vows, as an expression of contemporary mission in the world, and as pointing the church to the interdependence of all its members in the calling to perfect love.

This narrow way recognizes our human solidarity in sin. Within a dramatic interpretation of the Book of Revelation von Balthasar treats the problem of evil at the heart of the divine drama.[32] It is a matter for deep thankfulness to God that our solidarity in our fate should have been the means by which God's grace might show, by a deeper and more agonizing form of love, how deep his love might sink to draw us into free engagement with his blessedness. The divine drama therefore depicts and defines our common fate. There is an incompleteness to humanity in the face of death compounding the disturbing mystery of the souring of our human qualities and forces. There is a natural striving for salvation through encounter with

God, but this is only truly human in so far as the human being is ready to be granted its fulfilment as the divine gift of grace. To expect it on other terms is as much a *hubris* as to expect love in a human relationship on the basis of coercion.

Adam's choice was a failure to live by the standard of divine love, and thus a claim to autonomy over against God, an assumption of power involving deception, with that consequent turning-in-on-himself, Augustine's *incurvatio in se ipsum*. The drama twists and turns. Even as Adam falls from grace, God marks him with an invitation: he is 'called' – a mark of grace over against the growing power of darkness. But Adam's claim against God draws him further away in that undertow that characterizes evil.

But even yet the agony of the human situation is not yet fully evident. Only Christ on the cross, taking our place, reveals that. The cross stands in the long line of atrocities which stem from our inhumanity, the inadequacy and failure of human love. It declares before God the world's guilt. The cross is evidence of that original sin by which, through selfishness, humanity's grasp on grace was rendered harder still; it is also evidence of divine grace of which there was never any intermission, but only a transmission to a new and more effective form.[33]

If the narrow way recognizes our solidarity in sin, it also recalls the difficulty of the return route. This too involves death, our entry into the pattern of the Son's death and resurrection: 'Man participates in Christ's archetypal experience only by being raised outside of himself through sharing in grace and faith.'[34] It involves a task: 'Grace brings man a task, opens up for him a field of activity.'[35] It involves co-operation with grace, and the uncertainty of living by faith. For we are not passive participants in the divine drama. We are active participants, and this involves obedience and discipline, commitment and prayer. It involves growth and change: von Balthasar describes it in terms of a journey to the perfection of grace and love. Part of this is the secular political and social struggle, although von Balthasar is anxious that political liberation should be seen as only part of the gospel.[36]

We are caught up in the divine drama of grace, in which we are called to be the embodiment of grace, a people in whom the qualities of grace are evident. Nothing is more characteristic of von Balthasar than his interest in people of faith whose lives are evidence of divine grace. This shapes his use of the traditional theological terms:

> There is an objective name and it denotes the reality in itself, and this is grace: a sharing in God's own intimate reality; as sanctifying grace it gives us objectively a share in God's being; as 'actual grace' it enables us to live this reality and act with it. The other name is subjective and shows our consciousness of its presence; it is divine virtue (i.e. an aptitude, a capacity to turn ourselves towards God) and is thus the triad: faith, hope and charity.[37]

To summarize: von Balthasar understands the Christian life in terms of involvement in the divine drama in which the divine grace draws us at great cost and with incredible daring into a share in God's own mission and being. As we share in that grace and love, our response is one of wonder, rapture and praise, of joy in responding to God's glory in the journey towards perfect love and thus witnessing to God's eternal love for all humanity.

When we turn to the Wesleys the same nuances are present. It is no easier to find a satisfactory mode of presentation in their case than it was in the discussion of von Balthasar.[38] There are those who are convinced that 'responsible grace' provides an integrating focus[39] for the theology of the Wesleys, and that it would be proper to systematize their work around that centre. Others are less sure. Our method will be to use several cross-sections of the material. In this way the strength of the motif of 'grace and love evoking rapture' becomes evident and some important nuances begin to emerge.

John Wesley's language is proverbially straightforward and plain. It stands a very long way from the complex, figurative language of von Balthasar. Since part of the fascination of von Balthasar's work is that his style is an appropriate form for his content, John Wesley's very different literary milieu makes his literary style a good place to begin. Wesley was a preacher rather than a theologian and his concern with plain language was in the interests of clear, immediate communication. So we shall begin this section with Wesley material which is treated in different literary forms: John Wesley's *Sermon on Prayer* and his *Hymns on the Lord's Prayer*.[40] The sermon itself is concerned first with the right attitudes to prayer and with the Lord's Prayer as containing all our duty to God and man; the meditation branches out into a mosaic of references framed as a contemplation in the third person (If he is a father, then he is good, and he is loving, to his children) – its preface concerns particularly God's gracious work in creating, preserving (cf.Heb 4.16), justifying (freely by his grace, through the redemption that is in Jesus), receiving (as children by adoption and grace), and caring for all (the universality of grace), accompanied by typically Erasmian references from Iliad 1.544 as well as the biblical quotations: 'His mercy is over all his works' (Ps.145.9) and 'the Lord's delight is on them that fear him' (Ps.147.11). The main section of the meditation includes discussion of the text of the Lord's Prayer (e.g. of bread as the sacramental bread – 'the grand channel whereby the grace of his Spirit was conveyed to the souls of the children of God', and of the relation our being forgiven to our forgiveness of others); then the final Doxology – a solemn thanksgiving for the divine attributes of sovereignty and power, and a reminder that praise is due from every creature. The meditation is thus a florilegium of materials mainly from devotional and scriptural sources, and covering a wide range of references to grace (prevenient, saving, co-operating, sacramental and universal).

The hymns are direct address to God, bringing together phrases reminiscent of Milton and Dryden and, of course, biblical references, but above all a different association of words and phrases, distinctly evocative and affirmative in character.

> Father of all, whose powerful voice
>   Called forth this universal frame,
> Whose mercies over all rejoice
>   Through endless ages still the same.
> Thou by thy word upholdest all
>   Thy bounteous love to all is showed;
> Thou hear'st thy every creature's call,
>   And fillest every mouth with good.

The association of 'mercies' and 'rejoice' illustrates this evocative approach to language: that God's 'mercies over all rejoice,/ Through endless ages still the same 'not merely contrasts with the powerful creative word of lines 1 and 2; it also suggests that far from mercy involving displeasure or initial judgment, the joy of creation is expressed in unchanging, universal, merciful care for all, and for all time. This 'merciful care' is then expanded through the following lines: the creative word also sustains the universe, the care involves 'bounty', a love which extends to every individual creature in every practical need. The contrast between the creator's power and his love towards the creation (echoed in his distinction between the irresistible power of the creator and the resistible grace of the Spirit's work) becomes in verse 2 a contrast between the creator's exalted place and the worshippers' prostrate praise. The creator surveys all, hell included; the contrast of heavenly light and infernal gloom implies no limitation on God's might. God is sovereign over all; and the worshippers confess the attributes which from creation onwards have made him so. The third verse is a masterpiece of literary construction involving chiasmus, monosyllabic lines, with this final exclamation:

> Jehovah reigns! Be glad, O earth,
> And shout, ye morning stars, for joy.

John Wesley spoke of this style in his Preface to the 1780 book as simple and plain, suited to every capacity, but he also admitted that it might possess the true spirit of poetry, not just imitating Milton or Spenser, but poetry such as might quicken devotion, confirm faith and kindle love to God and man.[41] Wesley was treating form as suited to the reader rather than as suited to content (except in so far as integrity of style might be concerned), but this brief exploration indicates the way the warmer tones of his poetic style sustained the content.

A second cross-section concerns the Wesleys' references to humanity 'sharing in the divine life', their 'dialectical mysticism'.[42] This is a very frequent feature in the Wesleys' hymnody:

> Unsearchable the love
>   That hath our Saviour brought;
> The grace is far above
>   Or man or angel's thought;
> Suffice for us that God, we know,
> Our God is manifest below
>
> He deigns in flesh to appear
>   Widest extremes to join;
> To bring our vileness near,
>   *And make us all divine*:
> And we the life of God shall know;
> For God is manifest below.[43]

or,

>Made like him, like him we rise,
>Ours the cross, the grave, the skies.[44]

or

>Father of everlasting grace,
>Thy goodness and thy truth we praise,
>>Thy goodness and thy truth we prove;
>Thou hast, in honour of thy Son,
>The gift unspeakable sent down,
>>The Spirit of life, and power, and love.
>
>Send us the Spirit of thy Son
>To make the depths of Godhead known,
>>*To make us share the life divine.*[45]

'Sharing the life divine' emerges from scripture, from the life of the early church, from the Eastern Fathers such as Ignatius of Antioch,[46] Gregory of Nyssa, and the Book of Common Prayer. Sometimes it is in association with the Holy Spirit's work:

> Unless the soul shall in this world receive the sanctification of the Spirit through much faith and prayer, and be made partaker of the divine nature (through which it will be without blame and in purity to perform all the commandments) it is unfit for the kingdom of God.[47]

Dwelling in God, being transformed by Christ, sharing in the glorification of Christ, this is a transformation into the divine love, mystical, social, practical; and costly – since it is the work of Christ's love:

>Love divine, all loves excelling,
>>Joy of heaven to earth come down,
>Fix in us thy humble dwelling,
>>All thy faithfull mercies crown ...
>Jesu, thou art all compassion,
>>Pure, unbounded love thou art;
>Visit us with thy salvation,
>>Enter every trembling heart.
>
>Come almighty to deliver,
>>Let us all thy grace/life receive ...
>
>Changed from glory into glory,
>>Till in heaven we take our place,

> Till we cast our crowns before thee,
> Lost in wonder, love and praise.[48]

The third cross-section concerns the work of grace in the 'Order of Salvation', to which there is manifold testimony in the structure of the Methodist societies, the organization of hymnody, the Letters and the teaching of the sermons[49] (this applies to all the mature stages of John's life). There is, for example, the awakening of conscience as the Spirit's work of grace:

> There is no man, unless he has quenched the Spirit, that is wholly void of the grace of God. No man is entirely destitute of what is vulgarly called 'natural conscience'. But this is not natural; it is more properly termed 'preventing grace' (i.e. the grace of the Holy Spirit). Every man has greater or less measure of this, which waiteth not for the call of man.[50]

There is the pattern of preventing, convicting, enabling, justifying, pardoning, sustaining and sanctifying grace, with perfect love[51] the goal of the whole process.

One particular hymn from the section for 'Mourners Brought To Birth' rehearses the work of grace particularly clearly: 'Come, O Thou Traveller unknown'. It follows the sequence leading to the New Birth in the form of Jacob wrestling with God at Penuel. Its emphasis on the synergism of divine action and human response is reminiscent of von Balthasar's method.

> In vain thou strugglest to get free
> I never will unloose my hold;
> Art thou the Man that died for me?
> The secret of thy love unfold:
> Wrestling, I will not let thee go
> Till I thy name, thy nature, know.[52]

On the one hand there is the question 'Art thou the Man that died for me?', hinting, as in von Balthasar's presentation, at the need for God to have entered into human existence for grace to be fully effective. It also indicates the unbelievable quality of the divine grace that is operative in incarnation and passion. On the other there is Jacob's tenacity, commitment, determination, resolve expressed poetically in the refrain: 'Till I thy name, thy nature know'. The danger and the cost of the enterprise are registered. Its audacity is almost blasphemous:

> What though my shrinking flesh complain
> And murmur to contend so long?
> I rise superior to my pain:
> When I am weak, then I am strong.
> And when my all of strength shall fail
> I shall with the God-man prevail.

Line 4 is a reference to II Cor.12.10, to the glorious victories which wrestling believers in Christ can win – albeit with broken bones and halting thigh. And all this belongs within the stage of repentant faith, with evidence of divine grace from start to finish. The narrative evokes the wonder and strangeness of the divine activity, using the kind of intriguing subtlety we met earlier in von Balthasar. What is said by that narrative about grace is complex and many-facetted. It is like a world of divine resource seeking our progress toward new birth.

Our simple comparison is complete, as complete as can be presented in this brief article. The convergences between the two traditions are striking; and they are greater than might have been anticipated. In both sections we have found grace, understood as love, as the divine life, radiating through human life and history, and becoming, for those who are serious in their following of Christ, the very nature of their own existence, so that in their lives too the glory of God is returned in humble rapture to its source.

In conclusion I make three comments on the comparison. First, there is the value of von Balthasar's work for the modern re-assessment of the Wesley tradition. Here is a modern thinker who refuses to turn aside from the major contemporary problems of Christian thought, whether it is the overwhelming pervasive reality of evil, or the manifest injustice of innocent suffering, or whether it is the scepticism of some traditions of modern metaphysics or the challenges to Christian discipleship within contemporary society. He does not shrink from the profundities of Christian experience and the complexities of manifold disciplines of learning. His response on all these fronts is creative and in some cases epoch-making. In particular we might refer again to the important response which he has made to the challenges of idealism. Yet, in essence, the central theological thrust of his work affirms aspects of the foundations of Methodism which we have been in danger of jettisoning. This central point of a convergence between the Wesleys and a major contemporary theologian could be constructive for our future work. In particular, our concentration on grace has raised again the significance of defining human nature ultimately and therefore proximately also in terms of divine reality.

Second, there is the relation of both traditions to the 'historical method'. Characteristic of both traditions is a joyful and positive faith, welcoming the range of divine activity in the world, and this is an encouraging departure from some modern norms. But what would be the effect on them of making concessions to the historical method? Von Balthasar is of course fully aware of the historical method and has proved a superb exponent of it, for example in his work on Evagrius. He is concerned with detailed accuracy of presentation, as in his book of Karl Barth, where it is vitally important for von Balthasar that it represents Barth with exactness. There is a breath of suspicion, however, in some of his studies, as for example in his work on Gerard Manley Hopkins, that his categories introduce interpretative features into his subject matter which are characteristically von Balthasar. But it is in his opposition to the use of the historical method in biblical material that the main problems arise. In some cases he refers to biblical historians and uses their work. In *The Christian State of Life*, for example, he accepts as final Hengel's judgment on the uniqueness of the authority evinced by Jesus in calling his disciples – a crucially important case in the historical discussion regarding Jesus' self-consciousness, and one which von Balthasar uses as a basis for his argumentation in that book.[53] Since other historians and biblical critics (e.g. E.P. Sanders[54]) disagree with Hengel precisely at that point, and since there is no historical discussion of the issue in *The Christian State of Life* beyond a reference to Schürmann's research in the area, it is evident that von Balthasar's preference for Hengel's judgment is influence by grounds other than the historical.

One of these takes the historical element in Christian faith more seriously than many biblical critics do. For von Balthasar, as we saw earlier, recognizes in the events recorded in the biblical text and in the biblical text itself, not simply the route by which the divine revelation may be reached, but that form in the distinctiveness of which the ground of all, through the work of grace, appears. Fundamental to this approach is von Balthasar's theological aesthetics, by which he moves from the traditional understanding of how knowledge and faith relate, to a view based on aesthetic judgments. This claims that the eye of faith is opened by the grace of the object which it beholds;[55] the form is recognized as the appropriate medium of what it manifests, whether that form is the Jesus of history, or scripture or the history of the church.

Undoubtedly this is a most original development in theological work which carries with it implications of many kinds, not least for the future of biblical historical criticism. It must, however, be pointed out that the analogy of aesthetic judgments with theological enquiry is capable of being pursued in more than the particular way chosen by von Balthaser. If, for example, we discuss the nature of aesthetic judgment in the light of that medium of artistic expression in which form and expression are most closely related, namely music, it becomes evident that aesthetic judgment can be dependent on the very same system of historical enquiry which is evident in biblical criticism. For form in music can be, although of course need not always be, dependent on such technical historical skills.

A classic illustration of this is the interpretation of Bach's *Art of Fugue*. There is no performance of the work which can be independent of a whole sequence of judgments, including text-critical and historico-critical, raising even the issue whether or not it should be performed (ought it rather to remain an object of contemplation?).[56] There is no doubt that the aspects of aesthetic judgment to which von Balthasar alludes apply here. But additionally it has to be said that neither the form nor the appropriateness of form to its expression can satisfactorily be discussed in isolation from the historico-critical method, part of which involves here a basic uncertainty as to whether or not the form and significance of the music can be identified. What von Balthasar has done in his *Herrlichkeit* is to utilize creatively a most powerful analogy. But the contexts in which that analogy can operate deserve attention too and introduce new dynamics into the discussion.[57] To do this would have wide-ranging consequences but perhaps here is not the place to pursue them.

Third, the concentration on divine love as the true focus for all reality deserves to be noted as a contribution to contemporary debate within the Roman and Methodist traditions. We indicated at the beginning that there are key issues which divide the two traditions, for example the interpretations of the Petrine and the Marian dogmas. Von Balthasar's determination in following through his main focus into controversial areas, as for example he has already done in *The Christian State*, has produced remarkable results. I think, for example, of his recontextualizing of the subjective aspects of the ordained priesthood within this central perception of reality. If that were given greater currency again (it has biblical and historical justification) the traditions could move closer on institutional issues as they clearly have on fundamentals.

Von Balthasar's work is an enormous resource, and it is to be hoped that Methodists will be willing to draw on this in order to expound more adequately their own tradition. What has been said on the subject of grace hardly begins to adumbrate the possibilities in this single area. It is to be hoped that others will take up the study.

6

Experiencing Grace

Kenneth G. Howcroft

Methodism has often emphasized the themes of grace, Christian experience, personal and social holiness and the importance of scripture for Christian living. This essay explores how the world of the New Testament might relate to that of our contemporary experience, and uses the situation of Christians in the modern British city as a test case. In doing so, it outlines a process in which people may experience grace.

The appropriation of experience

It is rarely that I am immediately and clearly aware of what I am experiencing, and even on those few occasions subsequent events often make me revise my initial opinion. This experience might be the effect on me of such things as stimulus in the external world; my thoughts or rational judgments; my feelings or instinctive and intuitive judgments; my emotions; the deeper-seated drives, motivations and yearnings within me. In each case I start by becoming dimly aware of something pressing upon me. It is only when some word, image, concept or symbol comes into play that this blurred and shadowy experience starts to come into focus. Two things then begin to happen. On the one hand I allow myself to go further down into my experience and to appropriate it more deeply and more richly. On the other I discover that other people share experiences that are focussed by the same words and pictures. At one and the same time I discover that my experience is a particular truth for me, and part of a more general truth beyond me. As the images interact with my experience, the two together become 'my story'. In continually recounting that story I find that I encounter both myself and the world more fully.

A common and almost trite example of this in our culture is the experience of falling in love. Before it happens the things other people say and the words of popular songs may make us look for something to occur and we may even attempt to manufacture for ourselves whatever we have imagined the experience to be. Yet whenever it does happen we find that it is never the same as any expectations we might have developed. It is unfocused. We are just aware of something happening to us and within us. It is at this point that we find ourselves repeating lines of poetry or singing the corny songs which we so liked to despise before. The experience makes them come alive for us for a time in a new way. Somehow they help us to recognize the experience more clearly and accept it more fully. They also enable us to signal to others what is happening to us and to discover in return that similar things have happened to them. The words and the songs provide a common bond, a bridge which enables us to share this experience with others, giving and receiving. As we do that it comes into even sharper focus, and we are enabled to explore it and enjoy it (or own it, if it involves pain) more fully.

What is true here for individuals is also true for groups. For a long time there has been much religious and political talk of the poor, the outcast and the marginalized, particularly those in the inner city, as the 'voiceless'. People and whole communities experience unfocussed and therefore inarticulate thoughts, feelings, emotions and unconscious urges about themselves, their surroundings, and the lives they feel forced to live. They are unclear about these reactions, and so feel the pressure of them as something external and alien. They find it hard to own them as their own. Political and religious groups step into the picture and try to give a voice to these 'voiceless' communities. They provide their own concepts, images, symbols and analyses, but often seek to impose them as fixed ideologies. When this happens the voiceless feel not only uncertain and frustrated but also alienated and oppressed. Sometimes the only way of expressing the unfocussed and unacknowledged experiences shared in by these communities and their rejection of the languages imposed upon them by others turns out to be in rioting and violence.

There is, however, another way. It means getting involved

Experiencing Grace

with a group of people in a particular context, of watching, listening and working with them, and then offering them a whole range of ideas, pictures and concepts out of which they may choose the ones which resonate most with their unfocussed experience, be it to comfort or to challenge that experience. Through the chosen images and models the people become more aware of what their experience actually is and more capable of communicating it to others. They can thereby recognize people who share similar experience and identify potential allies or opponents. All in all they become more able to take responsibility for their own lives, make plans and carry them into action.

The awareness and acceptance of what is happening in us and among us thus comes through the interaction of a generally unfocussed experience and particular concepts and images. As we noted in the example of falling in love, sometimes the concepts predate the experience, sometimes they follow it, but we always draw them from areas about which we already have a greater apprehension. They will therefore always have a greater clarity than our unfocussed experience – although the interaction between the two will create a greater apprehension of both.

It is already apparent that these concepts and images cannot be seen as literally applicable descriptions, as if they were the same thing as the experience they help to form. Enormous distortions take place if this is not recognized. Because the words and pictures are drawn from outside the experience, they are necessarily different from it, and are themselves culturally influenced and bound by the particular contexts from which they are drawn. What happens is that some of them resonate with our experience and help us discover it in sharper focus, but only to a particular extent in each case. Although we begin by saying 'Yes, it is this ...' we find that if we push our application of the image too far we end up wanting to say 'No, it is not this ...' or rather, since we do not want to deny the greater clarity and reality which the image has previously brought, 'No, it is no longer this ...'. Thus if we are black people living in the inner city we may find that the idea of slavery helps us focus, own and articulate our experience there at first, but that there are times when it becomes unhelpful and even counterproductive.

The concepts and images are therefore used as metaphors and analogies which by their very nature say 'It is this ... and yet it is not this.'[1] The danger of this approach is that it can all become completely subjective and lose any ability for the truth claims or the reality of the experience to be tested. The images which we choose might be our own fantasies and the projections of our own imaginations produced to justify the reality of an experience which is itself fantastic. The only guard, and it is not a complete guard, against this is when the image or concept employed is itself obviously rooted in some corresponding or correlative reality. As I struggle to own and come to terms with my experience when my partner suddenly dies, coca-cola advertisements may help me think that things are going better, but a biography of someone who lost a limb is more likely to help me explore my loss correctly.

Thus when correlative concrete events are used as metaphors a greater objectivity is acquired and at the same time the images do not become imperialistic ideologies imposed on reality. Looked at in this way it is not surprising that the Christian story, with its claim to a concrete historical and incarnational base, has had such a powerful effect on people. We are here drawing on the work of David Tracy in *The Analogical Imagination*,[2] although he is mainly concerned with pointing the way to a religious pluralism. He does, however, describe how my experience may be either completely unfocussed or already partially focussed through interaction with one set of images as I start to recount 'my story'. He then points out that it is only when I allow my experience or story to interact with new metaphors that are themselves rooted in concrete reality, that I become able to recognize, own and appropriate my experience more fully as my concrete reality. At the same time I start to discover and own that reality to be part of a wider reality encompassing myself, others, the world, and, to a religious outlook, God. Thus Tracy can say

> With T.S. Eliot, I may even recognize that only after that heated conversation did I find that the self prior to the conversation had the experience but missed the meaning. Only by analogically reaching out to the hard concreteness of the other and through that expanding conversation to the proleptic concreteness of the whole, will any of us find that we arrive where we began only to know the place for the first time.[3]

A New Testament model of appropriating experience

This process is not unknown in the New Testament. A powerful example occurs in Mark's Gospel. At the heart of the Gospel in Mark 8.22–26, Jesus is portrayed as healing a blind man, who begins to experience seeing. What he sees are people but the vision is unfocussed and he can only get a grip on it by referring to a metaphor which has greater clarity for him: they are positively like trees, but at the same time the metaphor cannot be pushed too far because they are not completely like trees in that they are walking about. A second stage then occurs in which he moves on to appropriate his sight fully and clearly.

Mark's Gospel tells this story as an indicator as to how we are to interpret the account which immediately follows it. Jesus asks his disciples to articulate their own experience of him in contradistinction to other people's. Peter is able to begin to do this by drawing an image of the Messiah from his cultural tradition, but he quickly shows by his response to Jesus' comments about his destiny that his experience is still very unfocussed. Jesus helps him into further dialogue between the images and his experience until there comes the moment of the Transfiguration, equivalent to the second healing touch for the blind man, where he sees clearly and appropriates the experience fully.

This story sums up a basic theme of Mark's Gospel. In it Jesus constantly proclaims the kingdom (Mark 1.14–15), on the one hand through miracles and on the other through verbal proclamation. Mark 6. 1–6 shows that the two are intimately connected, for when the people reject Jesus' preaching they automatically appear to make it impossible for themselves to receive any miracles from him. However, whereas Matthew and Luke make it explicit that the miracles are manifestations of the kingdom (eg. Matt.12.28; Luke 11.20), Mark leaves them just as events to be experienced. The people are challenged to see that experience clearly for what it is and thereby appropriate it. Images are provided to help them do this partly through allusions to scripture and contemporary traditions, partly through the verbal proclamation of the kingdom. Yet Jesus rarely does even the latter directly. Instead he presents the kingdom in parables, which we might describe rather as extended metaphors than strict analogies. They are offered to help people focus and appropriate for themselves the experience of the kingdom to be found in the miracles or other events in their lives.

The parables can help, but need not necessarily do so.

Consequently Mark 4. 3–8 provides a parable to help the listeners get a grip on their experience of parables. The point is put in a more direct way in Mark 4. 10–12. The upshot of both is that for some people the parables reveal, helping them to see more clearly. For others they conceal, making them blind and unable to possess for themselves any crop of experience. The difference lies in how they utilize the image in approaching their experience.

Mark therefore shows Jesus proclaiming the kingdom in an indirect way which demands that people appropriate their own experience of it. The same process applies all the more concerning the nature and purpose of Jesus himself. His preferred way of speaking about himself in Mark is as 'the Son of Man'. This is a phrase sufficiently unclear for scholars still to be unable to determine exactly what it means. However, it appears less and less likely to have been a title, and more to have been a metaphorical figure of speech which could refer to Jesus himself and anyone else who might be connected closely with him and share his destiny.[4] It is not a phrase which makes a formal description or proclamation about Jesus. If anyone in Mark's story attempts that, Jesus immediately commands silence: Mark 1. 21–28 is paradeigmatic for the whole Gospel here.[5] Rather than assent to a proposition about Jesus, the people in the story are challenged to discover the truth about him by focussing and appropriating their own experience of him.

This brings us back to the incident at Caesarea Philippi. We should, however, first notice its links to the baptism of Jesus in Mark 1. 9–11. There Jesus appears to have a private experience in which the Spirit and voice act as symbols which help him focus his experience of being anointed by God (a Christ) and also of being in an intimate relationship with God (Sonship). This enables him (not without a struggle depicted in Mark 1. 12–13) to appropriate for himself what it is to be himself in relation to God. Exactly halfway through the Gospel at Caesarea Philippi (Mark 8. 22–9.8) the private experience at the baptism is widened to include Peter as the representative follower of Jesus. Jesus asks his disciples to put aside the direct assertions which others have proclaimed as truth. Instead they are to focus their own experience of him gained whilst watching his signs, listening to his parables and participating with him in life and the kingdom. In so doing, Peter discovers that in some real even if transferred sense this will involve him in the same process of crucifixion and resurrection as that to which Jesus himself has been led in appropriating the experience at his baptism (Mark 8.31,34).

However, although Peter owns this experience, he proves unable to live it out fully in the days before the crucifixion (Mark 14.26–72). In denying Jesus he falls away and in a sense becomes God-forsaken in a way which parallels that of Jesus on the cross. No amount of proclamation that Jesus has been raised will touch him, and indeed no message is given (Mark 16.8). Rather, Peter must go back to Galilee where it all began and begin the mission of the kingdom again on Christ's behalf. In doing so he will be able to focus his experience more fully and discover both that Christ has been raised and that he himself has been lifted up to new life and has entered the kingdom he proclaims.

Ultimately Mark's Gospel contains the challenge for people to appropriate for themselves the experience of God ruling in their lives and in the whole created order (the kingdom). It all centres on Jesus in that the challenge and the process begins with him and then widens to include his followers. Until now we have shown how Mark portrays the actors in his story undergoing the process of appropriation. It is obvious, however, that the Gospel also invites the reader or hearer to identify with those actors and undergo the same process. Thus, at the end of the Gospel (assuming that this was at 16.8) the challenge widens out to include the reader. We are shown that no directly proclaimed truth will assist us, and that we are challenged to encounter the risen Christ as we immerse ourselves in this work and mission and focus and own our experience of him, and through him of God's loving rule.

New Testament experiences of transformation

Mark's Gospel is paradeigmatic for the rest of the New Testament. We can perceive the New Testament accounts as the records of the way people struggled to appropriate their experiences of the events connected with Jesus of Nazareth, particularly those around the first Easter. Serious and careful questions will have to be asked about what actually happened then; if Christianity is truly an 'incarnational' faith then it will never be able to dispense with disciplined historical-critical study. But what the records give us is not just direct proclamation that 'Christ has been raised' but more often the tools and the images to discover, explore and own our experience of it. The stories show us people fluctuating between violent extremes of unfocussed experience, overwhelmed by anxiety, guilt, fear and death at one moment and by life, courage, forgiveness and peace at the next. In order to come to terms with these at all they have to turn to every set of concepts and images available to them. But these they use as metaphors, aware that not one of them is a literal description of the event or the experience of it. Each is employed in order to obtain a purchase on the experience, but none of them can be pushed too far before it has to be negated.

The prime example of this is Paul. He employs a bewildering range of words and pictures drawn from a vast range of sources, both Jewish and Hellenistic, both religious and secular. He picks them up and then puts them down again as quickly preventing others from pushing them too literally or too far with an emphatic 'no' (eg. Rom.6.2) We turn to some examples of this process in connection with the theme of the transformation of life. They are drawn mainly from Paul, but also from other parts of the New Testament.[6]

Whatever actually happened when Paul encountered some new reality in his life connected with Jesus of Nazareth, he gained the impression that he was starting to live in a new way. The image which helped him focus and own that experience was that of new creation (eg. Rom.8. 18–25; II Cor.5. 17; Col. 1. 13–20) and in particular new birth (I Cor.15.8ff.); John 3 employs the same image. At another point he had a sense of forgiveness and of being at one with God in a way somehow connected with Jesus. What helped here was the concept in both Jewish and Hellenistic culture that what enabled people to be forgiven and at one with God was a sacrifice. Jesus was therefore portrayed as some form of sacrifice, as we find for example stated in Romans 3.25ff. and then explored in great detail by the writer to the Hebrews. Yet much as Hebrews employs this image, it also insists that Jesus was not a sacrifice in any sense previously understood (see chapters 9 and 10). The image is a metaphor used to focus and appropriate experience: it is this, and it is not this.

At another moment the sense is of being liberated or freed. The focussing image here is of Christ being one who releases people from prison (Rom.3.24; I Cor.1.30; Col.1.14; Luke 4. 18–21). Sometimes the feeling presses heavily that someone has paid a great cost in achieving that release. Paul uses here the concepts which existed in various forms in the Jewish and

Hellenistic world of the freeing of a slave and the ransoming of a prisoner (eg I Cor. 6.20; 7.21–23; Gal.3. 13; 4.1–7). Interestingly amongst the variety of practice in these respects, either the slave's master or another party could pay the necessary price, or the slave could save up for it out of his personal allowance. Paul can therefore use a variety of expressions saying sometimes that God effects the release, sometimes Christ, sometimes an apostle, and sometimes that we have to play a part in the process for ourselves. Paul does not seem interested in the question much beloved by later theologians of to whom the ransom is paid. If he caught somebody pushing the image that far he would probably immediately say that at that point it became useless and inappropriate – 'no, it is not that'.

At yet other moments, the pressing but unfocussed experience seems to be of finding oneself in an easy and open relationship that encompasses the sense of estrangement and conflict with oneself, with others and with God (eg. Rom. 5.10ff; II Cor. 5.18ff; Col. 1.20ff – the image is later extended in Eph. 1.4–2.16). This involves a sense that experience is not just an individual matter, but concerns people in all their relationships, and that it also includes the corporate experience of whole communities and societies. The image employed here is that of a reconciliation being negotiated between two parties by an ambassador. This helps grasp the element of the process which involves a continuous dialogue between the parties. But it does not speak to that unfocussed feeling that people are different yet intimately connected, and that they are united in diversity yet diverse in their unity. Images employed to help focus that experience are those of the body (eg. I Cor. 12. 12–21) and the refurbished building (eg. I Peter 2. 4–8).

Paul and other New Testament writers therefore use images as metaphors drawn from concrete situations in their world in order to focus and appropriate fully their experience of transformation in their lives and in their world. It is noticeable that there are prior assumptions both that they are undergoing some experience of transformation in their ordinary lives and that this is somehow connected with the crucifixion and resurrection of Jesus of Nazareth. The writers discover that the images enrich their understanding both of Jesus himself and of their experience of him. When they invite us into their story to undergo the same process, the former assumption might be understandable, but the latter is often harder to establish. This means that a difficult preliminary stage has to be added to the contemporary process. It does not, however, invalidate the process itself.

Contemporary experience and scripture

The implication of the last paragraph is that there is an inherent difficulty in seeking to relate the images or world of the Bible to our contemporary experience. We have attempted so far to describe a process by which people explore and own their deep experiences of life. All attempts to work through this process have their own integrity and validity. Nonetheless, men and women of a religious outlook will claim that any experience in life is only appropriated at its deepest level when it is found to be dynamically related to God. Those of Christian persuasion will in turn see this essentially in terms of being related to the crucifixion and resurrection of Jesus. Yet it is increasingly hard to discern either how an historical crucifixion and resurrection can have a real effect on our contemporary experience, as some Christian traditions claim, or how, as others state, they are a continuing reality within it. On the wider front, there is a growing problem about how we can with any certainty discern any activity of God in life, and of how we can talk with any credibility of God at all. The more we speak of God-talk, in particular the language of scripture, consisting of images and metaphors, the more we open ourselves to the charge that all such talk is related to no objective reality, and is therefore fantasy and projected idealism.

We have, however, also attempted to show that the New Testament itself tells of the characters within its own stories undergoing just such a process of appropriating experience as we have outlined. This suggests that there might be a link between the biblical world and our own, and that the scriptures might provide us with a model for the process as well as some raw material in the form of images to be used in it. Nonetheless it does not of itself prove that the references to the divine in the experiences recorded in scripture are not projected fantasies.

We have, though, already noted that one guard against the images we employ being unreal fantasies comes about when those self-same images are drawn from concrete situations and then used analogically as metaphors. A degree of objectivity is thereby maintained in that we can test whether the concept or image which concerns us is rooted in a concrete situation. So far as scripture is concerned, historical-critical exegesis has a very important role to play in this. Yet what historical-critical exegetes have often appeared not to face is that if the historical event and its story are to touch us and affect our relationships with each other and with any God that there might be, then there must inevitably be an element of subjectivity in the matter. An event or a story might come to me, so that in a sense I am its object, but if it is to become my experience there is another sense in which I am the subject. Because historical-critical scholars have often seemed to neglect this, other readers have swung the pendulum to the opposite extreme and treated the images and concepts of scripture purely as paradigms. This can lead to a total subjectivity, which is as inappropriate as the supposedly 'objective' stance against which it reacts.

What is needed here is a form of contemporary-critical exegesis of our own experience – both the event of that experience and the story of it. Any experience is open to reality-testing. The testing is done both against other parts of our own experience, and against the experience of others. Any experience which we might focus and appropriate for ourselves with the help of the images of scripture will be open to this form of testing. Moreover the testing will be done through the medium of those images and concepts which are themselves held in common by ourselves and others. This is what the church has done over the centuries, testing a particular understanding of scripture and a particular experience against the understanding and experience of the whole Christian community, both as articulated contemporarily and as recorded historically in the tradition from the beginning.

This introduces an element of objectivity into the process, yet not a complete objectivity. The same images can speak in different ways to different people. Sometimes the church has declared that a particular experience and the articulation of it does not match the way that it perceives truth and reality, because the logic of that experience is not consonant with the logic of its own. The process of reality-testing here employs the further tools of the canons of reason. This is a right and proper thing to do. At times it might entail a single prophetic voice speaking out against the received wisdom of the community which is judged in later times to have articulated the truest experience and understanding. It is just such a stance which John Vincent seems to adopt in defining genuine Chrisitan experience. In summarizing research he states that

The person most likely to have a religious experience was a highly educated, well-to-do, elderly lady from a Welsh village, with a high level of psychological well-being. The person least likely to have a religious experience was an ill-educated, poor, young man from South Yorkshire, with a low level of psychological well-being.[7]

He then proceeds to assert that the experience of the former is invalid and a fantasy, whereas the latter's is real. His reasons for this are that the Bible shows God to be the God of the poor, the uneducated and the alienated, and that the story of Jesus shows that it is when people experience themselves to be forsaken and furthest from God that they are nearest to God.

We might agree that it is right and proper that this sort of experience should be affirmed. Yet should this be at the expense of denying the other kind of experience? In the present case, John Vincent seeks to affirm a position which has a long history in the Christian tradition. It has been articulated for centuries particularly within the orthodox churches in the form of negative theology. Moreover it is a major driving force in contemplative, mystical spirituality which claims that people move from a positive experience of God touching them to a negative one of themselves touching God's otherness. Both, however, are valid and people often fluctuate between the two. There is no logical reason, if it is valid to speak of God at all here, why it cannot be the same God who prompts both experiences. Which way people react will depend a great deal upon who and what they are at that moment. Ultimately wholeness should require that their experience encompasses both the positive and the negative strands. Sometimes the prophetic voice does indeed contradict a current received wisdom which is completely perverted and a total fantasy. More often the prophet is seeking to gain attention for a new position by setting it in antithesis to the old only for a synthesis to be made eventually between the two when it is shown that there is no logical incongruity between them. Such a synthesis is made if, once the logical impossibilities are carefully ruled out, people allow the images to work in both their positive and negative senses. This they can do with a degree of objectivity if those images are admitted to be historically rooted metaphors which can say both 'it is this' and 'it is not this'.

Soskice describes what we have termed 'historically rooted metaphors' when she states that the biblical stories are grounded in

> ... the experience of individuals and of communities which are believed to be experiences of the activity of a transcendent God. The language used to account for them is metaphorical and qualified, it stands within a tradition of use and is theory-laden, yet in so far as it is grounded on experience it is referential, and it is the theological realist's conviction that that to which it refers, the source of these experiences, is God who is the source and cause of all that is.[8]

Soskice restricts her concern to that of establishing that it is logically possible for religious language to depict a reality which is God without defining God. She therefore dispenses with the need to provide a proof for her conviction that there does exist a reality which can be termed God. Yet it would seem that she sees people arriving at such a conviction as they allow the experiences recounted in scripture to interact with their own experiences and experience the results:

> ... it is not simply that texts interpret us, they interpret our experiences; and it is not simply that we interpret texts, for we also interpret the experiences which they more or less obscurely chronicle.[9]

This is helpful, providing we recognize that it assumes that the realities of our own experience and that recounted in the Bible are of the same order, so that the process is one merely of forging appropriate links between the two. Of course, if the biblical material rings true as descriptions of forms of experience which are at least possible for human beings, then we can justifiably say that the references to the divine in them are at least worthy of attention. Yet Soskice's assumption goes beyond that, and seems to involve a kind of act of faith in which someone accepts that the religious language may depict a genuine reality which is God, and trusts that hypothesis enough to risk letting the images and metaphors of that language interact with his or her own experience and so discovering the validity and reality of that experience and also of God in the process.

Such a process has always been a presupposition of the Methodist tradition. It is about 'doing theology' or, as Wesley would put it, 'experimental divinity'. It deals with the interaction of scripture and our contemporary individual and corporate experience, and sees reason, tradition and context operating as ancillary tools. It claims that in the process of that interaction we discover that both our own experience and also the God described in the biblical texts are dynamic entities. The result is that as Wesley put it, drawing his theme from Romans 8. 16, 'The Spirit of God witnesses with our spirit that we are children of God.'

This process need not be completely random and subjective. We have outlined the various ways in which degrees of objectivity might be built into it. Ultimately it involves recognizing that our experience needs images to focus it, and that the images of scripture are about experience. It requires the development of an historical-critical exegesis that recognizes that we cannot be completely objective about the scriptural records because of the way these affect us, but that whilst accepting that we can strive for some objectivity. It also requires the development of a contemporary-critical exegesis of our own experience which seeks to distance us from our experience in order to test the reality of it, and yet recognizes that we need to allow ourselves to experience things subjectively. Above all, it involves making an act of faith in starting on a process which may lead to nothing, to ridicule, or to being proved wrong.

Experience in the contemporary city

All the issues outlined in the previous section are raised in an acute form in the particular case of Christian experience in the contemporary city. There is the same sense that the experience is overwhelming and yet at the same time uncontrolled and undefined; the same difficulty in bringing together biblical material and contemporary experience; the same question about how we can say that God exists at all, and if we do have reason to claim it, how we can reliably discern where God is active; the same need to immerse ourselves in a process in an act of faith that something dynamic will occur.

We noted in our first section that people and communities often feel overwhelmed by their experience of being in the city, and that this is magnified by the fact that they cannot properly focus or appropriate the experience. It is now widely held that there is a problem about living in the city. Following its 1987 election victory, the British Conservative Government declared that dealing with the 'problem' of the inner cities would be a major priority. Other political parties have made similar declarations. It is to be hoped that any social or political programme will not just be directed at eliminating symptoms, but above all at dealing with the causes of the problem. To do that will involve listening to the experience of the people living in the inner city, and that will involve assisting them in focussing, owning and then articulating their experience.

It is here that Christians have an important role to play. To do so they have to deal with the problem they perceive about their numbers. At one level, to people open to influence from scripture small numbers are no problem, as the New Testament stories of the early church, and the image of the leaven in the lump show. At another level, however, the numbers show how the churches recently have discounted and disengaged from the city. Although in the inner cities there may be more clergy in proportion to worshippers than elsewhere, the proportion of clergy and laity together in relation to the total population of the area rises dramatically the further out from the inner city area you go. This is not just because the inner cities have large populations of people from other faiths and cultures, for it is also true of nominally 'Christian' areas.

Nevertheless, where Christians are present in the inner city they share in the experience of the communities in which they are situated and have the opportunity to use the tools of their tradition to focus and own that experience more fully for themselves, and to share that process with those around them. We have suggested in the previous section what attitudes they will have to adopt to do this effectively. Yet this they almost always fail to do, preferring either to make incomprehensible pronouncements to contemporary experience in Christian code, or to deal in that experience alone without reference back to the Christian tradition.

Some recent attempts seem to start off in the direction which we would wish. In its report *Faith in the City*, the Archbishop of Canterbury's commission on Urban Priority Areas acknowledges a debt to liberation theologies coming from other parts of the world, and summarizes how it has observed this image of liberation helping people to grapple with their experiences and, having owned them, to act:

In Britain today it forces us to ask what it is (in the way of inherited attitudes and priorities) that may actually be preventing people from responding freely to that power which (we believe) is capable of transforming both their individual lives and the society in which they live.[10]

A major image used both in *Faith in the City* and in the impressive outworking of its principles within a particular context entitled *Faith in Leeds*, is that of 'Community-out-of-disintegration'. Both documents perceive disintegration and division occurring in the city in the economy, physical surroundings and institutions, and social relationships.[11] The image of community is presented as '... a means by which people can recover confidence, dignity, and some degree of influence over the conditions under which they are forced to live'[12] with regard to each of those three categories.

These images immediately recall those of the New Testament outlined in our previous sections. Yet there is little sign of any creative interplay between the experience and the tradition ... *Faith in the City*, tends to draw its images from secular analyses, particularly socio-economic ones. This is legitimate, for images have to be drawn from all sorts of sources in order to find the appropriate ones to focus any particular experience: the New Testament provides many examples. Nonetheless, unlike the New Testament, there is no sign of Tracy's analogical imagination being employed, of a dialogue occurring between these images and symbols and those of the religious tradition, even when there is a close correspondence between the two. *Faith in the City* contents itself with broad theological statements. *Faith in Leeds* attempts to go further by adapting a strategy from America.[13] This begins by outlining perceptions of experience, then moves on to social analysis and theological reflection before recommending and implementing a pastoral strategy which will later have to be evaluated in a way which clarifies and deepens the orginal perceptions of the experience. The intention here is impressive but the actual performance very variable. Sometimes the theological sections are little more than affirmations of wishes or assertions of dogma. *Faith in Leeds* has a sub-title, 'Searching for God in the City', but it does not lead us to this. Instead it ends with the assertion that the search occurs when people become involved in situations for themselves (p. 44). Similarly *Faith in the City* (p. 69) claims that 'an authentic theology can arise only as a response to each particular circumstance' and then declines to show us any examples of such reflection.

Why this reticence? The problem is connected with the fact that whereas in New Testament times it was part of the cultural and intellectual background to identify the divine in everything, today it is not. Some people in Britain are now two or three generations away from meaningful contact with the church or the use of religious language. Some Christians have responded by withdrawing into a religious ghetto and acting like the stereotype of the British abroad on the assumption that they only have to shout their own language louder to make foreigners understand. More difficult but more valuable in the long run is the attempt to become fluent in two languages and to translate from one to another. To do this we shall have to develop something like the approach outlined in our previous section.

It is particularly difficult to speak of the activity or work of God. Greg Smith [14] outlines four areas where the work of God might be discernible: numerical growth in the church; the transformation of the lives of individuals and communities; the development of Christian community; incarnational growth and influence on the world. Coming from a background in the London Evangelical Coalition for Urban Mission and the British Church Growth Association he proceeds to attack the Church Growth scholars for an unquestioning acceptance of empirical and statistical sociology in judging these matters. His own position is to attempt to develop an objective, descriptive sociology of religion which is also grounded in a biblical world view. Yet whilst denying that sociological and statistical statements are literal and simplistic truths he assumes that the statements of the Bible are. He is obviously unhappy with this but unable to break through it (p. 11). Here again the position outlined in our section on 'Experience and Scripture' would further his commendable purpose.

Smith ends with an image which helps him focus and appropriate the experience of being in the city when he cannot be sure that God is there and at work. It is that of incarnation:

> We need Christian pastors, evangelists, community workers and political activists to work with God to transform our cities, rather than armchair theologians to write about them.[15]

Similarly *Faith in the City* argues in Chapter 4 that the church in the inner city must be local, outward looking, and participating in the neighbourhood and community. Again, the image is an over-riding one for John Vincent:

> First there is the level of incarnation. We need to confirm ourselves in the areas of need. If we are not there, a few of us need to move there.[16]

Several caveats need to be registered about this use of the term 'incarnation'. The first concerns the danger of evacuating it of its theological and christological content by broadening it to mean any involvement in the structures of human life. The second concerns the presuppositions behind its use. They sound remarkably familiar. In 1887 the West London Mission of the Methodist Church was founded to respond with others to Mearns' 'Bitter Cry of Outcast London'.[17] It called and enabled groups of Christians to settle in the centre of London in order to reach out to the people there and interact with them. It was an exercise of those within the structure of society identifying and sharing with those beyond the pale. Yet today even if individual Christians still need to make a journey to join the outcast, the church to which they belong does not. Whereas at the end of the nineteenth century Wesleyan Methodism was considered to be part of society and public life, the churches today are themselves outcast and considered irrelevant to society in the general public eye. The media and politicians of right and left deny them any right to ask questions or comment on social and political issues, or corporate moral problems. The churches have become marginalized. Admittedly, they are the respectable marginalized, whereas others in the inner city are unrespectable. This distinction must not be glossed over. Yet both parties are marginalized, and there is already an enormous bond between them. However, the churches still come to the inner city as if they have to move from being part of society to being marginalized, and they therefore appear to be untrue to their own situation and experience. The result is that the help they offer is gratefully taken, but the givers are despised and rejected and often accused of being hypocritical because they are acting on presuppositions at variance with their true situation.

The third caveat concerns the modern tendency to use the term 'incarnation' as a modern shibboleth like 'the temple of the Lord' in Jeremiah 7. It often seems to be assumed that Christians just need to settle in the inner city and new life will automatically be brought about in them and around them. This involves a commendable act of faith, but unless they discover some appropriate image they will not be able to appropriate that new life that they believe God offers them. Hence they feel a sense of discomfort and disease which is not just a form of guilt about the failure of their mission. Somehow the image of incarnation as outlined above does not draw out and enable them to explore enough of their experience for anything dynamic to occur. Presence and interaction are not enough on their own, for they should be allowed to lead to transformation and life. In order to deal with the experience of being in the city we have a need for images which talk of bonds of solidarity and attachment, interaction, change and transformation.

Incarnation, transformation and bonds of attachment

The psychotherapeutic theory of attachment and its counterparts loss and disintegration sheds some light here. John Bowlby[18] describes how people attach themselves to significant figures and thereby gain the secure base from which they can go on to explore themselves and the world. Those whose primary attachments are broken by losses which are not properly grieved over, healed and integrated are in our terms left with unfoccussed experience that is not fully explored or appropriated. They prove unable to relate properly to themselves, to others or to the world.

Peter Marris[19] has extended the theory from individual to corporate and social relationships. He describes a Chinese university during the cultural revolution. The professors withdrew from conflict with the students who then factionalized into two sections and started fighting each other. Workers from Peking came and immersed themselves in the situation, slowly related to everyone, and then began to reflect their experience of what was happening to the various parties. This enabled everyone to understand the position and reconstruct the situation. The workers had come and immersed themselves in a particular context, and allowed themselves to enter the experience of the people in it. As a result, the professors and students formed attachments with the workers which gave the space and security to explore their confused feelings and the overwhelming experience they were undergoing. They felt safe enough to allow the workers to show them how they were behaving in the interactions between the various groups. As they became able to appropriate their own experience in this way, the members of each group began to relate better to the members of the other groups, until relationships on the campus were integrated again.

The theory shows that failure to appropriate experience leads to disintegration and dis-ease. Signs of adequate appropriation are when those symptoms disappear. Thus I can tell that you have owned the experience of your father's death when your episodic depressions and sense of impending but unfocussed tears diminish. We can claim that Europe has appropriated the experience of the Second World War when the cold war aggression between the parties involved ends.

According to Bowlby 'evidence is clear that, unless a therapist is prepared to enter a genuine relationship with a family or individual, no progress can be expected'.[20] In other words, the therapist has to 'incarnate' himself or herself in the experience of the patients, providing a secure bond of attachment and reflecting back to them how they behave in that relationship, and thus enabling them to appropriate their general experience of relationships and attachments more fully. Attachment is therefore not a static image, but a dynamic one lived out in the form of the therapist. The therapist is a form of living metaphor who can say 'yes, it is this and yet no, it is not this' and thus enable the patients to own their relationships with others more fully. Such is the strength of this theory and practice. Its weakness is that although the therapist enters the relationship of the client and has to be prepared to withstand intense and painful emotion, what is being shared belongs to the patient and not the therapist. It is therefore the secure who are reaching out to the outcasts, those who have supposedly appropriated experience to those who have not. As such, there is a danger of the patient being stigmatized as a 'patient', coming to feel dependent and powerless as a result, and eventually despising and rejecting the therapist as hypocritical. The problem echoes that for the churches outlined in our previous section.

Attachment, interchange and transformation in Christ

There is a New Testament image which talks of incarnation and transformation, of bonds of solidarity and attachment, of interaction and change; which operates in both individual and corporate spheres; which discovers an experience of God in human life and activity; and which centres on the crucifixion

and resurrection of Jesus of Nazareth. It is at the heart explicitly of Paul's writings and implicitly of Mark's Gospel (with its view of the disciples as the corporate Christ). It is the concept which Morna Hooker has explored in a series of articles and termed 'Interchange in Christ'.[21]
Examples of the concept are to be found in

Romans 5. 12–19; 6. 1–14; 8.3ff;
Galatians 3. 13; 4.4ff;
II Corinthians 5. 21; 8.9;
Philippians 2. 1–10; 3. 17–21;
I Thessalonians 5. 10

Their basic element is Paul's claim that Christ shared our human condition and experience so that we might share his. Hooker admits that her term 'interchange' can be misleading here. It is not a matter of simple substitution or exchange where Christ dies and Paul lives. It is not like the attachment therapist taking all the patient's painful emotion in return for giving that patient all of his or her experience of well-being. Paul insists that we only further our own experience by being in Christ (I Thess. 5. 10). What is in view is a participation and a sharing of experience.

Paul discovers that the image helps him focus all sorts of issues and experience. One concerns his experience of atonement or open relationship with God. There are certain logical constraints inherent in a relationship with God. Paul sees these codified in the Torah, and he also perceives that Jesus fulfils them. Since Jesus does, Paul does 'in him'. But human beings like to use the constraints in the Torah to manipulate and control others, rather than as the vehicles of God's gift, and so they engineer it that the Torah condemns Jesus: in this Christ participates in Paul's experience. But God vindicates Jesus in the resurrection, and therefore Paul as well – which explains Paul's experience. Paul discovers that the demands of the Torah are simultaneously affirmed absolutely concerning what it is to live with God, and relativized about how we can control others with them.

Central to these themes of condemnation and vindication, of being apart from God and living with God, are the crucifixion and resurrection of Jesus. The image of interchange enables Paul to focus his discovery that these occurred once and for all in history and yet continue to be worked out in his experience each moment. Similarly any experience comes to us in particular historical contexts, but the process of appropriating it is a continuing one.

Hooker shows that it is Paul's view that Christ attaches himself to our experience and that he then carries us forward with him, first to his death and then through that to his new life (Rom. 6). She notes that in going to his death and resurrection Christ goes to the ultimate in human experience and tastes it to the full. What she does not state directly is that since this experience is our experience, Christ carries us along to experience ourselves more fully. With him we find ourselves tasting the depths of aloneness, dereliction, disintegration, and God-forsakenness in which we are left with nothing that we can rely on in ourselves, in others, in the world and, so it seems, in God. Yet by still waiting on God, even with a reproach on our lips, we find ourselves for the first time fully open to be raised to new life.

Consequently another aspect of experience which the image helps focus is that of the need for a total reliance on God in all things, even when our obedience takes us towards suffering and death. When Paul shares experience with Christ, he discovers that his own mission helps him understand Christ's experience better, and Christ's mission helps him appropriate his own experience more fully. In II Corinthians 1, Christ's death leads to life for Christians, and Paul's afflictions lead to comfort and salvation for the Corinthians when they patiently endure the same sufferings. Similarly, Christ's resurrection leads to resurrection and glory for those prepared to suffer with him, whilst Paul's comfort leads to comfort for the Corinthians if they are prepared to share his sufferings

> It was in sharing Christ's situation of helplessness that he learned to share his hope in God (II Corinthians 1. 8–17). Under apparent sentence of death Paul was delivered from danger, and so, in a sense, brought back to life. The difference between the two experiences of 'interchange' referred to in II Corinthians, the one linked with Christ's death and the other with Paul's suffering, is that the second experience derives from, and is dependent on, the first.[22]

The same thing occurs when Christians repeat the pattern in their relationships with individuals and groups in the city. Coming to a complete vulnerability and openness to God ourselves we share peoples' lives and carry them along with us to experience that for themselves more fully. In that we and they become open to be raised to life.

Paul therefore discovers that he is swept into a process of becoming like Christ, and that this has an effect not just on his future state after death but also on his attitudes and behaviour here and now:

> ....he (Christ) was obedient; he emptied himself; he humbled himself; he became poor; he identified himself with the sinful and the outcasts. And so, in describing his own ministry Paul claims that he, too, has accepted all manner of humiliation and suffering for the sake of others; he, too, has accepted poverty and yet made others rich.[23]

Thus as we stand alongside people in the inner city we must be a community of openly broken people ready to identify with others in their brokenness and to share with them the process of allowing ourselves to be healed. In this we enable them to experience their own brokenness and their own healing to the full. What enables us to perceive and appropriate our own experience in this process more fully is the living image of Christ identifying himself with others, and emptying himself to the point where he was open to accept God's grace and be raised to life (Phil. 2).

Emptying ourselves to that extent, however, is hard to do unaided, and the new life we taste in adopting Christ's life-style is not an automatic reward or something which we can achieve for ourselves or for others. Central to the theme of 'interchange' is Paul's discovery that human responsibility and activity are an essential part of the process, and yet at the same time in, through and beyond all that, it is the activity of God. At one level Jesus gives himself up to death, rises to life, intercedes for his followers and shares his life with them. At another the same process is experienced as God handing Jesus over and then raising him to life. In participating in that with Christ, Paul starts to appropriate an experience of God whilst engaging in his own activity.

Paul puts the point another way by stating at one moment that the blessing which comes to everyone through one person, Christ, parallels the curse which came through one man, Adam. Yet at another moment he recognizes that it is not an exact parallel: Adam acted in separation from God, whilst it was actually God acting to bless people in and through Christ. The symmetry is further disrupted if, probably unlike Paul, we now recognize that Adam is a mystical representative figure, whereas Jesus is an historical figure. Yet what are the links between Jesus of Nazareth and the Christ in whom we interchange experience? Hooker's exegesis of Paul rests on the assumption that Paul considered it possible to have a real experience of relating to a Jesus Christ raised to life, and that the same is true for us. Paul talks of Christ being available for us in the Spirit, but how can we experience this today? Ultimately we are driven back to the need for an act of faith outlined in the section on contemporary experience and scripture. What seems to happen is that the image of Christ in scripture which has helped us deal with our experience more deeply now starts to gain a dynamic of its own and to carry us along with it. The metaphor becomes a living metaphor. It is as we walk down the road struggling to link our human experiences in the city with the images of scripture that the living reality of Christ is disclosed to us, sending us back to the city transformed to share the experience with others (Luke 24. 13–53). In this we are experiencing grace.

7

Surgical Spirit

David G. Deeks

The essay attempts to clarify a method of theological reflection. It starts from an every day experience in a waiting room of a doctor's surgery. The author then seeks to pursue the deep questions and challenges arising from the experience along two paths: the socio-historical analysis of assumptions about health and wholeness; and a search in the theological tradition for resources which illuminate the contemporary issues. The pastoral theologian's task is to establish creative interchanges between self-questioning, the needs of others and the scriptures. The purpose of this work is to suggest a way of life which is able to respond to the surprising grace of God.

Waiting

It was 5.30 pm on a Friday afternoon. I was sitting in the waiting room of the doctor's surgery. Twenty minutes had passed since I had presented myself at the window of the receptionist's office. By now there were seven other people in the waiting room. Two parents and a young child were to my right, about a metre distant; an elderly couple sat more or less opposite me in the circle of twenty or so chairs; and two individuals sat to my left, so that each of us was separated from the other by two or three empty chairs. The only sound came from the child and whispered exhortations from her parents to sit still and quiet. Three times during the twenty minutes our silence had been interrupted by a raucous buzzer and a flashing red light above the door. This was the signal from the doctor that she was ready to see her next patient.

I found myself reflecting on this arid experience. My thoughts and feelings were a kaleidoscopic jumble. At a distance from the experience I recall the following themes.

The sense of isolation. Here were men and women inhabiting the same space, but not communicating with one another. No one cared (or perhaps no one knew) how to take an initiative to bridge the chasms between us. We were bowed down by conventions, by cultural expectations, by fears (of invading privacy, or perhaps of catching some unspeakable disease). We had come independently to the surgery; our 'meeting' was fortuitous; but we had no way of engaging with anything we held in common. So what is it to be human?

> A pen appeared, and the god said:
> 'Write what it is to be
> man.' And my hand hovered
> long over the bare page,
>
> until there, like footprints
> of the lost traveller, letters
> took shape on the page's
> blankness, and I spelled out
>
> the word 'lonely'. And my hand moved
> to erase it; but the voices
> of all those waiting at life's
> window cried out loud; 'It is true.'[1]

The surgery to which I had come was part of a *multi-disciplinary practice*. In addition to a group practice of three GPs, there were on the staff a nurse, a chiropodist, a counsellor, a health visitor and a social worker. Here was a marvellous array of professional skills operating in a collaborative manner for the welfare of patients in the community. One of the doctors was qualified to perform minor surgical operations, and a room had been set aside and equipped appropriately. In some senses this health centre was like a scaled-down hospital. My initial hypothesis was that the assumptions about the meaning of 'health' which undergirded the work of the health centre were the same as those which operate in a large hospital.

Immediately, however, I noticed a difference. There was no equivalent at the health centre of a hospital chaplain. (I was quick to spot this because I am an ordained minister of the Methodist Church; in strange situations I inevitably look for people like me.) Indeed, as I looked around the waiting room and cast my eye over the multitude of posters advertising every conceivable voluntary and self-help group in the neighbourhood, I noticed that there was no reference anywhere to the churches. Has religion nothing to do with 'health' at this centre? Why have the churches been so indifferent to the emergence of inter-professional health agencies in local neighbourhoods? What is the role of faith in the process of healing?

I was conscious of considerable *confusion in me about my own role*. Everybody else in the waiting room was probably assuming that I was in some sense 'sick'. This was ironic because in fact I had called in at the surgery in the middle of a busy life as a minister simply to have an innoculation before going abroad. But even if I had been 'sick', I would presumably have been well enough to get to the surgery and therefore almost certainly well enough to be doing most if not all of my normal job. But on entering the waiting room was my work as a minister in suspension? What is it to be a pastoral person in such a situation, whether sick or well?

No one, I guessed, knew what my vocation is. I was wearing no distinctive clerical dress. Of course, I in turn had no knowledge of the other people in the waiting room – their family circumstances, their hurts and fears, their loves and hobbies, their questions about life's meaning and purpose, or their discoveries in their spiritual pilgrimages. We were truly strangers to one another. I was in a thoroughly secular environment where I could make no assumptions about a taken-for-granted language of faith. In Peter Kerr's suggestive phrase, I was 'playing away from home'.[2] I was in fact not playing at all. But I puzzled deeply over how I might become someone who could create an opportunity for communication, for sharing what truly matters to us, for exploring together symbols we have each found meaningful and creative in the struggle to make sense of life.

My inner confusion was aggravated by uncertainty about my social standing. Am I a professional person, who in my own eyes and in the eyes of others, belongs as a *minister* with the team of professionals based at the health centre? Or does a minister relate differently to people, more as a friend, in relationships where there is more mutuality, more sharing of experience, of failures and achievements?

As I reflected further on the matter, I became increasingly alienated from much of the health centre ethos. I sensed that my pastoral care fits uneasily with the technological, diagnostic and biochemical character of the doctor's work. I do not operate with 'clients' or 'patients' whose cases need to be managed according to well-tried procedures. In my work I want to stimulate insight and imagination; I want myself and others to dig deep, beneath the physical and medical aspects of life, beneath even the emotional turmoil of human relationships, dig into – I know not what, except that its mysterious unknownness allures me infinitely, challenges me uncompromisingly and promises not less than everything. But I have no over-arching vision to share and express. I find myself called to be an explorer, to live inventively with fragmentary glimpses of something wonderful and some extraordinarily complex raw materials (the rich, varied, puzzling, unmanageable experience of human beings – broken, fractured, incomplete, corrupted by evil and overshadowed by suffering and death). I want to work with what I experience and what people give to me, and in the shaping of it to see what emerges that might reveal the glory of God.

So the issue for me was not whether I was a professional among professionals, or whether I was a patient among patients; it was whether I could engage both professionals and patients in a common search for our shared humanness, and thereby for God.[3]

These reflections were racing around in my mind. But would they help me to *act* in any concrete way? What could I do which would represent the gospel? What could it possibly mean in this situation to be a loving and obedient disciple?[4]

The waiting room had provoked in me some profound challenges. First to be challenged was my image of myself and my understanding of my vocation. Flowing from that was a question about what it means to be human, and a challenge to my convictions about God. Challenges of such a kind are the rightful stimulus for pastoral theology.[5]

Analysing

Analyses from many disciplines in the human and social sciences can throw shafts of light on our current confusions about what it is to be a well human being. The most obvious starting point is the historical success of the natural sciences (physics, chemistry and biology). They now enjoy incomparable authority in the battle to overcome disease, extend the length and quality of life and eliminate handicaps. However inexact a science medicine

Surgical Spirit

itself may be, an understanding of medicine which is not scientifically based is inconceivable. With it have come widely prevalent assumptions about the biochemical nature of reality. These have been underscored by philosophical investigations since Descartes (1596–1650). He portrayed human beings as essentially discrete individuals; each individual was then further defined in dualistic terms, with a body which can be understood exhaustively by science as a sort of machine and a soul (the place of divine operations) which is utterly separate from the body.

Over the centuries since the Enlightenment dualistic thinking in the context of a burgeoning natural science has fastened attention on the body but left the soul a marginal, vague entity. The moral foundations of human behaviour and the aesthetic exploration of what lies at the edge of consciousness have become peripheral. Untold resources of human intelligence and of finance have been devoted to science and technology; the arts have been starved of public support; and questions of meaning, value and purpose have been reduced to private speculation unconnected to any serious public search for truth and reality. Our culture has become thoroughly secularized; and religious allegiance has become fickle – the inevitable outcome when religion is reduced to small numbers of committed individuals who band together in voluntary associations to pursue private interests.

Throughout the historical process of secularization there have been occasional flowerings of alternative perceptions to the dominant individualistic, materialistic and atheistic trends. Religious revivals have been of uneven significance, both numerically and in terms of their impact on the general culture. All seem to have fallen victim to the compartmentalizing tendency which locks God up in a separate sphere disconnected from the scientific, political and economic aspects of life. Formal religion has tried valiantly to provide a ritual focus where the insights of the Christian movement can meet creatively the subterranean and incoherent values of society at large.[6] But more often than not Christian values have been subverted so that the churches have found themselves giving religious sanction to what society wants and idolizes.

Observation and analysis of these processes have been the special prerogative of the social scientists. They have kept alive, often more effectively than religious groups, the reality of the corporate dimensions of human existence and the effects of social structures on human behaviour. Occasionally sociology has become wedded to an ideology like Marxism, to give coherence and strength to its insights over and against the prevailing culture.

Another example of a movement against some, at least, of the main historical trends is to be found in the psycho-analytic schools of psychology, from Freud (1856–1939) onwards. With no little controversy they have tried to keep on the agenda the role of emotions in human happiness; they have forced us to confront the power of sexual desires and of the irrational unconscious inhuman behaviour; and they have endeavoured to develop therapeutic procedures to help men and women to manage interpersonal relationships.

Elsewhere it has been the turn of philosophers to throw the occasional stone at the juggernaut of scientific humanism. Existentialism, for example, proclaimed the sole reality of the subjective self, which takes responsibility for its own decisions and actions and transcends the constraints of nature and history. Such emphases spawned a plethora of therapeutic movements concerned with self-awareness, self-affirmation and self-actualization.

Since the breakdown of the pre-Enlightenment *ancien regime*, both the pioneers and guardians of the predominant cultural trends and advocates of the alternative perceptions have struggled to entrench their positions in society. They have battled with each other for power and authority. The most straightforward way of achieving such ends has been the organizing of skills, bodies of specialized knowledge and disciplined activity into professions. What began two centuries ago as a structured form of altruism has become an unbridled lust for wealth, prestige and influence.[7]

Among the so-called caring professions, there can be no doubt that the medical profession takes pride of place, because it fits so neatly into the dominant cultural assumptions about what it is to be well and human. Those who work with complementary perspectives on health and healing have also achieved professional status, but with a lower standing (psychotherapists, nurses, community workers and so forth). Sometimes out of necessity and sometimes even by choice, doctors have granted other caring professionals (within limits set by the medical profession!) the opportunity of working with themselves in interprofessional teams.

In long-established multi-disciplinary institutions, such as the hospital service, there is a residual, marginal place for chaplains; in more recent developments, religious officials have no role whatsoever. Similarly some other minorities (osteopaths, practitioners of herbal medicine, acupuncture and the like) are normally considered to be beyond the fringe. Though to be fair to the total picture, there has been a concern, albeit among a small fraction of doctors, to develop coherent understandings of holistic medicine.[8]

Judgments about status seem to derive from two principal sources; power and basic assumptions. The manipulation of power by the powerful, to defend their position, is what keeps doctors well-paid and privileged, nurses lowly-paid and social workers overstretched and often vilified. This power structure has important implications in the formulation of public health policy. It enables senior hospital doctors easily to operate in both the private and the public health sectors and thus to ally themselves with a government keen to diminish the significance of the NHS. It enables the government also to impose the rapid transfer of mentally ill patients from institutions into the community, and easily to brush aside the complaints from psychiatric nurses and social workers of inadequate supportive resources in the community.

The connection between status and basic assumptions may be seen by reference to psycho-analytic traditions in psychology. Followers of Freud and Jung claim to be able to penetrate into the hidden recesses of the personality through analysis of dreams and the techniques of free association. Problems of interpretation abound. Analytical psychology is not a precise science. It is as much about the power of suggestive imagery as about predictable results read off from a coherent theory. The deeper into the mind the analyst ventures, the fewer seem to be the clear boundaries of the precise data. Within psychology itself psycho-analysis has been controversial. Opposed to the analytical schools stand the behaviourist traditions of Skinner, Watson and Eysenck, who have tried to give psychology the methods – and therefore the high status – of the natural sciences.

In consequence, psychotherapy and counselling have been Cinderellas in the public health service. Practitioners have had to win their way in society by free-lance activity. The result is their suburban and middle-class captivity.

My analysis of the situation behind my reflections in the doctor's waiting room has been in terms of the historical processes of secularization (with special reference to the rise of the natural sciences) and professionalization. The latter theme links into issues of politics and economics; it is intimately concerned with power and authority in society and with public policy. If the analysis is anywhere near right, it underlines the confusion in our society about what it is to be human and to be well. There is no agreed vision or spirituality which inspires and unifies our quest for healing, happiness and peace. So the people perish (Prov. 29.18), not least in our sense of impotence, ignorance and paralysis in the face of illness, severe stress and disaster. We have no trust in our own capacity to heal ourselves or to strengthen one another. We turn deferentially to the experts, whose god-like authority is believed to be omniscient and salvific. So disabled are we by our uncertainty of what we might strive for as human beings and so overawed are we by the anticipated competence of the professional helpers that we have nothing to say to one another in the ante-chamber of the great king's throne-room (i.e. the doctor's surgery). A terror intermingles with an intense eagerness to be in the presence, and reduces us to a quasi-mystical silence.

I am tempted by my analysis to act in a particular way. Why not rush out of the doctor's waiting room, put on what all would recognize as liturgical dress, and return to my seat? Surely that would represent the religious character of the silent group? It would be a gesture which might enable the dumb to speak. It would give me a clear role – but only as a priest of the high god 'GP'. Fundamentally I would have changed nothing. My true vocation as a minister of the gospel would have been prostituted. I would have become like Tom in Iris Murdoch's novel, *The Philosopher's Pupil*:

> Tom was in the state of restless obsessive nervous energy which drives people to meddle when they are too stupid to think clearly and too frightened to act decisively. What he needed was some sort of symbolical or magical act which concerned or touched his situation without running any danger of changing it. He wanted, as it were, to light a candle or recite a formula, he needed to busy himself about his state of mind.[9]

A deeper question has now surfaced: How can I as an *incognito* Christian mediate the reality of God and his grace to those who worship other dreams, values and meanings?

Theologizing

Centuries of formation within the Christian tradition lead us to think we know what to do to construct a theological response to the situation I have been trying to describe and understand. We must appeal to a doctrine. There must be a doctrine of health and a doctrine of what it is to be human which will make a critical judgment on our contemporary dilemmas. With enough wit and consultation, we must be able to see the implications of our doctrines, and act accordingly. And mother church tells me where to search for these doctrines, which are indeed claimed to be 'truths of salvation': they 'are set forth in the Methodist doctrinal standards' of the Deed of Union (1932).[10]

As far as health and healing are concerned the twentieth century has been fascinated by the Christian concept of 'wholeness'.[11] In the first instance wholeness is an encouragement to human beings to strive against all that constrains, blocks, dislocates, damages and thwarts human possibilities. It inspires us to cure ills, enhance life-opportunities (through education, travel, cross-cultural encounter and political action for justice, for example), and overcome handicaps and disabilities with technical interventions and ingenuity. It challenges us to test every apparent limit to our skills and abilities, to climb every mountain, to question what is taken for granted and to explore what is conventionally forbidden.

Secondly, 'wholeness' is clarified by distinguishing it from 'fullness'. In many areas of life we eventually rub up against irremovable blocks and non-negotiable limits. I may press as far as possible my capacity for intellectual enquiry, but I cannot fundamentally make myself, or be made, more intelligent than I am. I must accept graciously the boundaries that cannot be changed.

To accept a limit after a period of thorough probing is an inner attitude with many spiritual dimensions. It requires that fine judgment which acknowledges limitation in one area but keeps explorations in other areas open and hopeful. It expects that one faculty rudely damaged or impaired may stimulate another faculty into extraordinary achievements: otherwise, how can the blind sometimes hear so acutely? It distinguishes between those parts of the personality that shrivel or become defective fairly readily from those more inward emotional and spiritual dimensions which seem capable of almost limitless growth.

Ultimately, when many fixed boundaries *have* been encountered, it acknowledges that attitudes to circumstances matter more than the circumstances themselves. Thus personal wholeness becomes synonymous with maturity and wisdom, and is marked by qualities like trust, autonomy, initiative, creativity, a clear identity, relaxed intimacy and love, a commitment to the best interests of the succeeding generation, and integrity.[12]

Thirdly, wholeness involves integration, or the creating of harmonies: 'harmony between the many aspects of the human person (physical, mental, spiritual), between man and his fellows and his communities, between man and the natural order, and between man and the source of all value and being, God the Father'.[13]

The concept of 'wholeness' seems like wholesome doctrine. If there were space we could doubtless develop comparable statements of what it is to be human. (They would include discussions of maleness and femaleness, rational and irrational, conscious and unconscious, individuality and society, of psychomatic *gestalt*, of growth, development and processes of change, of culture and language.)

What, however, is the effect of restating doctrines? What difference do they make to our perception of the issues confronting us in our modern world, and to the ways we can respond to them? It depends on what sort of statements we imagine doctrines to be. At its lowest, doctrine has been thought of as a constantly repeated recorded message, issued with the authority of the church. Doctrine has claimed to give reliable solutions to recurring human puzzles. The obvious weakness and frustration of such an understanding is that it is impossible to interact with invariant doctrinal assertions. No personal growth and freedom can be won by listening to them.[14] Intellectual assent does not necessarily lead to loving actions.[15]

But not all is lost. Even recorded summaries and repetitive arguments can sometimes evoke in us a recollection of what we already know. They may stimulate memories long forgotten which represent something vivacious and good. Occasionally they may prompt us to recover sufficient confidence and inner resources for us to answer our own perplexing contemporary questions.

From another point of view, doctrinal formulations have been considered to be clear and consistent propositions which function like notes on the back of a record sleeve. Their intention is to sharpen up a person's capacity for listening to the music with greater attentiveness. Unfortunately they are just as likely to distract from that process and lead to an intellectualized *cul de sac*. And however elegantly the notes may be written, however informative and however productive of enlightened concentration they may prove, they can never be a substitute for listening to the music itself. Many people prefer direct engagement with the music, without programme notes and without a score. Who is to say they are not more thoroughly transfigured and transformed than those who mediate too much experience through the intellect?

For centuries the authority of doctrinal propositions was bolstered not only by the decisions of accredited church leaders but also, from Aquinas (1225–74) onwards, by the intimate marriage between doctrine and an agreed metaphysic. By the end of the nineteenth century the metaphysical assumptions of Christendom were neither known by nor credible to European society as a whole. The equation 'theology = doctrine' had broken down. We may note in passing that Methodism was born at the time when doctrinal theology had begun to be suspect; it is therefore not surprising that Methodists made few if any noteworthy contributions to the doctrinal tradition, but were largely parasitical upon the doctrinal deposit of the church of England.[16]

So is there any hope that we can respond positively to our contemporary dilemmas and concerns by appealing to doctrine – even doctrine which is dusted down as we take it off the historical and ecclesiastical shelf and perhaps given a new tone with a fresh coat of varnish? Only something genuinely creative, which engages directly with our contemporary situation as well as classical Christian insight and wisdom, will suffice.

Here we must pay attention to a third possible interpretation of the nature of doctrine. The total doctrinal deposit may be considered to be a mammoth work of art – a piece of architecture and construction of cathedral-like proportions;[17] or a related series of musical creations analagous to Wagner's *Ring of the Nibelungs*. If such were to be the case, exposure to the doctrinal tradition would be an enveloping aesthetic experience which conveyed the possibility of a disclosure of truly transcendental proportions.[18] New ways of seeing, experiencing and acting would be stimulated by participation in the doctrinal 'event'.

Unfortunately the church's doctrine cannot be regarded like

this simply by wishing it were so. It has not been the experience of most Christians that doctrine has been formulated so as to suggest new vision and fresh ways of experiencing things. It has, on the contrary, been familiarly received as a series of erudite intellectual discussions and sophisticated theoretical conundrums unrelated to the practical issues of life. Time and again commentators on the history of religious thought have pointed out the significant shift from the rich, unsystematic, daring and suggestive imagery associated with the birth of religious movements (as in the Christian scriptures) to the arid, theoretical and dully comprehensive formulations of later generations of intellectual leaders who were as much concerned with social control as the struggle for truth.

Until a genius emerges (as indeed has happened from time to time in Christian history) who can reconstruct Christian doctrine as an epic poem, we need to find ways of using creatively the best fragmentary resources we possess. A pastoral theologian wants to assist a lived faith, in obedience to the gospel. He or she wants something more profound than doctrine as normally conceived, however sensitively the historical formulations may be rephrased and expounded. A pastoral theologian wants the music of heaven to be heard, the very heart of God releasing its Spirit of love into our existence.[19] To achieve this aim in our contemporary society he or she has to return to the basic method and resources which have characterized a theological reflection on experience in every generation.[20] Of course, such methods and resources lie behind the statements of traditional doctrines. But it is often difficult to discern the process of manufacture in the finished product.

A pastoral theologian therefore interprets his or her task – to continue with musical metaphors – as the construction of a trio, whose voices converse and jarr, clash and interact in the search for exquisite tunes and harmonies. If we could hear such ethereal sounds we would become men and women with a new consciousness, our own hearts full of Christ and of love.

The first voice in the trio is like the piano in relation to the violin and the 'cello: it has a range, a potential volume and a capacity for rich chords which are far in excess of the other two instruments, individually or together. This first voice is the scriptures. When we have done all our digging into the scriptures, as we must, using every available critical and hermeneutical tool to help us unlock the secrets of these ancient books, we discover that principally the Bible is an incredibly rich resource for the imagination. Here are story, myth and parable; here are metaphor and symbol; here are poetry and the distilled, elliptical sayings of the wise.

These imaginative resources suggest pictures of an ultimate environment of meaning, value and purpose for the whole universe. The predominant themes which keep on appearing, or half appearing, with subtle variations, are these:

Jesus (who was crucified) is the living One;
the saving events of Exodus and of the resurrection of Jesus are
   celebrated because they lay bare the foundations of the whole
created order;
   men and women, inspired by the Spirit of God within them
and among them,
   gladly share responsibility in radically new communities
marked by
   justice, peace, freedom and hope.

So the 'ultimate environment' which the scriptures hint at is a new world which somehow or other intervenes in the confused and ambivalent world we know only too well. In a word, the NT in particular is eschatological: it witnesses to a God who came uniquely and finally in Jesus of Nazareth, and who continues to come with all his grace to everything that exists, from the future. His coming and his grace meet even non-negotiable limits like death and create miraculous possibilities of openness, communication and relationship.[21] The test of our having glimpsed this vision is found in a particular experience: we are stimulated to pray, yearn, beseech, appeal, ache until it hurts for the final coming of God's glorious new era; we feel compelled to reach out, touch and consume whatever embodies the coming Messiah. 'Your kingdom come, your will be done' (Matt. 6.10; 26.39).

The second voice in the divine trio is the sound of our neighbour, and particularly the cry of the poor. In his novel *Siddhartha*, H. Hesse describes what it meant to his hero to be listened to by the old and experienced ferryman Vasudeva:

It was one of the ferryman's greatest virtues that, like few people, he knew how to listen. Without his saying a word, the speaker felt that Vasudeva took in every word, quietly, expectantly, that he missed nothing. He did not await anything with impatience and gave neither praise nor blame – he only listened. Siddhartha felt how wonderful it was to have such a listener who could be absorbed in his own life, his own strivings, his own sorrows ... Disclosing his wound (the loss of his son) to his listener was the same as bathing it in the river, until it became cool and one with the river.[22]

It is of the utmost significance – here is the influence of the scriptural tradition – to note that occasional, unexpected and fleeting encounters with a neighbour are the normal means God uses to act kindly towards us through other. The highlights of the Gospels are provided by those who cross the stage of Jesus's ministry only once, and briefly, and find salvation (Mark 2. 1–12; 5.1–43; Luke 7.1–17); in Mark's Gospel, certainly, the disciples who stay with Jesus throughout misunderstand (8.17–21), fail (10.35–45) and forsake him (14.17–21, 32–41, 66–72).[23]

Consonant with this stress is the observation that the Bible itself is largely a collection of writings. By its very form it encourages the disciple to live creatively in the here and now, to grasp the opportunity of the present moment, to give undivided attention to this particular individual who has unexpectedly, without warning, and often at a point of considerable inconvenience, knocked on my door. This is true obedience. It is preferable to long-term strategies, neat and tidy bureaucractic procedures and well-oiled management methods.

The third voice is the sound of myself, of my inner life. I need to be able to listen to what lies beneath the surface, to the repressed fears, hurts, jealousies and anger, to the irrational and largely unconscious complexes and instinctive drives. I need to hear honestly my own desires and concerns; I need to know what it is I want more than anything else, what truly motivates me when the self-image projected towards others (even those who know me intimately) no longer hides what is at the root of my being. Ultimately I must strain my ear to catch some distant, and maybe distorted, echo of the God whose longings spring from unfathomable depths beneath my being. H. Hesse wrote of Siddartha: 'Above all, he learned from [the river] how to listen, to listen with a still heart, with a waiting, open soul, without passion, without desire, without judgment, without opinions.'[24] This is the skill and the state of being in which prayer becomes possible. Shaped by the evocative symbols of the scriptures, its content is:

> Enlarge, inflame and fill my heart
> With boundless charity divine.[25]

In response to such a prayer, God's Spirit bursts forth from the transcendent depths and recreates the personality from within, converting defensiveness into openness, reaching out in humble service to the neighbour and the coming kingdom.

Pastoral theology, I conclude, has more to do with spirituality than the niceties of doctrinal precision, as normally understood; it gives rapt attention to what is deep, mysterious, suggestive and open-ended before it deflects its energies into either the study of historical precedents or philosophical speculation. It is therefore more like artist's work than anything else.[26] And just as art is nothing unless it expresses itself as form in a medium (paint on canvas, sculpture, notes on a staff, words on a page), so pastoral theology is nothing unless it is linked integrally to pastoral action.

It was the genius of early Methodism to notice that the background formation of a pastoral theologian develops best in a small group. The cell is the most creative context for attending to each of the three 'voices' by itself – the Bible study group; the group which raises consciousness of the needs of the poor and the oppressed and analyses their plight with the aid of the human and social sciences; and the experiential, self-awareness group. The cell is also the environment in which the 'free conversation' between these three voices can generate its distinctive results: shared understandings, mutually enriching insights, and the release of the divine Spirit creating holy obedience in practical living.

The sting, however, is in the tail. Groups usually fail to live up to such high expectations. They are hard to sustain as creative interpersonal encounters. Conversations are as likely to produce fierce arguments, inflict unforgivable hurts, or overwhelm participants with a sense of futility, boredom and aimlessness as to stimulate vision and discipleship. The brokenness, confusions and discords or wider society invade the group and undermine it. Group members feel powerless to confront the fall-out of history and of the dehumanizing social institutions which are characteristic of urban society. So groups collapse, with not a little guilt infecting the memories of their former members.

Such harsh realities do not necessarily lead to despair about Christian nurture in small groups. They can stimulate realistic expectations and a mastery of the dynamics of group behaviour. In the Methodist tradition, with a memory of bands and classes operating creatively but little contemporary experience or commitment, special attention needs to be given to overcoming inertia and the guilt of past failure. But progress will be slow and fitful. These are barren days for artists and therefore for pastoral theologians. We can legitimately interpret our situation in terms of the people of Israel wandering in the wilderness for forty years. The prosaic defeats the imaginative. The ecclesiastical institution absorbs more and more of our time and energy, organizing us to serve its interests. Yet through all this misdirected activity and confusion, the struggle to hear God's music and relay it to the world must go on. What is at stake is the discovery of a new spirituality for our Western culture.

God's future and coming kingdom will reveal that long-awaited spirituality – a clear and comprehensive vision of human life in all its depth and mystery, in communion with God. Now, however, is the day of small things; and sometimes what we think we see are only mirages, illusory images of the promised land.

'Since we cannot get what we like, let us like what we can get.'[27] We can drench our critical faculties and imaginations in the scriptures, which point us to Jesus, the Icon of God and of a full and well human life. And we can act, however constricting and unpromising may be the circumstances. 'The prison life suddenly seemed to her the best life of all. It was large enough for love. So it was large enough.'[28]

Acting

In the waiting room (or was it in my imagination, anticipating my next visit to the doctor's surgery?) I decided I has spent enough energy observing, analysing and thinking. I had gazed at the scene long enough, as if it were detached from me. I decided now to enter the situation, to become involved with the seven others, to sympathize.

I unearthed from my past memories of illnesses and injuries which had taken me to doctors' waiting rooms as a patient. I recalled how I felt. I recollected fears and modest distress; I remembered considerable frustration because my well-laid plans for my life were being interrupted or the pace of my life was being altered. I thought about the times when I had been angry at being sick, irrationally so on occasions. I reflected on the many experiences (inflicted on others much more than on me) when I had had to confront the arbitrary, unjust and destructive nature of illness and injury. What sort of universe is it in which some suffer so appallingly?

My digging into my own story of being unwell was not a morbid self-indulgence. It was a self-conscious act of empathy with at least some others in the waiting room. I was offering my memories and reflections into the empty space in the middle of the circle of chairs, to form bonds of common understanding, and to purge myself of self-concern. Only by knowing and denying myself could I give to others a more disinterested love.

I was now able to look freshly and without any sense of voyeurism at each person in the room in turn. I listened attentively to the messages which poured silently out of their eyes, the furrows on their brows, their lips, hands and feet. The messages were often garbled, but sometimes were clear. Always they were drenched in strong emotions, and shot through with deep questions – questions about meaning and purpose, questions about themselves. In tentative ways I could even share their suffering and hear their cries. In some sense or other we had become sisters and brothers.

With all the concentration and integrity I could muster, I held everyone in the presence of God – the God who was already present, unknown, hidden and mysterious, in each of us and among us. I silently prayed us into the divine love which was welling up from transcendent depths to meet us as grace and life and hope.

I agonized over my continuing silence and my physical and emotional isolation. I wanted to reach out and touch at least some one else. I heard banging in the back of my mind the sage's conviction, 'A word in season, how good it is!' (Prov. 15:23). But what to say and how to say it, in a pluralist society, among strangers?

The little girl took out of her mother's plastic bag a toy xylophone. She sat down near her parents' feet, banged the instrument and made an unpleasant, tinny noise. Her mother immediately told her to stop. The little girl rose, toddled towards me, placed the xylophone on my lap and handed me the hammer. 'Make nice music, and make us happy!' she demanded.

In her initiative, before I held my hand over hers and helped her play a recognizable tune, I had already heard the music of heaven. We are indeed members one of another. And if experience confirms what the scriptures regularly proclaim, that we are ministered to by little children, it is small wonder that acts of love, however small, can cover a multitude of sins (Peter 4.8), and the word of a poor wise man can save a city under seige (Ecc. 9.13–17). Hence I recover my conviction: imaginative pastoral care, enmeshed with deepening self-knowledge and sensitive reflection upon scriptural spirituality, can transform a culture, and make us all human and whole.

8

The Catholic Spirit: The Need of Our Time

Ralph Waller

The increased hostility between the various schools of thought within the churches calls for a new exploration of the idea of the catholic spirit. John Wesley's sermon on 'The Catholic Spirit' provides some theological indicators which are relevant to this task. He gives a glimpse of four insights which together make a major contribution to a theological understanding of the catholic church. These insights are: 1. the idea of doctrinal development, 2. the church centred on Christ, 3. the church as a community, 4. the diversity of the catholic church. The essay explores these themes. It also points to another strong point in Wesley's theology where he recognizes that a true catholic spirit cannot be retained in the narrow confines of the church but must reach out and include the whole family of humanity.

There have been two clearly-defined movements in the British churches over the last quarter of a century. The first has been a growing understanding between the denominations: while hope for official organic unity in the churches has receded, mutual acceptance and friendly relationships between the churches have developed during recent years. The second has been the growth of hostile factions within many of the denominations: this can be seen in the Church of England over the issue of women in the priesthood, or in the Roman Catholic Church on matters of birth control and married priests, or in the Free Churches between the traditionalists and the charismatics.

It is surprising that, at a time when denominational boundaries are being more easily crossed, there is an increasing polarization between the various schools of thought and ecclesiastical affiliations within the different denominations. The resulting conflict is one into which all the members of the church are being drawn. For it is a dilemma confronting all those who wish to follow Christ that they have to take a place in one of the many sections of the universal church, and by so doing become identified with a definite body of doctrine and a particular form of church practice. All Christian groups by their very nature rest more or less on this sectarian basis and have a tendency to place considerable stress on the dogmas and rites which distinguish them from all the others, rather than emphasize the beliefs and aspirations they hold in common. This process has resulted in a narrowing of perspectives and a tendency to exaggerate ecclesiastical issues.

In analysing the present state of the church it is much easier to see what is wrong than it is to prescribe a cure. However, initial steps towards that cure can be taken by recognizing that the best talents and insights of the various expressions of Christianity should not be locked up and insulated in the different schools of thought, but that there is a need for free and open dialogue between them all. Every since the Reformation there have been those who have encouraged this open approach to other Christians; among their number would be included Richard Baxter in the seventeenth century, John Wesley in the eighteenth century, John James Tayler and James Martineau in the nineteenth century, and Arnold Lunn and Oliver Lodge in the twentieth century. Anyone in pursuit of this ideal would want to acknowledge a debt to all of them as well as to Dr Arnold and Bishop Hampden. There is no easy solution to the problem of sectarianism facing the modern church, but the writings of these men can provide some foundations from which to start. In particular John Wesley's sermon on 'The Catholic Spirit' does supply theological indicators which if followed through could be relevant to our contemporary situation. The sermon was first preached at Newcastle in the autumn of 1794 and it shows that Wesley following the nonconformity of his mother and of the seventeenth-century divine, Richard Baxter, came to believe that the Christian faith could never be fully encapsulated in any form of words. He recognized that people's apprehensions, experiences and temperaments were very different, and that these differences produced varied dogmatic conceptions of the faith; moreover Wesley held that, while it was important for everyone to follow his or her own inclinations in regard to the truth, these should not be the cause of hostility against those holding different views.

> Every wise man will allow others the same liberty of thinking which he desires they should allow him; and will no more insist on their embracing his opinions, than he would have them to insist on his embracing theirs. He bears with those who differ from him, and only asks him with whom he desires to unite in love that single question, 'Is thy heart right, as my heart is with thy heart?' . . . I do not mean embrace my modes of worship, or I will embrace yours. This also is a thing which does not depend either on your choice or mine. We must both act as each is persuaded in his own mind. Hold fast to that which you believe is most acceptable to God, and I will do the same. I believe the Episcopal form of Church Government to be scriptural and apostolical. If you think the Presbyterian or Independent is better, think so still, and act accordingly. I believe infants ought to be baptised; and that this may be done either by dipping or sprinkling. If you are otherwise persuaded, be still so, and follow your own persuasion. It appears to me that forms of prayer are of excellent use, particularly in the great congregations. If you judge extemporary prayer to be of more use, act suitably to your own judgment. My sentiment is, that I ought not to forbid water, wherein persons may be baptised; and that I ought to eat bread and drink wine as a memorial of my dying Master; however, if you are not convinced of this, act according to the light you have. I have no desire to dispute with you one moment upon any of the preceding heads. Let all these smaller points stand aside. Let them never come into sight. 'If thine heart is as my heart,' if thou lovest God and all mankind, I ask no more: 'Give me thine hand.'[1]

This sermon shows a remarkable breadth of sympathy on Wesley's part towards those who advocated a very different churchmanship from his own; it also has important implications for Arminianism, in that if it is possible for all to be saved and come to a faith in God, then the outward expression of that faith will be very varied owing to the different outlooks and temperaments of individuals.

Wesley gives a glimpse of four insights which together make a major contribution to a theological understanding of the catholic church. These insights are: 1. the idea of doctrinal development,

2. the church centred on Christ, 3. the church as a community, and 4. the diversity of the catholic church. The first two ideas, of doctrinal development and the church centred on Christ, show that for Wesley the basis of Christian fellowship was not agreement on doctrine but an allegiance to the person of Christ. The second two concepts, of the Christian community and its diversity, are indications of Wesley's belief that the church was not simply made up of individuals but in its essence has a communal nature which is enhanced and enriched by diversity and variety. These four insights if expanded could provide a useful starting point for a theology of the catholic church.

The development of Christian doctrine

It would be incorrect to suggest that Wesley had a clear idea of the development of doctrine in the modern sense, yet his belief that the Christian faith could not be fully expressed in words alone is a forerunner to modern ideas of development of doctrine. Moreover his view of orthodoxy expressed vividly in the *Plain Account of Christian Perfection* (1748) adds weight to this contention, as can be clearly deduced when he writes: 'Orthodoxy, or right opinions, is at best a very slender part of religion, if it can be allowed to be any part of it at all.'[2]

A realistic study of any major denomination of the church would show that it does not consist of like-minded people who all hold the same doctrines in common. Within any one denomination, or indeed, within any local church, there will be a wide variety of beliefs and opinions. There is much to commend Wesley's view of giving up the idea of a Christian orthodoxy, and abandoning the belief that there is, or needs to be, collective agreement on matters of doctrine by the members of a church. Rather than start from the catechism, it would be better to start from the assumption that all belief and speech about God is figurative. This starting point arises from the conviction that religious truth is concerned with the infinite, which goes beyond human experience and language, and therefore cannot be fully comprehended by the human mind. Thus our truest beliefs are not the truth, but simply our modes of representing the still absent truth to ourselves. All these modes are symbols of the great reality; sometimes they will represent a kind of 'poetic truth' of apprehension which is different to reason. But our thoughts about God are substitutes or approximations for the actual truth which our finite minds cannot comprehend.

This sense of all our ideas about God being mere approximations is not just because our finite minds cannot fully comprehend the infinite, but is also due to the fact that revelation has to be received by our own faculties, and in this process is subjected to human inference, language, and interpretation. The same process of interpretation are at work here as when two competent students research the records of the primitive church and one finds a hierarchy of spiritual officers, while the other finds an equality; both are seeking the truth and both believe that they have found it.

A further degree of error is introduced into doctrine when we try to articulate the truth that we have grasped. There are two processes between revelation and doctrine: revelation has to be received by the human faculties, and it has to be expressed verbally before it becomes doctrine. Between revelation and doctrine lie the fallibilities of human apprehension and human language. As a consequence of these two processes the resultant doctrine is only an approximation to the original revelation.

Another factor which influences changes in doctrine is the continual change in society. My grandparents were born within a decade of Darwin publishing his *Origin of Species*, and although the church where they worshipped looks substantially the same today, in almost every other aspect of life there have been revolutionary changes; in conditions of living and working, in the worlds of thought and invention, as well as in political and social structures. Some churches have survived because they have changed with the times, even if they were often reluctant to change and blind or short-sighted to the challenges they faced. In changing times the church always faces the dilemma of either refusing to change and thereby taking the risk of becoming ineffective, or of accommodating itself to modern cultural values and thereby risking triviality and secularization. However in a changing world the Christian faith continually needs to be restated; for example ideas and expressions which set the trend in the sixties may look hopelessly out of place in the eighties. Tip-up seats and churches which look like cinemas are no longer the order of the day. Similarly the idea of portraying Jesus as a clown already seems rather dated.[3] Conversely the advancement of the women's movement has raised important issues for Christian doctrine and practice.

If we believe that doctrines not only change but have to change, there are several implications that need to be high-lighted for the church facing the closing years of this century. Every person who thinks deeply about his or her religion will have a theology and develop a doctrine as a means of clear and definite intellectual access to it, and as a way of showing how that religion relates to the wider world. While such a process is essential for the individual, it must not permanently lock the church into a doctrinal cul-de-sac. Doctrines which we inherit from the past and treasure in the present should not be seen as immutable, but rather viewed as transient modes of religious thought, meeting some deep present need but open to continual modification from new and higher influences. If the intellectual apprehension of a particular form of doctrine is made a condition of membership of the church then some of the finest Christians of all ages would be excluded. It has been one of our great mistakes in the twentieth century to assume that Christianity is identical with our own dogmatic conception of it, as if the true and living gospel could exist in no other form. Christian unity will never come about by the triumph of one form of doctrinal Christianity over all the others. But it could come about if we accepted Wesley's point that while people differ over doctrine, at the heart of their Christianity they are essentially one. James Martineau, the nineteenth-century theologian argued that if you sink deep into the inner-most life of any Christian you will touch the ground of all.[4] Many people, for example, can heartily sing Watts's hymns while disagreeing with his unitarian tendencies, or pray the prayers of Anthony Bloom while rejecting his interpretation of the creed, or can be moved by Bonhoeffer's *Letters and Papers from Prison* without accepting the whole of his theology. You do not have to be a Congregationalist, or a Lutheran, or a member of the Greek Orthodox Church to appreciate the spirituality of these Christian people. How often has the experience of Wesley been ours, that when we have found ourselves in conversation with someone from a different ecclesiastical tradition and we have freely exchanged our thoughts, there was at bottom a deep spiritual sympathy between us; though the language we employed was so different, our religion which built up our inmost life, which took us to God and Christ, was substantially the same. It is impossible not to feel in such moments that although in this world we meet at separate communion tables, we are nevertheless fed by the same bread of life.

Christianity is a progressive venture of faith, kept on course by the person and character of Christ, and cannot be limited by detailed theological agreement which is impossible to achieve. This understanding of doctrine goes hand in hand with the concept of the church as a living community which is open to growth, change and development. The church can be likened more to a living forest with sap rising in its branches than to a stone obelisk with eternal rules and regulations carved upon it.[5] An important feature of the Christian church is its sense of continuity, and there is a danger that this continuity could be broken by the church becoming locked into a fixed doctrinal position. The church has an unbroken continuity with the past from which it must not be cut off, but also a present responsibility not to limit the doctrinal expression of future generations. Faced with the problem of guarding continuity, the church can choose between two alternatives: it can prohibit the development of thought, or it can provide for it, and treat that development of thought as a blossoming of its very life and essence.

It is unlikely that Christian unity will ever be achieved by doctrinal agreement between different schools of thought. And it is certain that a true catholic church can not be formed by expelling minorities whose doctrine deviates from that of the majority. Opposition to a doctrinal basis for a catholic church is grounded not only in the fact that doctrines are partial and transitory insights into truth, but also arises out of the belief that communities are not essentially made by agreement on rules and regulations, but by shared memories and thoughts, desires, sympathies and love. At the heart of catholicity lies no dogmatic system, but spiritual affections towards God and towards humanity. This is the key principle for a truly catholic church: a union of holiness and love, founded on and inspired by Jesus Christ.

Jesus Christ is central to the church

In his sermon on 'The Catholic Spirit' Wesley asks a central question, 'Dost thou believe in the Lord Jesus Christ?' For Wesley the centre of the church is Jesus Christ and the discussion of the church starts from this point. The church is defined by its centre, Christ. The very word 'church' invariably assumes discipleship to Christ. It is not the story of Jesus, nor his picture, nor his doctrine that is central to the church, but the person of Christ himself. Where the person is supposed to be unreal the faith cannot be real. To the relationship between master and disciple both parties are indispensable; and if the master vanishes into a figment of the imagination, then the disciple slides into pretence. But it is Christ whose personality can be seen in what Karl Barth called 'the mirror of the narrative' who is the inspiration of the church. Moreover Christ is the external standard of all that is sacred and holy against which individual beliefs, experiences and interpretations can be tested. He is the one who prevents religion from being merely a private and subjective belief; he brings harmony into it and reaffirms the true inner revelations of God.

To such a statement two objections can be raised from completely opposite points of view. One would argue that such a definition of the church is too wide and too vague; and the other would argue that it is too narrow and too exclusive: one maintains that there can be no effective practical Christianity without a definite dogmatic creed to which all must subscribe; the other holds that a truly catholic church ought not to limit itself to Christianity but must embrace a wider theistic belief, including Judaism, Islam and Buddhism. Both of these objections deserve some consideration.

Those who hold that to define the church by its centre, Jesus Christ, is too broad and too vague must face up to the question: who, on a narrower definition of the church, is to be excluded? For if any exclusive definition is to be applied rigorously then undoubtedly many of the greatest Christians down through the centuries would be refused admission. If Bishop Phillpotts's tests had been widely applied, there there would have been no place in the nineteenth century for a Tillotson, a Butler, a Berkeley, or a Lowth. Similarly if Mr Ian Paisley were to draw up the membership of the church then half the members of the universal church would be struck off the books overnight; one wonders if Bishop John Robinson or Mother Teresa would survive if some of the extreme sects of the church were allowed to enforce their views of church membership. Such an exclusive attitude is not only against the spirit of Christ, but would have the practical affect of impoverishing the life of the church; its libraries would be thinned, its literature would be savaged, and its rich and varied hymnody would be depleted.

If the criticism is that a church centred on Christ is far too narrow and restrictive, then it needs to be stated that we are not trying to undervalue the great religions of the world, nor wanting to withhold partnership from any who worship the living God. But this essay is on 'the church' and the historical use of the word 'church' is important for understanding its role today. The original Greek, *ekklēsia*, took on a new meaning when Christians started to meet together. The church is a gathering of the Lord's disciples and denotes nothing before or beyond the range of his community. Without Christ the community would cease to be a church. St Ignatius put this theme in words of great significance: 'Where Christ is there is his church.'[6] The church can be defined as a circle with the centre, Jesus Christ, but it is also a circle without a clearly defined circumference which would make it exclusive, or indeed without any segments that would separate the denominations. All the reference points are taken from the centre, Jesus Christ. This open nature of the church arises from the fact that Christ is the head; he unites his disciples and awakens them to the presence of the family of God.

The church as the Christian community

This approach to Christian doctrine may leave the impression of being concerned simply with the individual and his relationship to God, facilitated through Jesus Christ. This is not the case. The church also has to be considered as a corporate body, with a strong sense of the Christian community. Wesley's phrase, 'If thou lovest God and all mankind, I ask no more: Give me thine hand,' is symbolic of this fellowship. One could argue from a theological basis, and from a practical point of view, against an individualism which undermines the corporate nature of the church. On theological grounds it can be argued that a Christian's life is not his or her own to do with as he or she wills, but that we belong to a holy society, and have a responsibility towards other members of the community. It must also be recognized that the individual's conscience and inner feelings are not the only factors that determine Christian behaviour; respect is also needed for the consciences of others.

From a practical point of view, it can be mantained that very few people thoroughly believe or disbelieve alone by themselves, but that they usually need the sympathy of others to confirm their own inner feelings. If our beliefs and feelings are not confirmed by others then we might well begin to suspect that we are deluded. In this way faith is not simply an individual property, but is much more a process of catholic consent. Religion can never be a purely individual experience between the worshipper and God; it is much more a relationship connecting individuals with each other and with God.

The Christian church is not limited simply to an earthly fellowship, but contains an historical community of former generations linked to those living in the present, and a community in heaven which is joined to Christians on earth. This total church community is made possible by Christ and held together by him. St Paul's thought of one family distributed between heaven and earth (Eph. 3. 14–15) is a key theme for the doctrine of the church. It is Christ who unites those in heaven and on earth in one family, and it is his spirit which draws people together in the community of the church. Any serious study of the church produces an awareness that much has been inherited from the past and that we owe a debt to great Christians of former ages. This continuity is found especially through the singing of hymns and psalms that have been left by former generations as a record of their communion with God. Through them we can identify with the confessions and struggles and desires of those who lived in a previous age, and gain inspiration from the past.

It must be one of the great characteristics of the Christian church that it is an inclusive society. James Martineau drew an analogy between the church and a great choral work which involved the whole of humanity; the disciples of Christ alone knew the words, but the voices of the 'great and good' of every age richly mingle as supporting instruments, filling in the melody.[7] On this view the church is not seen as standing over and against the world but in partnership with the highest aims of humanity. This non-exclusive nature of the church springs from an understanding of the nature of Christ, and his concern for all people. Those who hold this model of the church refuse to place a circle round Christ's disciples or even round all the 'great and good' people throughout history: for this fraternity is not exhaustive. Beyond this company a vast and various crowd of people is scattered, and no line must be drawn which they are forbidden to cross. Christ will not remain the head of the whole family if its outcast members are simply excluded.

The authority for such an inclusive church comes from the earthly life and teaching of Jesus. Any exclusive form of Christianity would be a denial of the spirit shown by Jesus and indeed, could be a rejection of those whom God has received. If it is the character of the religion of Christ to be open, then a

Christian necessarily has an affinity with all devout and righteous people, irrespective of nationality and belief.

The catholic church and its diversity

The idea of catholicy within the church ought to begin with the observation that there are real differences in people's perceptions of the Christian faith, and that these differences actually enrich the faith. Wesley encouraged his hearers not to give up beliefs which apparently tended to divide the Christian church, but he instructed them 'hold you fast to that which you believe is most acceptable to God'. These are not superficial differences, or the results of unfortunate accidents, but they lie in the very nature of humanity and are intrinsic to the life of the church, which would be immeasurably impoverished without them.

This true union among Christian people does not depend upon similarity of thought but will often include a wide variety of opinion. In the same way as in magnetism unlike poles attract each other, so too in this union those who hold diverse views can live in harmony and sympathy with one another. It is this principle that distinguishes natural society from artificial association; the former, springing from the impulse of human feelings, brings together elements that are unlike but which compensate for one another and produce a real and living unity: the latter, directed to specific ends, combines like with like and thus multiplies a mere fraction of life by itself, resulting only in an exaggerated partiality. Many of us could illustrate this factor from our own lives, being conscious that our deepest obligations, as learners from others, is often to writers not of our own denomination. This practice of drawing from a wide catholic background is also influential in worship. Athough Wesley did not agree with Toplady's theology he still included his hymn 'Rock of Ages cleft for me' in his hymn books.

Not only should individuals acknowledge the diversity of backgrounds to which they are indebted, but churches also should be aware of the varied roots and influences from which their tradition has developed. Christians holding diverse views are not simply formed into the catholic church by the process of unlike poles attracting one another: Christ is the centre of unity and it is faith in him which brings together people of different outlooks, races, classes and educational attainments. It is faith in him which throws together unlike ingredients which civilization has sifted out from one another. Every true church reproduces the unity which the world had dissolved. Because Christ is not divided but equal to the whole of our humanity, the partial truths which we have grasped need to be held in relation to the whole. Believers, by keeping a reverent eye fixed on the person and spirit of Christ, cannot but find their partial apprehensions corrected and enlarged and in his holy presence the divisions of Christianity fall away.

Conclusion

The issues we have discussed, the development of doctrine, the church centred on Christ, the communal aspect of the church, and its diversity arise out of Wesley's view of the catholic spirit; but it is also one of the strong points of his theology that he recognized that a true catholic spirit cannot be retained in the narrow confines of the church but must reach out into the wider community. Towards the end of his sermon he wrote of the Christian:

> But while he is steadily fixed in his religious principles, in what he believes to be the truth as it is in Jesus; while he firmly adheres to that worship of God which he judges to be most acceptable in His sight; and while he is united by the tenderest and closest ties to one particular congregation – his heart is enlarged towards all mankind, those he knows and those he does not; he embraces with strong and cordial affection neighbours and strangers, friends and enemies. This is catholic or universal love. And he that has this is of the catholic spirit.[8]

The truly catholic spirit must reach out beyond the church into the wider world. Learning, refinement, enlightened views, a liberal spirit, and love, however valuable in themselves, are of little purpose if they do not spread beyond the circle in which they have arisen and flow out into the world, blessing the whole family of humanity.

9

Logic, Chronology and Context in Theology

Martin L. Groves

The first part of this paper underlines the importance of order in both theology and common Christian discourse. It suggests that the method, or ordering, of our theology carries with it its own interpretative burden. This point is illustrated with reference to various issues of concern to theologians, evangelists, spiritual directors and all who seek to articulate the Christian faith. The second part of the paper considers four contexts within which theology is practised and argues for a structure of priority within them. The purpose of these suggestions is to offer a method which avoids the dangers of theological liberalism, without retreating from any of the social or intellectual challenges of the day.

The problem

What should we speak about first of all? Where we begin is a matter of some importance. Unless other people can see that we begin where they are, they may not want, or be able, to follow. Yet there is little time to waste, and often it is only our first word that is heard. The sermon illustration is remembered, but not the point that was being illustrated, far less the conclusion of the sermon. If we are to be honest and if we are not to be misunderstood, then our first word must be as true as the last; but the problem is that the first word may not bear the same weight or significance as the last. Part of the reason for this is that our religious experience has changed us. We are no longer what we once were. Since we have been changed by the processes of love and history a problem arises as to how we can give a true account of what we once were. In order to make ourselves understood it may be necessary to tell the story of our lives, but the story is about God and not about ourselves. The purpose in telling the story is to give God the glory. And where shall we end? Perhaps we will end up in love with God for his own sake; ie., for what he is in himself. But how do we explain that kind of love to others? In the nature of the case there is no explanation or justification of such love, save in the description of the beloved. So how shall we proclaim the crucified Christ who is nonsense to some and folly to others? And if the object of our faith is never explained, interpreted or justified; if there are no apologetics, then what is to stop dogmatics becoming dogmatism and what will save us from obscurantism? Once we start looking for points of explanation and commendation such as might appeal to a listener, have we not begun to appeal to his cognitive self-interest? And is that not the antithesis of loving God for his own sake? More striking is the appeal that evangelists sometimes make to self-interest, when they seem to offer Christ for the benefits that he will confer on the individual and his soul. Social theologians are also sometimes heard appealing to our collective self-interest as they offer the Christian faith for the social improvements that it will bring. What then is the place of the self and of self-interest in the practice of Christianity? Is the practice of Christianity a selfish pursuit? Is it something one does to do oneself some good? Or is it something one does to do God some good? These are questions that require a methodological as well as a substantive answer. It is part of the purpose of this paper to suggest that a useful tool in this inquiry is to distiguish between logical and chronological priorities in our Christian discourse. By a logical priority I mean that which assumes most importance within the total pattern of Christian experience, belief and discourse. By a chronological priority I mean that which has, or ought to, come first in the sequence of Christian experience, belief and discourse. When such a distinction is made I suggest that we will have a clearer view of the self in relation to God and perhaps be able to better order our theology and our spiritual lives. What follows is an attempt to reflect on some of these methodological issues from within a Methodist theological context.

The issues

What priority should we give to our own spiritual experience within the divine economy? Should we speak first of all about God, or should we begin by speaking about what God has done

Logic, Chronology and Context in Theology 159

for us, and how Christ has loved us and how that has changed us? The first thing that happened was that we discovered God coming to meet us in Christ. Then we discovered God loving us, forgiving us and accepting us. It was these discoveries that changed us and gave us our interest in God. This was the history of how we became interested in God for himself and not for us. How is this to be reflected in our Christian discourse? Shall we begin with 'personal testimony' or with adoration and praise?

Following the Wesleys' spiritual experiences in and around the year of 1738, Methodists have had a strong interest in what Wesley called experimental or, as we would say, experiential religion. There is an oversimplified account of John Wesley's life which is taken to be the pattern for every Methodist and indeed for every true Christian. First there is a period of searching, often within a religious context, then there is the experience of conversion which is closely associated with an experience of the free, unmerited and forgiving love of God, and then there is the remainder of this earthly life spent in evangelical pursuits, the principal method of which will be the retelling of one's own story; the story of what God did for me at the point of my conversion. The Methodist then spends the first part of his life seeking spiritual experience and the second part retelling the story.

But there is a problem. For to dwell on oneself in this way, to dwell on the benefits and blessings accruing to oneself on account of an original spiritual experience, runs the risk of destroying its significance and meaning. The original spiritual experience was significant because it was an experience of God and not myself. To dwell on the fruits of conversion and its associated spiritual blessings is, from an evangelical point of view, likely to be counter productive since it will presumably only reinforce the very self-interest and selfishness which is the opposite of the goal of the Christian life; that is the love of God for his own sake. The selflessness of authentic Christian spirituality is evident in the work of both Wesleys.[1] It is a recurrent theme of Charles Wesley's hymnody, sometimes taken to a point which some have found unacceptable:

> Confound, o'erpower me by Thy grace,
> I would be by myself abhorred.
> All might, all majesty, all praise,
> All glory, be to Christ my Lord.

> Now let me gain perfection's height,
> Now let me into nothing fall,
> Be less than nothing in thy sight,
> And feel that Christ is all in all.

The point is that love is essentially transitive. It requires an object. Without an object we cannot understand what love means. Without an object love cannot be practised. The same is true of faith. The fundamental orientation of the Christian life is not at issue. The problem is one of method; that is to say when we are talking and writing about our faith, where do we begin? Should we begin with God or with ourselves? Around this methodological question cluster a number of related questions, most of which are formally discussed in the ordering of systematic theologies but also have to be answered in common Christian discourse and will have been implicitly answered in the preaching of every sermon.

Shall we begin by speaking of God's being in itself, or shall we begin by speaking about the revelation he makes of himself? Chronologically we knew nothing of God until he chose to reveal himself to us. Our knowledge of God began and begins with revelation. But what God reveals is himself. It is he who is the object of our interest, affection, love and he is the principal subject of our discourse. Logically God's being precedes his self-revelation. Chronologically, God's self-revelation precedes our knowledge of his being. Should ontology take precedence over epistemology or vice versa? Where shall we begin?

W.B. Pope, the most systematic Methodist theologian of the nineteenth century, began his three volume *Compendium* by writing 230 pages on the nature of revelation claiming that 'The term Revelation ... is at once the most elementary and most comprehensive word of our theological system.'[2] Although Pope had written at the beginning of his book that 'God is the source and the subject and the end of theology'[3] he had soon qualified this observation by noting that:

> Theology is mainly concerned with the things of God as they are related to man and his destination. This proposition implies the capacity in our nature to receive Divine truth; indicates both the extent and limits of its range as revealed especially for man; and explains the essentially human character which is impressed on its form and invests it with a profound human interest ... [4]

After having dealt with revelation Pope wrote on the doctrines of God, Creation, Providence, Sin and discoursed on Mediatorial Ministry, all before he turned to the doctrine of the person of Christ. How was it that Pope was able to speak about so many things and say so much about God before he spoke of Christ? And what is the significance of Pope's prior interest in revelation and method? How is it that theologians come to be writing about theological method even at the feet of the crucified Christ?

The interest in method arises in a number of ways. Bernard Lonergan began his work *Method in Theology* with the observation that ' ... when the classic notion of culture prevails, theology is conceived as a permanent achievement and one discourses on its nature. When culture is conceived empirically, theology is known to be an ongoing process and then one writes on its method.'[5] Methodism was born and flourished in the empirical environment of the eighteenth and nineteenth centuries. Methodism's own interest in felt religious experience and all the fruits of holiness in both body and spirit was a product of and a catalyst to the empirical and pragmatic intellectual environment of the age.

The empirical philosophy that is able in a self-conscious manner to recognize (as well as create) an environment of cultural change also creates the conditions of spiritual insecurity. One is naturally the more afraid of an unknown future, for success and survival in today's world does not guarantee success or survival tomorrow. The fear of an unknown future is frightening and militates against substantive theological propositionalism. Methodist theological interests have been in response to this environment. The distinctive themes of the universality of the gospel, the assurance of forgiveness, and the perfectability of holiness and love, provide the dynamic spiritual security for a situation of cultural insecurity. The emphasis is on practice rather than theory and on method rather than propositional statement.

If this was part of the work of Methodism in the cultural environment of its first two centuries, the contemporary need is of the same kind, only greater. Not only the technology, but all the machinery and hardware is assembled for the annihilation of life; a planetary holocaust. Technological and cultural change is so fast that the future is more than ever unknown. It cannot be assumed that today's theological truism will be true, or intelligible or useful in the future and so it is important to discover a method in theology and in the Christian life that will enable us to be as sure as possible and as critical as possible throughout the process of change. This is necessary not just for ourselves and for the comfort of our souls but for others if we are to be understood outside those communities that share our language and order. Our being understood depends not only on what we say but on how we say it.

> When Christ says, 'There is an eternal life', and when a theological student says, 'There is an eternal life': both say the same thing ... both statements are, judged aesthetically, equally good. And yet there is an eternal qualititative difference between them.[6]

The interest in theological method should not be thought of as a soft option amongst theological disciplines nor as a kind of retreat from saying anything about God or the world. Theological method is the grammar of our religious discourse. It arises in the context of our speaking about God and the world, amongst ourselves and also in the course of our evangelism. Understanding the distinction between logical and chronological priority in the language of the Christian faith will enable a dialetic which will keep the Christian story open to bear tomorrow's interpretation. But does this mean that it is necessary to learn a language and a grammar before the gospel can be heard or proclaimed?

Under the influence of Karl Barth, twentieth-century theologians have been inclined to begin their systematic theology with an account of the revelation God gives of himself in Jesus Christ. Twentieth-century theology and spirituality have until very recently had a pronounced christological focus. In popular Methodist piety this christological focus was given appeal by preachers in the school of Leslie Weatherhead. But even if we agree to begin by speaking about Jesus, we have to decide whether we will start with his person or his work. Systematically the question is, should christology precede soteriology or *vice versa*? Spiritually the question is, do we love Jesus because of who he is or because of what he does for us? That is also an evangelical question. It is close to the question about whether we begin by speaking about God as he is in himself or for what he does for us.

In the relationship between christology and soteriology, the methodological issues, particularly the question of where we should begin, assume such importance that the boundaries between method and dogma are pushed aside. On the one hand it is necessary to begin with the account of Christ's death and resurrection, for it is this, particularly his resurrection, which establishes his divinity and 'proves' that he was, 'after all', the Son of God. Had he not been raised from the dead, it would be difficult to say (merely on the basis of his life and ministry) that this Jesus was the Son of God. On the other hand, unless one comes to the events of the first Easter with some knowledge of Jesus' past and a predisposition towards acknowledging his divinity, then it is hard to see why the resurrection should be viewed as anything more significant than a phenomenological abnormality. Part of the importance of this debate is that the starting point governs the interpretation of its conclusion. So McLeod Campbell attempted to sufficiently explain and define atonement through an exposition of the incarnation, whereas in the *Cur Deus Homo*? Anselm answered the question about incarnation with an exposition of atonement.[7] These were the matters under discussion in Scott Lidgett's seminal Fernley Lecture of 1897, *The Spiritual Principle of the Atonement*.

It could be argued that where one begins in all these cases depends on one's interpretation of human nature and in particular on the judgment that is made concerning the character and extent of human sinfulness. If the human character in all its faculties is so distorted and diseased, it may not be possible for us to recognize God as he is, or even as he comes to us in Christ. It may be that our perception, insight, imagination and cognitive faculties are so poor that we see Jesus but do not recognize him as the Christ or as God until something has been done to heal and clear our vision. If that is the case, then we must begin with confession and atonement as a precondition of the approach to God. Only when God has done his work putting us right with himself will we see his glory in the new-born Christ. Such would be the chronology of our spiritual experience, and it is likely that our interest in the mechanism and effects of this atonement on ourselves would remain at the fore of our theological and autobiographical interests.

But it would seem that not everyone has such a sense of the importance of sin. On the contrary, it is argued by some, from the history of their own spiritual experience, that it was the vision of God (which came in myriad ways and various degrees) that awakened the self to its need for restoration and atonement with God. Those with this spiritual history find it more natural to begin with adoration than testimony, more understandable to begin with thanksgiving than with confession. The liturgical implications of this discussion should be plain. Shall we place confession and absolution before the reading of the Gospel as in the Methodist Service Book or after the Gospel and the Ministry of the Word as in Rite B of the Alternative Service Book?

Assuming for the sake of argument that we have decided to begin with ourselves, this matter of whether our spiritual history begins with a positive experience of God or points to God through the negative experience of our sinful self, still needs to be answered. The traditions of positive and negative theology can be traced throughout the entire history of Christianity. Paul Tillich finds these different traditions in the spiritual life:

> One can distinguish two ways of approaching God: the way of overcoming estrangement and the way of meeting a stranger. In the first way man discovers *himself* when he discovers God; he discovers something that is identical with himself although it transcends him infinitely, something from which he is estranged, but from which he has never been and never can be separated. In the second way man meets a *stranger* when he meets God ... Essentially they do not belong to each other.[8]

Tillich goes on to comment, there are differing epistemological implications that follow from these two traditions or starting places. Beginning with the vision of God and the certainty of being in relation to God, positive theology and spirituality always has a struggle to determine the basis of a critical determination of right and wrong. Whilst on the other hand, negative theology and spirituality having begun with such a profound sense of alienation and judgment can speak with confidence only of the need and longing of the soul for God. As to his real being only probable statements can be made.

It seems unfortunate that we should be so dependent on a prior and presumably secular assessment of the human condition before we come to order our theology, especially since its order will be intimately related to its character and conclusions. After all, how much is gained if having begun in a state of alienation our religion takes us through confession and atonement to leave us with only the hope of judgment, or having begun with engagement it leads us through adoration and thanksgiving to a stage of communion? The danger is that we end up more or less where we began.

Ending up where we began is a danger to which we are all equally subject whatever our political or theological orientation and yet those who seek to develop a self consciously contextual theology appear to be more vulnerable than most if only because they state their starting and finishing points more honestly and more clearly than many! John Vincent commends what he imagines to be the basic method of contextual theology to Methodists. The method, he writes, is this:

1. A social, economic and historical analysis of the situation.
2. A search for the biblical and historical stories and paradigms.
3. A statement of the present 'will of God' in terms of policy for the situation.
4. Practical action in mission, politics, life-style.
5. Assessment and restatement in the light of the action.[9]

It is the starting point of this method that is of interest here. To what extent is it possible to begin with a social, economic and historical (one could add psychological or environmental etc.) analysis of the situation? If it was possible to complete such an analysis, why bother then to go in search of biblical stories and paradigms? Is it not precisely because we are unable to make a satisfactory analysis of the situation in purely social, economic or historical categories that the matter of theology or religion arises? Furthermore is it not likely that we will have already read our assumptions about the 'will of God' and his policy for the situation into the original analysis? Why should our theology be so subordinate to secular analysis? Is this not a case of the world setting the agenda for God? Is this not the methodology of liberalism? The danger is that by beginning with a secular analysis we end up with the same analysis washed over with a tint of piety. Social change happens in a more revolutionary and more divine manner than this and our analysis needs to be more rigorously theological.

This case raises the more general question as to whether we should begin with explanation or mere declaration? Shall we begin with apologetics or dogmatics? If we begin with apologetics, do we not evacuate religious language of its content? If it is possible to say what we mean in the language of the world, why bother with religious language at all? If one has to explain

Christianity by reference to that which is not Christianity, is it better not to be a Christian? This is the problem behind many sermon illustrations. Since it is held by many (Methodists especially) to be so necessary to explain the things of God by reference to the things of the world, it is not surprising that some of the people remember the illustration better than whatever was being illustrated, and still others decide that it is better to remain in the world of material intelligibility since it is the key to even religious truth! How can the apologist be other than a rationalist and a liberal? This was the concern that led Newman to declare that 'faith is, in its very nature, the acceptance of what our reason cannot reach, simply and absolutely on testimony'.[10]

But what is the alternative but mere dogmatism and obscurantism? How do words which are never translated or interpreted bear any significance at all? What saves them from being nonsense? And what will save us from seeming to be unconcerned and unloving towards the world to which the word is spoken? These are questions which Methodists might well explore in the context of worship. More often than not it has been a genuine evangelical concern for the world that has led to a liberal style of homiletics. A concern for the social, moral and bodily welfare of society and its individuals has sometimes reduced the sermon to a moral homily. The evangelical desire to explain and transmit the faith in the modern world has sometimes reduced the sermon to an apologetic treatise. An overarching desire to make the word as practical and as intelligible as possible can become counter-productive. The attempt to be as lovingly practical as possible can result in us failing to offer the means by which the moral goals which are offered may be attained. The attempt to be as lovingly intelligible as possible has resulted in us failing to enable a new word from God to be heard, or to say anything more than that which was already understood. The doxological result of this is that our worship has of late been characterized by a banality, a mundanity and a lack of transcendence. Naturally we have no interest in dogmatism, far less obscurantism, for its own sake. Neither should we do anything to turn our back on the material predicament of society. But is hard to see why we come to church unless it is to address and be addressed by God. It may be that the human element in worship is to approach the edge of the mystery, lovingly leading the world to the brink of its own understanding, with the expectation that God will speak his own word and fill the dark of our dogmas with the substance of his own meaning. Even so, it should not be imagined that the relationship between aplogetics and dogmatics is an easy one to determine.

Speaking then of method and Methodism, the question arises as to the place of the Methodist Church within the Catholic Church. On account of Methodism's peculiar beginnings and uncertain relation to the Church of England, Methodists have always had to give attention to matters of ecclesiology. Again it transpires that questions of order and method are of concern, not just for the sake of tidiness, but because they carry a substantial interpretative burden. When writing and speaking about the church, where do we begin? The starting point will reveal the ecclesiological presuppositions of the author. One could start with the early church. In his book *The Holy Catholic Church, the Communion of Saints*, Benjamin Gregory, the Fernley Lecturer of 1873, shared a static Vincentian ecclesiology with the early Tractarians. Or, sharing Newman's later ideas on development, one could choose to tell the history of the church from the beginning to its issue in John and Charles Wesley. Some see the Methodist Church as a reform movement within the Church of England and so begin their account of Methodist ecclesiology with the state of the Church of England at the beginning of the eighteenth century.

The starting point of our ecclesiology does not need to be historical or chronological. In his essay on *The Place of Methodism in the Catholic Church* Herbert Workman began with a reference to the work of the Spirit, paused to reflect on the sociological establishment of Methodism before discoursing at length on the idea of Methodism and its development within the catholic church. Workman represents a considerable tradition within Methodist ecclesiology which claims nothing for Methodism which cannot be claimed for the whole catholic church. He began with the creed,

> Credo in Spiritum Sanctum,
> Sanctam Ecclesiam Catholicam,
> Sanctorum Communionem

and ended,

> We believe, as did the earliest fathers: Where Christ Jesus is, there is His Church. And in the story of Methodism only the blind and irreverent can fail to discern the presence and

power of the Master. For us as for St Ignatius: 'Our charter is Jesus Christ; our infallible charter is his cross, and his death, and his resurrection, and faith through him.'[11]

Before Workman, Pope's ecclesiology had similar characteristics:

> The words used by William Burt Pope to designate Methodist theology, and continually illustrated in his *Compendium of Christian Theology* are 'scriptural', 'catholic' and 'orthodox'. This is the hallmark of Methodist theology: the theological assertion of Church status, with the denial that methodism is a sect. As part of the One, Holy, Catholic Church, Methodists have a contribution to make to ecumenical theology. Methodist theologians wrote Christian theology – not Methodist theology, if this means a truncated version of Christian belief.[12]

The method and style of systematic theology exhibited by Pope illustrates the kind of denominational theology pleaded for by Stephen Sykes in his book *The Integrity of Anglicanism*. Sykes, in the Anglican context, engages in the argument about the extent to which a denomination ought to have its own distinctive theology, beliefs and method. He argues that there is (or at least there ought to be) a recognizable Anglican theology and a theological method to go with it, but that such a theology is the work of individual theologians writing catholic and orthodox theology alongside ecumenical theologians from other traditions. Pope's work was and is recognizably Methodist, particularly in its treatment of the doctrines of assurance and sanctification and his treatment of the administration of redemption, but all of that is only in the course of a thorough-going catholic systematic theology.

This is the ecclesiological version of the question already posed. Shall we begin with ourselves or with God? Now the question is, shall we begin our ecclesiology with reference to the whole catholic church or to the Methodist part of it? Methodism is a comparatively recent issue in the history of the catholic church, and yet for Methodists it has been the place of their baptism, the point of their first entry into the catholic church. Where shall be begin? The position is (or should be) no different for Anglicans or Roman Catholics or Presbyterians. Methodist history, however, has meant that Methodists have been less inclined to fall into exclusive notions of themselves as belonging to and constituting the one and only true church. The material facts of Methodist church history have helped to remind Methodists that the primary and constitutive characteristic of any church is its relation to Christ in the power of the Spirit.

The view we have of our church and its position within the whole catholic church will influence our approach to ecumenical developments. Ought a church to enter into ecumenical conversations with the leading idea that its life is perfected in sacrifice and self-sacrifice after the example of Christ and so be prepared to put aside its past, 'I would be by myself abhorred' and abandon all, 'Now let me into nothing fall' for the sake of the unity of the body of Christ? Or should we say that this our church has been the sacrament and the very means of our participation in the body of Christ, his church? After all, it is not as though we are individual Christians who accidentally happened to find that we had inherited this denomination with its buildings, practices and other assets. In the experience of Methodists, this poor, Victorian, lower-middle-class elderly institution has been and is the holy catholic church, the body of Christ, the place where the sacrifice has been offered and received and the entire unity of the church has been discovered in its relation to Christ.

In ecumenical conversations, should we speak first about our riches or our poverty? Should we speak about an existing unity that we have in Christ, despite all our denominational differences? Or should we begin with the scandal of our separateness from each other? How is it possible to speak of any real union in Christ, when we do not recognize each other's ministries, do not share in the eucharist, and have little or no day-to-day business with neighbours who belong to other denominations? But if we cannot speak of such an existing unity in Christ, on what basis can we proceed? For one option which is not open to us is to imagine that we can create a new united church. It is in the nature of a church that it can be neither created nor invented. Similarly so with church unity. The church is given to us by Christ and is created and renewed in the power of the Holy Spirit. As we have discovered that we cannot manufacture the means of our union with God or indeed with each other so we cannot manufacture a church. The church is that point in space, time and society where and when we find ourselves in union with God and each other through Christ and in the Spirit. Method is important in ecumenical theology, because ecclesiology is about order (where we begin and where we end) and not about invention.

Before leaving the area of ecclesiology, it is interesting to note that, after two introductory paragraphs on methodology, Schleiermacher began his systematic theology with a preliminary examination of the church. His proposition was that 'Since Dogmatics is a theological discipline, and thus pertains solely to the Christian Church, we can only explain what it is when we have become clear as to the conception of the Christian Church.'[13] It is a thought which has chronological integrity since our interest in dogmatics only arises in the context of the church and at the point of encounter with God. But to begin a systematic theology with a definition of the church would seem to some to be putting the cart before the horse. The rigorous ontology of F. D. Maurice probably has more natural appeal to the English theological mind.

> I have said that I believe in God the Father and in Jesus Christ His Son, and in the Holy Ghost; after that in the Holy Catholic Church. That I have understood to stand in His name, to have no existence apart from it. If I am to believe in the Church first and then in God, I do not know what the Church is; I do not know how it came into existence or what function it can have.[14]

Maurice was here reviewing Newman's *Grammar of Assent* and it should not be overlooked that the priority given to the church by Newman and the Tractarians was the primary instrument in the reformation of the Church of England in the nineteenth century. In any case, Maurice was not saying that it was possible to believe in God apart from the church, rather that it was not possible to believe in the church apart from God.

Issues of method arise out of the tension between ideas and facts, ontology and epistemology, between logic and chronology. But it is this same tension or dialectic which creates the dynamic space for our encounter with God. It is one of the mechanisms which we find at work in the sacraments. In the sacraments of the church we are thrown backwards and forwards between the event and its interpretation, between the being and the believing, between order and experience, until the dialectic is mysteriously resolved in the person of God and we ourselves are forgotten in the divine encounter. Method in theology describes the history and nature of our relationship with God.

The context

So far I have attempted to do little more than stress the importance of method in theology, particularly drawing attention to the matter of what should be put first. I have suggested that the order given to a systematic theology or to any piece of Christian discourse will not only betray the *a priori* interests and presuppositions of its author but will also affect the interpretation of its conclusion. These thoughts have been suggested and illustrated by raising various issues concerned with the starting point, priorities and direction of religious discourse. Whilst most of these issues arise in the course of determining an order for a systematic theology, it is clear that logic, chronology and method have an importance in Christian practice that goes beyond that limited task. Unless we are able to recognize and order the different levels of logic and chronology in Christian discourse, we will not be able to say what we mean. It is likely that our religious language will have collapsed into the language of pure idealism or materialism and be inadequate to describe the form of human relationships or the character of our relationship with God. In raising these issues I have no doubt indicated some of my own theological preferences, but have advanced no general theory of theological method. Such a task is in any case beyond the scope of this paper. Nevertheless, it may be possible to make some more positive and constructive suggestions that bear on the area of method in theology.

It has been fashionable over the last fifteen years to speak about contextual theology. In the early 1970s the Latin American liberation theologians developed a self-conscious interest in the social, economic and political context within which the Christian faith is practised and its theology done. This interest arose out of a strong appreciation of the historical nature of revelation and also out of the natural concern for relevance and intelligibility. Methodological reflection on the practice of theology, especially in revolutionary situations or situations where the Christian community is alienated from the political and economic establishment, has produced an awareness of the importance of context in determining the interpretation of Christian theology. And that in addition to the obligation of the Christian community to make its proclamation of the word of God in such a way that it can do its lovingly creative and redemptive work in the world. None of this is original or controversial. That context makes a difference to theology is evident from the New Testament itself and is a presupposition of much New Testament study. What is more interesting and controversial is to establish how the context will be described and determined, and precisely how it affects the content and methods of Christian doctrine and theology.

It is no easier to determine the proper context for doing theology than it is to make a satisfactory secular analysis of the situation and environment in question. It is the determination, analysis and interpretation of the context that is (after all) the problem. Looked at from one perspective we could say that this was the only and entire task of theology; that is, to determine the context in the light of the being and purposes of God.

I want to suggest four of the contexts within which theology is done. They are concentric, they overlap each other and refer to the same reality, but they generate different ways of speaking about that reality. The order in which they are treated is important.

Theological reflection within the divine-human relationship

Instead of speaking of God as the subject of theology it might be better for us to think of all our theological reflection as happening within the context of our relationship with him. Instead of speaking of the establishment of a relationship with God as the goal of Christian piety, it might be better to think about the working out of our salvation in the context of God's presence, love and judgment; that is, in the context of the divine relationship. God is himself the context of our life, religion and theology. Context implies relationship and it is this relationship which constitutes the whole environment as well as the beginning and end of Christian discourse and theological reflection. John Macmurray, one of the most unappreciated English theological thinkers of the twentieth century, gave detailed and at times original consideration to the primacy of the relational in Christian theory and practice in his Gifford Lectures of 1953/4 on *The Form of the Personal*. Towards the end of the second volume he wrote, 'Consequently, the theological question is improperly represented in the form "Does God exist?" It must be expressed in the form, "Is what exists personal?"'[15] Prior to this Macmurray had argued that to be in relationship is constitutive of persons and personality.

To begin by speaking of God as the first context of theology has ontological integrity since God existed before creation.

Semantically it may be a truism, but it is necessary to restate the proposition to correct the impractical and undesirable suggestion that theology should begin with a (presumably secular) analysis of the 'world'. It is necessary to restate the proposition since, with whatever motives and interests we may have begun our interest in God, now we are interested in him for himself. The case of one who began to be (or who still is) interested in God on account of what it was hoped God would do for him, is not precluded by this approach. The assertion that God is the first context of theology, and that all Christian discourse takes place within the context of the divine-human relationship does not depend on any particular chronology of Christian motivation or experience. The question of whether we begin our evangelism, apologetics and theology with ourselves or God is approached from a new angle. To begin in this way helps us to realize that it is not possible to talk about ourselves or God other than in relationship with each other. Something of this insight is given in the opening passages of Martin Buber's book *I and Thou*. 'There is no I as such but only the I of the basic word "I-Thou" and the basic word "I-It".'[16]

A further implication of interest to both methodology and piety concerns the difference between belief in and belief about. Christian discourse and theological method must be able to distinguish between belief in a person and belief about a proposition. Narrow empiricism has tended to concentrate more attention on the 'belief about' question, with the result that Christians have often understood the question of belief in God to be a question about the existence of God. The methodological debate is about whether it is possible to hold a belief before it is proved to be true and certain; before it is understood and explained. John Coulson has argued that this is the claim that Newman made in *The Grammar of Assent*. Coulson goes on to suggest that whether or not Newman's grammar of assent had integrity for his day, the situation today has changed. From the standpoint of a pluralist and secular culture 'the demand is that what we believe must be, in the first place, not doxologically or dogmatically credible, but rationally adequate'.[17] The apologetic and evangelical demands made on us by a secular culture may make it necessary to begin by explaining our belief, but surely that must be a chronological and not a logical priority. In the exercise of theology it is necessary to explain belief, but the explanation cannot be understood until it is believed. Explanation may precede belief, but belief will always precede understanding. *Credo ut intelligam.* This is because God himself forms the first context of our theological reflection and Christian life.

Our faith is in divine persons, not in our generalization; faith in a Being whose thoughts we cannot measure or compass, but in whom we live, and move and are; faith in Him who has promised to guide us into all truth.[18]

Theological reflection in the context of worship

If we begin with God, or if we begin our theological reflection mindful that it is conducted in the context of the divine-human relationship, it follows that our Christian discourse will be conducted in a doxological environment. Having begun with a sense of being in God and believing in God it is reasonable to suggest that the character and method of our response will have the form of worship. This idea has recently received systematic treatment from Geoffrey Wainwright in his book *Doxology*.

There are a variety of ways in which it makes sense to speak of worship as a context of theology. In the first place we are accustomed to the idea of meeting God and of being met by him and of being in his presence when we are at worship. It is when we are worshipping and at worship that our thoughts and spirits are most occupied with God. So John Henry Newman wrote in his sermon *Holiness Necessary for Future Blessedness*:

> Heaven, then, is not like this world; I will say what it is much more like, – a church. For in a place of public worship no language of this world is heard; there are no schemes brought forward for temporal objects, great or small . . . Here we hear solely and entirely of God. We praise Him, sing to Him, thank Him, confess to Him and give ourselves up to Him and ask his blessing. And therefore, a church is like heaven; viz. because both in the one and the other, there is one single sovereign subject . . . God brought before us.

We have no business at worship in church other than to be in communion with God. It is God's presence incarnate in Christ in the here and now which makes a church and which transforms us into worshippers. As Christians we are who we are when we are in church, at worship and in communion with God. Put another way, if the eucharist is the environment or context in which we are both evidently and really in the presence of God, then the doxological and eucharistic environment of a church ought to provide the context and form of life in the world. This was F.D. Maurice's thought in a much quoted passage from *Theological Essays:*

> The world contains the elements of which the Church is composed. In the Church these elements are penetrated by a uniting, reconciling power. The Church is, therefore, human society in its normal state; the world, that same society irregular and abnormal. The world is the Church without God; the Church is the world restored to its relationship with God, taken back by Him into the state for which He created it.[19]

Worship, as in church, is the context and form of our response to God. It was so in the beginning at Epiphany; when the wise men first saw Christ they worshipped. It is believed that it will be so in the end. The fourth chapter of the book of the Revelation to St John contains the vision of creation consumated in an act of worship. Wainwright concluded his book with a verse of Charles Wesley:

> Finish then thy new creation,
> Pure and spotless let us be;
> Let us see Thy great salvation,
> Perfectly restored in Thee;
> Changed from glory into glory
> Till in heaven we take our place,
> Till we cast our crowns before thee,
> Lost in wonder love and praise.

A lively sense of the doxological context of Christian belief reminds us of the way in which we use, understand and believe in the creeds and the scriptures. In both cases worship is the primary and normative environment for them to be spoken, heard and understood. The speaking, hearing and understanding of them is done in the presence of God, their meaning is dependent on the contemporary reference to God. The scriptures describe the historical environment of the revelation of the presence of God and illustrate the manner of the human response to that promise. The creeds offer a form for the expression and confession of our belief in God. They are not, in the first place, inventories of the components of spiritual reality as it is believed to exist by Christians and religious people. When

Christians say 'We believe in God the Father Almighty...' what they mean is that their believing takes place in the presence of God and in the context of the divine-human relationship. Belief that God exists is included within such a confession, but is neither the beginning nor the end of Christian faith. Wainwright notes that the creeds 'have provided a hermeneutical grid through which the believer could interpret both the ampler witness of scripture and the church and also his own religious stance.'[20] Or as John Coulson has suggested,

> ... to have correct beliefs must be distinguished from knowing or holding the truth. What we hold, we hold – in the primary sense – not as propositions, but *doxologically*, that is in the prayer of praise, memory and hope – from which doctrinal or metaphysical forms are but inferences.[21]

One could say that the creeds and the scriptures in their doxological context serve as sacramental vehicles through which God reveals himself and his word. It is in the moment of revelation that they are given meaning, and it is that meaning which then interprets the world for today.

There are other methodological and epistemological implications that follow from recognizing that the doxological context is normative for theological reflection and for Christian discourse. Light is shed on the inter-action and relationship of certainty and humility in the Christian life. Worship presupposes a kind of certainty. Celebration, adoration, confession, thanksgiving and praise happen only in the context of an assured relationship. It is precisely out of this assured relationship that the Christian life derives its confidence. In particular it is this assured relationship that provides the freedom for criticism and self-criticism. It is because Christian certainty is in God and not in ourselves that it is possible and indeed necessary to be self-critical. 'The humility of adoration protects ... (theology from) ... the overweening pride of having comprehended the eternal truth of God by means of human words.'[22]

There are certain things which one does not say or think in church and there are certain ways of thinking and speaking which one does not use in worship. That is to say there is a kind of reserve which is associated with worship. Again it has to do with a sense of the presence of God. It may be analogous to the difference in how we speak of someone in his or her presence and how we are tempted to speak of the same person in his or her absence. Or perhaps it is like the reserve shown by a lover in speaking of the beloved to a third party. The reserve that we practise in worship and in church should be exercised in our common Christian and theological discourse. Those Christian traditions that have begun with a sense of the importance of the Word of God have sometimes fallen short because they have spoken and written and preached as though it was necessary to speak vicariously for God, as though God himself had suddenly become mute since some earlier revelation. Authentic Christian discourse will be of the kind and in the style that allows God to speak his word between our words and through our words. If it is rude to talk so much as to exclude another from conversation, it is hell for us so to treat God. Similarly, when in the presence of another we do not speak as though we knew the length and breadth and every little mechanism of that person's soul, neither should we speak that way of God. It should be noted that this reserve derives not from agnosticism, but from a profound sense of the fullness of the presence of God. The analogy is the reserve that characterizes our discourse when held in the presence of another. It is a silence which is different from the uncertain silence that issues from scepticism or ignorance or in the absence of our subject. The reserve that characterizes our discourse comes from having discovered that however vital and sacramental and necessary words are in the declaration of love and faith, there is still more to love than even they can say. To carry the fullness of its meaning the word of God became flesh and dwelt among us.

The doxological context of Christian faith and language sheds useful light on another question which has often been approached without regard to matters of chronology and priority in Christian discourse. Having, as it were, given up on the question 'Does God exist?', Christian apologists have turned more hopefully to the question 'What difference does it make that God exists?' Some have tried to exploit the evangelical potential of the anticipation that Christian faith might make a difference to the life of an individual. But if worship is the normative context for the practice and articulation of faith, then it becomes clear that an interest in the anticipated results of Christian faith and belief should be treated with caution. In worship and in the spiritual life celebration and thanksgiving assume priority over intercession and petition. I went to church to celebrate my wedding not, in the first place, because I thought it might make a difference to my life, but because I felt compelled to declare my love for my wife and to celebrate that love with others. It is so with the Christian faith in its doxological context. Having encountered the love of God, that love demands that it be declared, proclaimed and celebrated (as happens in worship) without regard to the consequences.

Theological reflection in the context of society

The third context of theological reflection, Christian discourse and the practice of the Christian life, is the social context. The reality that is here referred to is the same as was spoken of in the previous two contexts. But now the view of the context has changed and this changed view affects our use of Christian language. It is not as though society exists apart from the life of God and his relationship with the world. There was society amongst the persons of the Holy Trinity before there was creation. We can understand creation as the issue of the loving relational activity of the persons of the Trinity. It is in the nature of love to give itself to another and human society owes its being to the divine society. Ontologically we can say that there is divine society and because there is divine society, there is human society, and human society is not something apart from the life of God. Logically divine society precedes human society and human society is subordinate to it. Methodologically we cannot speak (as we often do) as though our knowledge of or interest in society precedes our knowledge of or interest in God. Indeed we must find ways of making it clear that our interest in human society is subordinate to our interest in divine society and also contextually subordinate to the doxological environment of the authentic response to God.

This subordination should not be thought of as unloving, reactionary, far less anti-social. The life of all human society is contained within the divine-human relationship. Human social relationships are not merely analogous to the divine-human relationship; they are the means through which the divine relationship is realized and God reveals himself. Christologically the case is that God did not become like a human being in Christ, but that he became really human in him. This insight precludes the common homiletical method whereby the preacher begins with a human and social introduction as mere preparation or illustration for the divine truth that is to follow. Neither will it allow us to postpone our interest in the world until such time as the world has conformed itself to our model of the kingdom of God. For there is a common model of Christian thinking about the world (share in various ways by the political left and right) that God's current involvement in the world through Jesus Christ is confined to the church, and God will be present and active in the world at large only when his kingdom has come. There is an important semantic sense in which this may be true, but it often interpreted as implying that God is presently powerless or at least chooses to be inactive beyond the sociologically defined boundaries of the confessing Christian community.

Neither should the subordination of the social to the doxological context be thought to imply an aesthetic preference for choral evensong over the revolutionary struggle. Worship is the form of the human and social response to God in his relationship with the world. Again it includes within itself the whole life of society. The liturgy is the method of cultural action for socialization. In adoration is the visionary anticipation of the perfected life of the world in the kingdom of God. In confession is the whole of social criticism. In the proclamation of the gospel and the ministry of the word is all the means of conscientization and social transformation. In thanksgiving, eucharist and communion is the practice of true community. This community is a divine society formed out of the common relationship of all its parts with God. Being formed by God and constituted in his presence this community bears the marks of equality, freedom and peace and is a real prolepsis of the final condition of all society in the kingdom of God. In intercession is the whole of our commitment to the renewal of the world's society in the kingdom of God.

Different liturgies present different social programmes. As different theologies are reflected in liturgical variety and produce that variety, so Christian social praxis will not be uniform. But that is not the point. The point is that our speaking about God and the Christian faith is always done in a social context, for the life of society is included with the life of the God who created, redeemed and is perfecting it, and our worship describes the form of Christian social praxis.

Theological reflection in the context of the work of God

So much attention has of late been given to the question 'What difference does it make?' that it will seem strange to some that I should have left the social context of theology to this late point and have said almost nothing constructive about the evangelical context of Christian discourse. For broadly speaking, the question about the difference made by the Christian faith has been answered in one of two ways. Either it has been answered in terms of the development or transformation of society; or it has been answered in terms of the development or conversion of the individual soul. To describe the transforming effect of the gospel on society as a whole, or on the individual soul has sometimes been thought of as the main, if not the only, task of theology. Within the Christian community there has been a division and an argument over which of these interests should take priority. Whilst much energy has been burnt up in this debate, both concerns are subject to the same danger if given unqualified priority in the structure of Christian thought and practice. The danger is that of theological liberalism. To be interested in Christianity only for what it is imagined it can do for society is theological liberalism and was perhaps the principal weakness of English Christianity in the middle part of this century. But to be interested in Christianity only because of the benefits it is supposed it can confer an individual soul is equally liberal and is the principal weakness of recent developments in popular piety. By liberalism in theology I mean the tendency to confuse heaven and earth in such a way that earth is made the standard by which heaven is criticized; the tendency to confuse God and his creature, with the result that God is judged by his creature; the tendency to confuse the kingdom of God with contemporary society is that the kingdom of God is (at worst) described as the society we have already or (at best) as the society some of us hope for.

The first problem with this liberalism is its descriptive inadequacy. That is to say it fails accurately to describe God and heaven. The second problem is that it cannot achieve its own ends. An overwhelming interest in the social implications of Christianity is methodologically inadequate since it can offer to society only what it has derived from society, at best society's own aspirations for itself. Such an approach can never be truly revolutionary. Similarly, an overwhelming interest in the fruits of religious faith for the individual; health, healing, peace, eternal life, salvation, does no more than offer an individual a description of his malady reversed in a mirror of hope. Such an approach and such an interest cannot supply the mechanism of self-improvement. It tells the individual only what he himself would like to become for his own good. It does not tell him what God would like him to be. This is a problem which has equal relevance to Christians interested in evangelism and Christians interested in spirituality.

It seems then that a theology that begins with an interest in social improvement, or evangelism, or holiness, soon finds itself involved in a practical difficulty which on reflection amounts to a theoretical contradiction. The practical difficulty is, to what extent should one, in any of these three areas of Christian practice, appeal to self-interest? The theoretical contradiction is, how one can describe Christian practice in a way which has apologetic credibility and evangelical appeal (that is to say, how can one describe Christian practice in a way that makes compelling sense?) and be true to the insight that the Christian life is life lived and died for another. The problem is precisely, how do we 'proclaim the crucified Christ', a message that is offensive and nonsense?[23]

In view of this difficulty and contradiction in the areas of Christian social concern, evangelical and spiritual activity, it is the more important for us to speak about the state of the work of God. *The Constitution, Practice and Discipline of the Methodist Church* requires all Circuit Meetings to consider the state of the work of God (Standing Order 555). It may be helpful for us to assume the work of God to be the fourth context within which we do our theology and conduct our Christian discourse.

Again it is important to stress that there is one reality, and in speaking about four contexts for the Christian life I am speaking of four levels within that reality, four ways of viewing it. The work of God was fully present in the first context, for God's first work was to make everything that is and to establish a relationship with it in Jesus Christ. The work of God was also to be discovered in the second or doxological context, since God created the world 'to share his own life and happiness for ever'[24] and worship is the form of the human response to God. In the third context it was asserted that the sustenance of social relationships is the work of God himself and society has no life of its own apart from this work of God. And so when we come to those areas of Christian life and activity most commonly associated with voluntary human activity, namely evangelism, spirituality or sanctification and Christian social responsibility, it is proper that, even at this stage, we should begin with the work that God does in these areas. Before we propose an initiative in any of these areas we should ask what has God already done and what is he presently doing? Only then is it sensible to ask what should we be doing? After the event it will be recognized that the primary agent of evangelical activity was the Holy Spirit since only God can incorporate one to himself. In the nature of the case only the Spirit can sanctify. Equally, only God can establish his kingdom; if I did it then it would be my kingdom not God's. The work of God is the fourth context of theological reflection and Christian discourse.

Implications

Do these methodological proposals imply a form of life that is quietist, pacifist and discouraging of responsible human activity? Are we to be like Moses who, when the people were in the midst of their exodus from slavery and were about to be cornered and attacked by the Egyptian army with their backs against the Red Sea, advised them to do nothing, saying 'The Lord will fight for you, and there is no need for you to do anything'?[25] If so, some will say that this is a reactionary theological method. Is the suggestion that we should be so interested in the being, person and activity of God that we allow ourselves to be the docile pawns of the power politicians of the world?

Such might be the result of these suggestions if that was the will of God. If it is in fact the case that God himself has little interest in the world and is not lovingly involved in transformative business with the world, then our interest in him, in the way suggested, would be 'other-worldly' and mystifyingly disengaged from the politics of society. But this is not the God of the Judaeo-Christian faith and tradition. When the Christian tradition focusses its attention in whatever way (methodologically, theologically, or in prayer) on God, it does not fix its gaze up into the sky. For the first word of God was to declare his love through a material outpouring of himself in the act of creation. The second word of God was to speak the word of his material presence at the nadir of the human experience, namely at the point of crucifixion when the creation would have destroyed itself in the destruction of the source of its being. The third word of God is to perfect the union of himself with his creation in a final declaration of the loving and truthful word, which is the point of judgment.

At each point when God speaks his word it is spoken to another, for the sake of the other and within the material predicament of the other. But this inquiry has for the most part been concerned with how we should order our Christian discourse. Quietism is excluded, since it is in the nature of love to declare itself; as in creation, as in the word of judgment, and as in a wedding. When we speak our word, it too must be spoken to another and for the sake of the other, and from within the material predicament of the other. If we take account of the context, then first of all the word is spoken to and of God. Secondly, it is a word of worship; of praise, confession, adoration and thanksgiving. As it is spoken from within the world and to the world it cannot help but transform the world and to speak this loving word is the work of God.

Postscript: The Freedom to Respond

While it was no part of our discussion that we should produce a coherent argument, a reading of these papers in retrospect leads us to attempt to produce a coherent statement of the implied theology. Our discussions frequently led us to recognize the congruence of our thinking, even where there was apparent conflict: the written document seems to underline this perspective.

Our human experience is best understood in terms of creation rather than accidental happening or simply universe. Our increasingly perspicuous accounts of the world model our experience of it, but do not challenge necessarily our overall perception of it as creation. Indeed in relation to God one is pointing to his freedom to make, and in relation to humanity the freedom to respond. In Arminian terms the way is therefore open for us to see all humanity as open to God and capable of responding to him. Indeed the doctrine of creation implies such reciprocity.

We have therefore to rethink any understanding of salvation which would imply that it was effected unilaterally by God and was not a collaboration of creator and creation as is implicit by the way we think about God in relation to the world. One model for this would involve human beings having the capacity to give to God, even to enrich him by their experience. Any such thought runs against some traditional reflection upon God within the Christian tradition, particularly perhaps that which involves an objectification of God as the one alone, who exists apart. However, to think of God at all involves us in the attempt to objectify, and it is a mark of human capacity to respond to God that we are able to do so. Of course one needs to be sensitive to the fact that in objectifying any individual model one may betray one's own freedom to think creatively, for in the Christian tradition losing our freedom is to threaten God's freedom, since the freedom of God and the freedom of humanity are interdependent. Our freedom to respond to God means that we have to be new to thoughts about God, if God is to be given space in our lives; if we do not give this freedom to him he has no opportunity to enable us to respond freshly to his love. God's freedom to be himself, quite independent of our conception of him, means that it is by giving the whole of our attention to him that we can find our freedom. This is apparently paradoxical, but God is the one to whom we can give the whole of our attention without losing the freedom to be ourselves. Indeed it is his nature to give himself so as to enable others to be: it is what the Christian means by 'God'. He precisely makes space for the other: and thus creation is always enabled to be and to become through God's grace.

Such models or stories of God have to be appropriated by human beings; for it is by such responsiveness to the active presence of God that creation takes place. Yet there is plenty of evidence in the contemporary world to indicate that we humans find it difficult to own our experience, to appropriate it as our personal life-story. The biblical tradition offers interesting examples, the understanding of which may get us started on the process for ourselves. But the process of incorporating experience, of responding to God's grace requires that we come to terms with the pain of waiting, the death that may accompany 'analysis' before new life is possible for those who share a new vision. Perhaps not surprisingly the occasion which often prompts one to accept one's experience is a surprise, an 'accidental' event which on other grounds we may later understand by undeserved grace.

Methodist ecclesiology offers no limits to the ways in which a Methodist tradition may incorporate such an understanding of God as the one who is available, self-giving, the one who makes room for genuine free response by the other. But where do we begin? Perhaps by looking at three possible active conceptions of the common core of what is involved in being human, namely the worship of the church, the community of humanity and the work of God. For by attending corporately to the reality which is God, we rightly both affirm and threaten our understanding of him and thus open ourselves to a vision of his beauty. By accepting the searchings of our fellow human beings, their doubts, aspirations, courtesies and fears, we acknowledge the ambiguous responsiveness of the human condition, and by attempting to share in the work of God through our sensitivity, new behaviour and making space for others, we affirm his presence.

In this developing idea we can see the crucial importance for the Methodist tradition of affirming the freedom of humanity the freedom of God and the universality of his grace.

There is hardly an attribute of humanity which requires greater emphasis at the present moment than freedom, though one must recognize that while freedom is a good horse, one must ride it somewhere. With regard to the human situation as characterized by the Christian understanding of creation the concept is a relational term. Human being is free in relation to God; every aspect and development of that freedom which is of the essence of what it is to be free as a human being comes from the human relation of creature with the creator. It is because God makes room for human being that human being can grow and flourish. The fullest expression of this is found in God's commitment of himself in Christ, which therefore is of course also paradoxically the true instantiation of what it is to be human. Christ's willingness and desire to give his whole attention to God frees him to be himself in relation to his neighbours. Through love of him the disciples find themselves made aware of the fragility of their own understanding and drawn to the one who offers himself for them; it is Christ's willing obedience to death that concentrates the attention of the world on the creator, and shows just how costly and creative the creator's love can be.

This whole response to God therefore threatens any merely human system or structure or objectification of a model. They are all relativized and shown to be things for which human beings can be responsible. Human beings are free if they so decide, if they so act in relation most particularly to their own creations. But it is crucial that one does recognize that one is free before one can be free. In the contemporary world political creeds, economic impossibilities, scientific predictability, the apparent completeness of descriptions – all these claim an absoluteness of obedience which threatens the liberating obedience of man to God on which alone his freedom and the realization of the true nature depends. It can be seen how in the life of Christ himself this threat is most profoundly stated by the religious traditions and ecclesiastical structures. Their very 'goodness' tempts them to overreach themselves and to domesticate rather than enable. It may well be that God has chosen the Christian community as a means of offering his grace and safeguarding that community for the future, but that very thought should put us on our guard against any suggestion that the actual structure is necessarily the only structure that could emerge as a means whereby the Christian community manifests and shares the grace of God. What we have to ask ourselves now is where – in the church, in the community, in political life, in economic affairs, in our aesthetic experience – the freedom of God is actually enabling us to be free? What, within the whole range of contemporary human experience, marks and develops our true humanity? And each Christian person must ask of herself or himself where lies freedom of response in relation to the vision of God.

Traditional theology has wanted to affirm the absolute freedom of God in choosing to create. There were no conditions or restraints on God; there was no one to please. He made because it was his nature to want to do so. The freedom of the Father was in the beginning a freedom for and with the Son, and the free expression of the Holy Spirit's love. From the beginning then, and in creation, the freedom of God is relational. God is free, if absolutely, nevertheless free for another.

What characterized his freedom in the beginning continues to characterize it throughout the history of the universe and throughout human history. It is a freedom of resource, an originality of response, such as the poet or artist may show. The freedom which he exhibits, a freedom of imagination and action, in no way fetters the world. Indeed it is only through such imaginative and gracious activity that the possibility of human freedom arises again. Human freedom is therefore a gift of God, and reflects the nature of the giver. Only by accepting that freedom ourselves do we enable the freedom of God to find fullest expression. The grace of God makes being possible, and makes being in freedom possible.

To be free to make space for others God has to know himself, and know that he is willing to take responsibility for himself and for others. In this respect his freedom is different from ours, since we are by nature unsure of our competence to undertake responsibility and must learn how to accept our freedom. It is a mark of the absoluteness of God's gracious, free-giving of himself that he is able to depend upon our recognizing that we have the freedom to give or deny space to him, despite the cost involved. He enables us to confirm the freedom which is his. His freedom is both judgment on us and a door of hope.

In our relationship with one another we are tempted always to place limits on what is possible. We give up hope because we do not see the redeeming features in our neighbour or we lack the imagination to reconstruct a future which would transform the present or because we do not have the will to keep on trying. When the Christian tradition affirms the universality and prodigality of God's grace it affirms that God's relationship with the world is characterized by no such limitations. Every circumstance, every event is an opportunity for God to be himself and thus to prompt human beings to accept responsibility for the world and for themselves in relation to him. God cannot be defeated or threatened. He is willing to bear the cost himself of this commitment of himself. Our understanding of the relationship of creation is such that we believe human beings are also like God able to make space for the other and thus to affirm another's freedom in relation to us. By so doing we respect God's person in his creative role and thus share in his work for the world. But the pain of this can be unbearable, unless one keeps one's attention on God and draws strength from the vision of him and unless one wills to have one's behaviour transformed by his presence. God's grace is not a soft forgetting of the past, but a life-giving forgiving and renewing of the present. Thus our own giving of ourselves involves a repentance and a re-direction of our behaviour.

What is true of individuals is also true of communities, and this raises other and more difficult questions. But God's grace meets all the structures of our human society. Institutions, those most conservative of human associations, may likewise be transformed and renewed through His Spirit.

When a Christian tradition thinks about God it creates possibilities for its own future, and offers a new perspective on its past. This is just the kind of way in which we, by proposing models, try to take responsibility for ourselves. There are many encouragements, in intellectual developments, aesthetic creations, and moral insights, in our contemporary society. Is it possible that the Methodist Church could so take responsibility for her past as to make a new future which would serve a wider Christian community and the whole purpose of God for his world?

Notes

1. *Science and Theology from an Arminian Perspective*
    1. For a fuller account see A. W. Harrison, *The Beginnings of Arminianism*, University of London Press 1926, chapter V.
    2. The story is told well in John Gribbin, *Genesis*, Dent 1981.
    3. An interesting discussion will be found in Hugh Montefiore, *The Probability of God*, SCM Press 1985.
    4. A good discussion of the anthropic principle as a scientific principle may be found in P. C. W. Davies, *The Accidental Universe*, CUP 1982.
    5. P. W. Atkins, *The Creation*, W. H. Freeman 1981.
    6. C. Darwin, *The Origin of Species by Means of Natural Selection*, Watts & Co, London 1859.
    7. See for example the discussion in John Maynard Smith, *The Theory of Evolution*, Penguin ^{3}1975.
    8. A detailed exposition of scientific creationism is E. H. Andrews, *God, Science and Evolution*, Evangelical Press 1980. The case against is well argued in Philip Kitcher, *Abusing Science*, Open University Press 1983.
    9. There is a good discussion in D. J. Bartholomew, *God of Chance*, SCM Press 1984.

2. *The Poet of Salvation*
    1. Harry Williams, *Some Day I'll Find You*, Mitchell Beazley 1982, pp. 212f.
    2. Harry Williams, *The True Wilderness*, Constable 1965, p. 8.
    3. Cf. Harvey Cox, *The Seduction of the Spirit*, Wildwood House 1974, p. 323; 'Few people ... today reject faith because it seems unreasonable. They reject it, or rather ignore it, because it does not seem to touch or intersect their own experience.'
    4. Paul Tillich, *Systematic Theology*, Volume 1, Nisbet 1951, reissued SCM Press 1978, pp. 14, 16.
    5. Paul Tillich, *The Religious Situation*, Meridian Books, NY 1956, p. 85.
    6. Paul Tillich, *Systematic Theology*, Volume 2, Nisbet 1957, reissued SCM Press 1978, p. 194.

7. Cf. Schubert M. Ogden, 'What is Theology?' in *Perkins Journal*, xxvi, 2, Winter 1973, p. 2: 'theology presupposes as a condition of its possibility the correlation of the Christian witness of faith and human existence ... [T]his witness exists only in correlation with human existence, for which it claims to be decisive.'
8. Ibid., p. 3.
9. Schubert M. Ogden, *The Point of Christology*, SCM Press 1982, p. 4.
10. Cf. Ruth Page, *Ambiguity and the Presence of God*, SCM Press 1985, chapters 2 and 3.
11. Cf. ibid., pp. 65ff; David A. Pailin, 'Theistic Verification' in *The Living God*, ed. D. Kirkpatrick, Abingdon Press, Nashville 1971, pp. 48–75; '"Credo ut intelligam" as the Method of Theology and of its Verification' in *Analecta Anselmiana*, Band 4, Minerva, Frankfurt 1975, pp. 111–129.
12. Ogden, *The Point of Christology*, p. 4.
13. Ogden, 'What is Theology?', p. 3.
14. Cf. Augustine, *On Christian Doctrine*, Book II, ¶60.
15. Samuel Taylor Coleridge, *Confessions of an Inquiring Spirit*, ed. H. Hart, A. and C. Black 1956, pp. 42, 64; cf. pp. 78f.
16. Rom. 5 9; I Cor. 1; 21, 18.
17. John Wesley, *The Standard Sermons*, ed. E. H. Sugden, Epworth Press 1921, Volume I, pp. 42f., 120.
18. Cf. David Hume, *The Natural History of Religion*; Sigmund Freud, *Totem and Taboo* and *The Future of an Illusion*.
19. Rom. 8. 31.
20. Cf. Karl Barth, *The Epistle to the Romans*, OUP 1933, pp. 8, 36ff, 80, 282, 383; *Church Dogmatics*, I/1, T. & T. Clark 1936, pp. 224f.
21. Tillich, *Systematic Theology*, Volume 1, p. 8.
22. Ibid., pp. 70, 72.
23. Ibid., p. 76.
24. Ibid., p. 68.
25. Dietrich Bonhoeffer, *Letters and Papers from Prison*, The Enlarged Edition, SCM Press 1971, p. 327.
26. Cf. The hymn 'O The bitter shame and sorrow' by Theodore Monod.
27. Gustavo Gutiérrez, *A Theology of Liberation*, SCM Press 1974, p. 307.
28. John [Pearson] Lord Bishop of Chester, *An Exposition of the Creed*, Fourth edition, London 1676, p. 362.
29. Alfred North Whitehead, *Process and Reality*, ed. D. R. Griffin and D. W. Sherburne, Free Press, NY 1978, p. 343.
30. Sigmund Freud, *The Future of an Illusion*, translated by W. D. Robson-Scott, revised and edited by James Strachey, Hogarth Press 1962, pp. 40f.
31. Ibid., p. 53.
32. Printed in *The Listener*, Volume 78, no. 2016, for 16 November 1967.
33. Alfred North Whitehead, *Religion in the Making*, CUP 1927, p. 144.
34. Eccles. 44. 9.
35. Albert Camus, *The Plague*, Penguin 1960, p. 5.
36. Friedrich Nietzsche, *Thus Spoke Zarathustra*, second part, in *The*

Portable Nietzsche, W. Kaufmann, Viking Press, NY 1954, p. 198.
37. John Calvin, *Institutes of the Christian Religion*, James Clarke 1953, Volume 1, p. 207.
38. Schubert M. Ogden, *The Reality of God and Other Essays*, SCM Press 1967, p. 35.
39. Ibid., p. 37.
40. Whitehead, *Process and Reality*, p. 346. When Whitehead says that God 'does not create the world', he is recognizing the contributions of the creatures in determining what becomes actual.
41. Ibid.
42. Cf. Charles Hartshorne, *The Logic of Perfection*, Open Court, Ill. 1962, p. 252.
43. Alfred North Whitehead, 'Immortality' in *The Philosophy of Alfred North Whitehead*, ed. P. A. Schilpp, North Western University Press, Evanston and Chicago 1941, p. 698.
44. Hartshorne, *Logic of Perfection*, p. 242.
45. Ibid., pp. 252f.
46. Ibid., p. 256.
47. Pierre Teilhard de Chardin, *Le Milieu Divin: An Essay on the Interior Life*, Collins 1960, p. 104. Although Teilhard de Chardin developed his ideas independently of the work of Whitehead and Hartshorne and so is not to be regarded as a conscious follower of 'process' thought, the understanding of the relationship between God and the world in Teilhard de Chardin and in process thinkers has interesting basic similarities.
48. Søren Kierkegaard, *The Sickness unto Death in Fear and Trembling and The Sickness unto Death*, Doubleday, NY 1955, p. 216.
49. This is in a private letter dated 28 July 1986 taking up points in the treatment of immortality in my *Groundwork of Philosophy of Religion*, Epworth Press 1986.
50. Teilhard de Chardin, *Le Milieu Divin*, p. 26,; cf. p. 34.
51. Whitehead, *Religion in the Making*, pp. 142f.
52. Hartshorne, *Logic of Perfection*, p. 257.
53. Whitehead, *Process and Reality*, p. 346.
54. Most process thinkers would hold that all occasions of reality have an element of choice in the determination of their actuality but I do not want to get involved here in the problems of a panpsychical understanding of reality.
55. Whitehead, 'Immortality', p. 695.
56. Ibid., p. 697.
57. Whitehead, *Religion in the Making*, pp. 143ff; cf. 'Immortality', p. 694.
58. Cf. David A. Pailin, 'Humanity, History, and the Activity of God' in *Process and Reality: East and West*, Japan Society for Process Studies, Nanzan 1984.
59. Whitehead, *Process and Reality*, p. 346.
60. Ibid and note on p. 413.

3. God and Spirituality: On Taking Leave of Don Cupitt

1. G. E. Lessing, 'On the Proof of the Spirit and of Power' (1777) in H. Chadwick, *Lessing's Theological Writings*, A. and C. Black 1956, p. 55.
2. G. E. Lessing in H. Chadwick, op. cit., p. 53.
3. David Hume, *A Treatise of Human Nature* III.I.I. in edition by L. A. Selby-Bigge, OUP 1888, p. 468.
4. D. Hume in Selby-Bigge edition, op. cit., pp. 468–9.
5. D. Hume in Selby-Bigge edition, op. cit., p. 469.
6. G. E. Moore, *Principia Ethica*, CUP 1903, p. 7.
7. R. M. Hare, *The Language of Morals*, OUP 1952, p. 46.
8. R. M. Hare, op. cit., pp. 80f.
9. R. M. Hare, *Freedom and Reason*, OUP 1963, pp. 89, 195.
10. B. Williams, *Morality*, CUP 1972, p. 13; G. J. Warnock, *The Object of Morality*, Methuen 1971, pp. 1–2.
11. Eg. G. Wallace and A. D. M. Walker, *The Definition of Morality*, Methuen 1970.
12. D. Cupitt, *Taking Leave of God*, SCM Press 1980, p. 67.
13. Ibid., p. 14.
14. Ibid., pp. 21ff., 72.
15. Ibid., p. 84; also *Crisis of Moral Authority*, Lutterworth 1972; reissued SCM Press 1985, pp. 69ff.
16. D. Cupitt, *Taking Leave of God*, p. 43.
17. Ibid., p. 84.
18. Ibid., p. 43.
19. Ibid., p. 39.
20. R. Hepburn, *Christianity and Paradox*, Watts 1958, pp. 208–9.
21. D. Cupitt, op. cit., p. 8.
22. Ibid., p. 9; Cf. also p. 96.
23. Ibid., 11. The individualism implied by this passage is, however, qualified on p. 80.
24. Ibid., pp. 3–4.
25. Ibid., p. 13.
26. Ibid., p. 125.
27. Ibid., pp. 39, 66.
28. Ibid., pp. 84ff.
29. J. H. Hick, *God and the Universe of Faiths*, Collins Fount 1973, 1977 p. 24.
30. It is true of course that some words have both descriptive and value meaning. Examples are words such as 'saint' and 'rogue'. Arguably the descriptive meaning of the words 'courageous' and 'foolhardy' is similar, the main difference between them being in their value connotation. The fact, however, that our language does not always follow the distinction between fact and value does not in itself undermine the validity of this distinction, since in our analysis of these words we can clearly distinguish the value from the descriptive meaning.
31. Eg. 'Moral Beliefs' in *Proceedings of the Aristotelian Society*, LIX, 1958 and 'Goodness and Choice' in *Proceedings of the Aristotelian Society*, Supplementary Volume XXXV, 1961.

32. Eg. D. Emmet *Rules, Roles and Relations*, Macmillan 1966, pp. 53–4.
33. D. Cupitt, op. cit., p. 44.
34. A. C. Ewing, *Second Thoughts on Moral Philosophy*, Routledge and Kegan Paul 1959, pp. 48, 77. Cf. also A. C. Ewing, *The Definition of God*, Routledge and Kegan Paul 1947, pp. 148–9, 151, 172.
35. I.T. Ramsey, 'Towards a Rehabilitation of Natural Law' in I.T. Ramsey (ed), *Christian Ethics and Contemporary Philosophy*, SCM Press 1966, p. 389.
36. H. Oppenheimer, *The Character of Christian Morality*. Free Press 1974, pp. 42–3.
37. Ibid., p. 42.
38. H. Rashdall, *The Theory of Good and Evil*, OUP 1907, Vol. II, p. 260.
39. A. Farrer, 'A Starting Point for the Philosophical Examination of Religious Belief' in B. Mitchell (ed), *Faith and Logic*, Allen and Unwin 1957, p. 26.
40. Rom. 12.1
41. P. Tillich, *The Shaking of the Foundations*, SCM Press 1949; reissued Penguin 1962, pp. 155ff.
42. D. Cupitt, op. cit., p. 82.
43. Cf. L. Gilkey, *Maker of Heaven and Earth*, Anchor 1965, p. 4.
44. Cupitt might object to this on the grounds of 'disinterestedness' being a central value for his spirituality (D. Cupitt, op. cit., pp. 68–9, 77). It is not clear, however, that disinterestedness – if it excludes any kind of concern for one's own well being – is incontestable as a spiritual value (cf. H. Oppenheimer, *The Hope of Happiness*, SCM Press 1983). Furthermore, it is not clear how Cupitt relates this disinterestedness with his concern for salvation (D. Cupitt op. cit., p. 101).
45. This relative autonomy allows our convictions regarding moral values and an appropriate spirituality to have an important influence in the other direction upon our theological beliefs themselves. Indeed, the part ethical reflection has played in theological reformulation over the past two centuries is very profound.
46. D. Cupitt, op. cit., p. 9.
47. Ibid., pp. 2, 19, 85.
48. Ibid., pp. 14, 68.
49. K. Ward, *Holding Fast to God*, SPCK 1982, pp. 41–2.
50. D. Cupitt, op. cit., pp. 19–20.
51. Ibid., p. 14.
52. Ibid., p. 87.
53. Ibid., p. 14.
54. Ibid.
55. Ibid.
56. Ibid., p. 82.
57. D. Cupitt, op. cit., p. 119.
58. As was argued classically by John Oman in *Grace and Personality*, CUP 1917. In his earlier book *Crisis of Moral Authority*, p. 42, Cupitt appears to accept this.

4. The Trinitarian Model of God

1. Bruno Bettelheim, *Surviving and Other Essays*, Thames and Hudson 1979, p. 93 (essay entitled 'The Holocaust – One Generation Later').

2. Cf. James Griffin, *Well-Being*, OUP 1986, for a discussion of the concept of Well-Being, together with the valuable bibliography there provided.

3. A full bibliography would be a volume in itself. However, account should be taken of the difficulties of Maurice Wiles who regards the doctrine as unintelligible and Geoffrey Lampe who regarded it as an understandable historical mistake, though one which should certainly not now be repeated. Against this, serious attention needs to be given to K. Barth, K. Rahner, J. Moltmann, H. U. von Balthazar and E. Jungel, all of whom take the doctrine to be necessary to the coherent statement of Christian theology and of crucial cultural importance. Amongst recent British writers on theology, David Jenkins, *The Glory of Man*, SCM Press 1966, *The Contradiction of Christianity*, SCM Press 1978; J. P. MacKay, *The Christian Experience of God as Trinity*, SCM Press 1983; David Brown, *The Divine Trinity*, Duckworth 1985 and (of an older tradition) L. Hodgson, *The Doctrine of the Trinity*, James Nisbet 1943 will all be found illuminating and useful.

4. There is a vast literature here too, especially in philosophy, much of which is interesting and relevant. Yet the discussion has been conceptual rather than substantive and left on one side the question of human nature. In this latter respect there is illuminating work by Mary Midgley, *Beast and Man*, Harvester Press, 1979 and R. M. Unger, *Passion: An Essay in Personality*, Free Press 1984. However, it is the novelist, the poet, the film maker and the painter who often have most to offer. In another context the same point was made by H. E. Root in his contribution to *Soundings* ed. A. R. Vidler, CUP 1962, p. 18.

5. An interesting discussion along these lines will be found in Fergus Kerr, *Theology After Wittgenstein*, Blackwell 1986, especially Chapter 1. The further interest of this volume centres on the thesis that it was Wittgenstein's intention precisely to attack the Cartesian tradition and to affirm the appropriateness of subjectivity as a philosophical category. Hence, of course, the crucial importance of Wittgenstein's attack on private language and the inappropriateness of the interpretation of Wittgenstein's assertion that religion was a 'form of life' to mean that it therefore did not stand in need of justification. For Wittgenstein anything of significance was public and stood in need of justification.

For a valuable critique of mathematics which nevertheless is full of the excitement of mathematical enquiry where appropriate, see Philip J. Davis and Reuben Hersh, *Descartes' Dream*, Harvester Press 1986; it is a successor to their equally interesting, *The Mathematical Experience*, Harvester Press 1981.

6. It is true that heirs of the Hegelian tradition have from time to time sought to personalize the Absolute, but the difficulties that have there emerged have given strength to the thesis attributed to Descartes and to his influence rather than diminish it.

7. Gareth Moore OP, 'Transubstantiation for Beginners,' *New Blackfrairs*, December 1986, p. 535.
8. Stuart Sutherland, *Jesus, God and Belief*, 1983, argues that failure to continue taking the problem of evil seriously has rendered theological enquiry and religious belief alike irrelevant. Yet theology is crucial to human well-being because it offers a perspective 'sub specie aeternitatis', which is embodied *par excellence* in the life and teaching of Jesus Christ. The key to the failure to apply theology to the problem of evil is the loss of an appropriate concept of the self. The history of the hermeneutic of self-denial in the Christian tradition would be an interesting study.
9. Charles Taylor, *Philosophical Papers I, The Concept of a Person*, p. 112–3, partly quoted in Kerr, 25–26. pp. op. cit.,
10. Cf. P. T. Geach, 'Omnipotence', *Philosophy*, 1973, 48, pp 7–20; R. Swinburne, *The Coherence of Theism*, Clarendon Press 1977, pp 149–161.
11. Antony Flew, 'Divine Omnipotence and Human Freedom', *New Essays in Philosophical Theology* ed. Antony Flew and Alasdair MacIntyre, SCM Press 1955, pp. 144ff.
12. In this context it is appropriate to ask to what extent the neglect of the aesthetic has hampered discussion in contemporary philosophical and theological enquiry. Certainly the aesthetic raises distinctive questions about the nature of time and the criteria and methods which it is appropriate to bring to bear on the judgment of whole systems. These points are crucially developed at length in H. U. Von Balthasar, *The Glory of the Lord*, 7 volumes, T. & T. Clark, translation in progress. For philosophical discussion see also, for example, Susanne K. Langer, *Philosophy in a New Key*, Harvard University Press 1942; Eva Schaper (ed.), *Pleasure, Preference and Value*, CUP 1983, especially the essays of J. McDowell and P. Pettit; Anthony Saville, *The Test of Time*, Clarendon Press 1982.
13. For an introduction to the vast literature on God and evil, see J. Hick, *Evil and the God of Love*, Macmillan 1966.
14. S. Sutherland, *Jesus, God and Belief*, Blackwell 1984, especially chapters 1 and 2.
15. Tertullian, *Adversus Praxeam* (c.217) ed. with commentary and translation, SPCK 1948.
16. For historical discussion of patripassionism see J. K. Mozley, *The Impassibility of God. A Survey of Christian Thought*, CUP 1926.

For useful philosophical distinctions see R. E. Creel, *Divine Impassibility: An Essay in Philosophical Theology*, CUP 1986. For a survey of recent work see W. McWilliams, 'Divine Suffering in Contemporary Theology', SJT 33, 1980, pp. 35–54.

The contemporary interest in the question has been stimulated by process theologians, e.g. C. Hartshorne, *The Logic of Perfection*, Open Court 1962, and C. Hartshorne, *The Divine Relativity*, Yale University Press 1964.
17. P. W. Atkins, *The Creation*, W. H. Freeman 1981.
18. R. Dawkins, *The Blind Watchmaker*, Longman 1986.

5. Grace, von Balthasar and the Wesleys

Abbreviations

AoB *The Analogy of Beauty*, John Riches (ed), T. & T. Clark 1986.
C   *Communio*, International Catholic Review.
CSL *The Christian State of Life*, Hans U. von Balthasar, tr. Sister Mary McCarthy, Ignatius Press, San Francisco 1983.
GoL *The Glory of the Lord* – Herrlichkeit, tr. Fessio, Riches et al, T. & T. Clark 1982.
H   *Herrlichkeit*, Hans U. von Balthasar, Johannes Verlag, Einsiedeln 1961.
HP   *Hymns and Psalms: An Ecumenical Hymnbook*.
KB   *Karl Barth*, Hans U. von Balthasar, Johannes Verlag, Einsiedeln 1976.
NG   *Nature and Grace*, Henri de Lubac, Ignatius Press, San Francisco 1984.
P   *Prayer*, Hans U. von Balthasar, tr. Graham Harrison, Ignatius Press, San Francisco 1986.
QR   *Quarterly Review*.
RGG *Religion in Geschichte und Gegenwart*, 3rd edition.
SM   *Sacramentum Mundi*.
TD   *Theodramatik*, Hans U. von Balthasar, Johannes Verlag, Einsiedeln 1978–
TRE *Theologische Realenzyklopädie 22*.
vBR *The von Balthasar Reader* tr. Daly and Lawrence, T. & T. Clark 1982.
WJW *The Works of John Wesley*, OUP 1983.

1. Philip Watson, *The Concept of Grace*, Epworth Press 1959; Geoffrey Wainwright, *Calvin and Wesley*, Uniting Church Press, Melbourne 1987; Tomáš Špidlík, *The Spirituality of the Christian East*, Cistercian Publications, Kalamazoo 1986; RGG; TRE (Gnade); also Note 7 below.
2. KB pp. 353ff.; vBR pp. 17ff.; NG pp. 81ff.; GoL I pp. 295ff.; also Note 28 below.
3. Albert Outler, *John Wesley*, OUP, New York 1964.
WJW Vol 1 Sermons I, Notes pp. 56f. & 66ff.; also AoB 10.
4. CSL p. 273; GoL I pp. 287 ff. 371; AoB 207.
5. CSL p. 221; For grace in the context of 'mission' CSL pp. 73ff.
6. CSL pp. 201ff.; TD II.2 pp. 269ff.; GoL I p. 564; AoB pp. 105ff. and the literature cited there.
7. SM pp. 415ff. On this problem H III.1 pp. 939ff.
8. GoL I pp. 34ff.; see also H III. 1 p. 939; H III.2.2 pp. 286ff.
9. GoL I. p. 140.
10. H III.2.2. pp. 363 ff. esp. p. 404. On Freedom and Grace GoL I p. 417; TD II.1 pp. 284ff; IV 90f., 368; H III.2.2 p. 289; on Sovereignty and Grace CSL p. 80; on Judgment and Grace H III.2.1 pp. 15ff; on Covenant and Grace H III.2.1 pp. 147ff.; on Obedience and Grace H III.2.1.p. 143; on Law and Grace CSL pp. 213ff.

Notes

11. P p. 39.
12. GoL I p. 229, esp. pp. 230ff. on 'experience' and grace.
13. AoB p. 2; CSL p. 337, and p. 392 on the specific character of the Christian calling.
14. CSL p. 29.
15. Cf. The prior context of the quotation from GoL I p. 140; CSL pp. 32ff.
16. GoL I pp. 435ff.
17. AoB pp. 22ff. on *Cordula* pp. 67ff. Cf. GoL I pp. 154, 163.
18. GoL I pp. 18ff..
19. H III. 1. p. 963.
20. AoB p. 49; GoL I pp. 167ff..
21. Cf. The following context of the quotation from GoL I p. 140.
22. TD II. 2 pp. 463ff.
23. AoB pp. 53ff.
24. TD II. 1. 21ff.
25. On being chosen and sent to perform within the divine drama cf. TD II.1 p. 13 and II.2.136ff..
26. GoL I p. 313.
27. TD II.1 p. 286.
28. John Zeitz, 'God's Mystery in Christ: reflections on Erich Przywara and Eberhard Jüngel', C 12 (1985) pp. 158ff.
29. GoL I p. 140.
30. AoB p. 198.
31. AoB pp. 201f..
32. TD III pp. 15ff..
33. TD III pp. 125ff.; also CSL pp. 67ff.
34. GoL I. p. 264.
35. CSL pp. 74 and 72f.
36. NG p. 117.
37. NG p. 42.
38. WJW Sermons Vol. 1 Sermons I pp. 55ff..
39. Randy Maddox, 'Responsible Grace in Wesley's Theology', QR 6 (1986) p. 24ff.
40. WJW Vol. 1 Sermons I pp. 572ff.
41. WJW Vol. 7 p. 44 & 73ff.
42. William Cannon, *The Theology of John Wesley*, Abingdon Press, Nashville 1946 p. 61.
43. HP 109 v.3
44. HP 193 v.4
45. HP 300 v. 2
46. Tomáš Špidlik, *The Spirituality of the Christian East*.
47. John Wesley, *A Christian Library* Vol. 1 p. 145.
48. HP 267
49. I am indebted to the Revd Tom Albin for his research on this area.
50. WJW Vol. 3 Sermons III p. 207.
51. Philip Watson, *The Message of the Wesleys*, pp. 131ff and 195ff.

52. WJW Vol. 7 No. 136 p. 251.
53. CSL p. 13.
54. E. P. Sanders *Jesus and Judaism* SCM Press 1985 p. 240.
55. AoB p. 144; TD II.1 p. 95.
56. The subject deserves a bibliography in its own right: Important works are; van Panthaleon van Eck, *J. S. Bach: Critique of Pure Music*; Gustav Leonhardt, *The Art of Fugue: Bach's Last Harpsichord Work*; Adel Heinrich, *Bach-Kunst der Fuge*; Christof Wolff, *Current Musicology*, xix 1975, pp. 47ff.; Gregory Butler, *Musical Quarterly*, lxix, 1983, pp. 44ff.; Wilfrid Mellers, *Bach and the Dance of God*.
57. Nicholas Lash, 'Ideology, Metaphor and Analogy', *The Philosophical Frontiers of Christian Theology* ed. Brian Hebblethwaite and Stewart Sutherland, CUP 1982, p.88; 'to "leave the story-teller to himself" would be to leave Christian practice – unconstrained by historical, literary and philosophical criticism – exposed to the risk, endemic to all autobiography, of "self-indulgence and even dishonesty"'.

6. *Experiencing Grace*

1. See Sally McFague, *Metaphorical Theology: Models of God in Religious Language*, SCM Press 1983, building on the work of Paul Ricoeur. Janet Martin Soskice's attack on this point in *Metaphor and Religious Language*, Clarendon Press 1985 p. 89 is not required by her major concern to insist that religious metaphor depicts reality and is not a fantastic construct.
2. David Tracy, *The Analogical Imagination*, SCM Press 1981.
3. Ibid., p. 452.
4. Barnabas Lindars, *Jesus, Son of Man*, SPCK 1983.
5. There is a long history of scholarly dispute over 'The Messianic Secret'. Space dictates the simple offering here of a viewpoint.
6. A longer study would attempt to trace the history of these images.
7. John J. Vincent, *Into the City*, Epworth Press 1983, pp. 116–7.
8. Soskice, op cit., p. 159.
9. Ibid., p. 159
10. *Faith in the City: A Call for Action by Church and Nation*, Church House Publishing 1985, p. 64.
11. *Faith in Leeds: Searching for God in our City*. Leeds Churches Community Involvement Project 1986, p. 42.
12. *Faith in the City*, p. 58. See also chapter 3, paragraphs 19–28; chapter 4; chapter 12. 27–55.
13. J. Holland and P. Henriot, *Social Analysis Linking Faith and Justice*, Centre of Concern, Washington DC 1981.
14. Greg Smith, *In the Inner City: How can we Tell if God is at Work?* Handsel Press/British Church Growth Association, Edinburgh 1986.
15. Ibid., p. 24.
16. Vincent, op. cit., p. 136.
17. Philip S. Bagwell, *Outcast London: a Christian Response*, Epworth Press, 1987.

18. John Bowlby, *The Making and Breaking of Affectional Bonds*, Tavistock Publications 1979.
19. Peter Marris, *Loss and Change*, Routledge and Kegan Paul 1974, pp. 169–170.
20. Bowlby, op. cit., p. 155 and generally pp. 145–156.
21. Morna D. Hooker, 'Interchange in Christ', *JTS* ns 21, 1971, pp. 349–61; 'Philippians 2.6–11' *Jesus und Paulus* ed. Ellis and Grässer, Göttingen 1975, pp. 151–64; 'Interchange and Atonement', *BJRL* 60, 1978, pp. 462–81; 'Interchange and Suffering' *Suffering and Martyrdom in the New Testament* ed. Horbury and McNeil, CUP 1981; 'Interchange in Christ and Ethics, *JSNT* 25, 1985, pp. 3–17.
22. Hooker, 'Interchange and Suffering', p. 78.
23. Hooker, 'Interchange in Christ and Ethics,' p. 10.

7. Surgical Spirit

1. R. S. Thomas, 'The Word' in *Laboratories of the Spirit*, Macmillan 1975, p. 3.
2. P. Kerr, 'Playing Away', *Theology*, September 1985, pp. 374–382.
3. E. Schillebeeckx, 'God's concern is man's concern: man's concern is God's concern.'
4. P. Winch, in an essay entitled 'Who is my Neighbour?' in *Trying to Make Sense*, Blackwell 1987, chapter 11, draws from the parable of the Good Samaritan the necessity of a practical response to encounters with our fellow human beings.
5. W. Pollock, *Selection for Ministry in the Church of England*, ACCM 1986; J. Navone, 'The Question-Raising Word of God' in *Theology*, July 1987, pp. 288–93.
6. B. Reed, *The Dynamics of Religion*, Darton, Longman and Todd 1978.
7. A. Russell, *The Clerical Profession*, SPCK 1980; B. Heeney, *A Different kind of Gentleman*, Archon 1976; A. V. Campbell, *Moderated Love*, SPCK 1984; W. F. May et al., *The End of Professionalism?*, Department of Christian Ethics and Practical Theology, Edinburgh 1985.
8. P. Pietroni, *Holistic Living*, Dent 1986; there is a weekly column entitled 'Body and Soul' in the 'Society Tomorrow' supplement of *The Guardian* newspaper.
9. I. Murdoch, *The Philosopher's Pupil*, Chatto & Windus 1983, p. 503.
10. *Constitution, Practice & Discipline of the Methodist Church*, e.g. SO 578.
11. A good example is the Methodist Conference Statement on 'The Church and the Ministry of Healing', 1977.
12. These attributes refer to the positive elements in the eight struggles which E. Erikson identifies as the typical psychosocial stages in the normal life-cycle.
13. 'The Church and the Ministry of Healing', para. 5.
14. J. Bronowski, *The Visionary Eye*, The MIT Press 1978, p. 36; 'Knowledge which another man supplies is always a constraint; every addition to your own knowledge is a liberation.'
15. G. Gutierrez, *We Drink from Our Own Wells*, SCM Press 1984, p. 107:

'Statements that never go beyond principles are naive and in the long run lead to self-deception; they are a way of evading history – the place where our fidelity to the Lord must find expression at the present time.'
16. John Wesley regularly appealed to the liturgy and homilies of the Book of Common Prayer, e.g. *Works* 8, pp. 102ff; 13, pp. 197f.
17. J. Bronowski, op. cit., pp. 45–56.
18. I. T. Ramsey, *Religious Language*, SCM Press 1957.
19. 'I do not believe in an art which is not forced into existence by a human being's desire to open his heart' (Edvard Munch).
20. F. Young, *Can These Dry Bones Live?*, SCM Press 1982; H. Rack, *Epworth Review* 9, September 1982, pp. 43–48.
21. W. Pannenberg, *Anthropology in Theological Perspective*, T. & T. Clark, 1985.
22. H. Hesse, *Siddhartha*. Peter Owen Ltd, 1954, pp. 83f, 105.
23. C. Burdon, *Theology*, March 1987, pp. 89–97.
24. Ibid, p. 85.
25. Charles Wesley, *Hymns & Psalms*, 767, verse 4.
26. 'Is art really a priesthood that demands the pure in heart who must belong to it entirely? (P. Cezanne); 'Metaphysical minds occupy themselves too much with abstractions to be able to share and taste to the full the pleasures of art, which always supposes an interchange between the soul and real external objects' (O. Redon).
27. Spanish proverb.
28. I. Murdoch, *The Unicorn*, Chatto & Windus 1963, p. 149.

8. The Catholic Spirit: The Need of our Time

1. John Wesley, *Standard Sermons* ed. Edward H. Sudgen, 2 vols. Epworth Press 1921, II, 139–40.
2. *Standard Sermons*, II, 128.
3. See Colin Morris, *The Hammer of the Lord*, Epworth Press 1973, pp. 89–101.
4. James Martineau, *Studies of Christianity*, London 1858, p. 12.
5. An image used by James Martineau; see James Martineau, *Suggestions on Church Organisation*, Manchester 1888, p. 28.
6. Herbert Workman, *The Place of Methodism in the Catholic Church*, Epworth Press 1921, p. 104.
7. James Martineau, *Endeavours after the Christian Life*, London ^{9}1892, pp. 460–61.
8. *Standard Sermons*, II, 145.

9. Logic, Chronology and Context in Theology

1. Albert Outler and others have drawn attention to the importance of the year 1739 in John Wesley's biography. It was then that he 'submitted to be more vile ...' and began his outdoor preaching with a selfless disregard for his own status or welfare. A. Outler, *Evangelism in the Wesleyan Spirit*, Tidings, Nashville 1971.

Notes

2. W. B. Pope, *Compendium*, London ²1880, p. 36.
3. Ibid., p. 2.
4. Ibid., p. 5.
5. B. J. F. Lonergan, *Method in Theology*, Darton, Longman and Todd 1972, p.xi.
6. Søren Kierkegaard, *Of the Difference between a Genius and an Apostle*, 1847, cit. John Coulson, *Religion and Imagination*, Clarendon Press 1981, p. 33.
7. John McLeod Campbell, *The Nature of the Atonement and its Relation to Remission of Sins and Eternal Life*, Macmillan ⁴1873.
8. P. Tillich, *Theology of Culture*, OUP 1970, p. 10.
9. John J. Vincent, *OK, Let's be Methodists*, Epworth Press 1984, p. 66.
10. J. H. Newman, *Rationalistic and Catholic Tempers Contrasted*, republished in *Essays Critical and Historical*, London ⁹1890.
11. Herbert Workman, *The Place of Methodism in the Catholic Church*, Epworth Press 1921, p. 104.
12. W. Strawson, 'Methodist Theology 1850–1950,' in *A History of the Methodist Church in Great Britain*, Vol. 3, Epworth Press 1983. A modern example of this style of ecumenical Methodist ecclesiology is Rupert Davies, *What Methodists Believe*, Epworth Press ²1988.
13. F. Schleiermacher, *The Christian Faith*, T. & T. Clark 1968, p. 3.
14. *Contemporary Review*, Vol. XIV, 1870.
15. John Macmurray, *Persons in Relation*, Faber 1961, p. 215.
16. Martin Buber, *I and Thou*, T. & T. Clark 1971, p. 51.
17. J. Coulson, op. cit., p. 42.
18. F. D. Maurice, *The Claims of the Bible and of Science*, London 1863, p. 61.
19. F. D. Maurice, *Theological Essays*, London ⁴1881, p. 343.
20. Geoffrey Wainwright, *Doxology*, Epworth Press 1980, p. 192.
21. J. Coulson, op. cit., p. 39.
22. W. Pannenberg, 'Analogie und Doxologie', cited in G. Wainwright, *Doxology*, p. 282.
23. I Cor. 1. 23.
24. Herbert McCabe OP, *The Teaching of the Catholic Church. A New Catechism of Christian Doctrine*, Catholic Truth Society 1985, p. 5.
25. Ex. 14.14.

www.ingramcontent.com/pod-product-compliance
Lightning Source LLC
Chambersburg PA
CBHW062037220426
43662CB00010B/1542